D1140590

993342832 8

WITHDRAWN

TESTING TIMES
IN PURSUIT OF THE ASHES

Also by Andrew Strauss

Coming into Play

TESTING TIMES

IN PURSUIT OF THE ASHES

Andrew Strauss

with Scyld Berry

HODDER &
STOUGHTON

GLOUCESTERSHIRE
COUNTY COUNCIL

9933438328	
Bertrams	02/11/2009
AN	£19.99
QY	

First published in Great Britain in 2009 by Hodder & Stoughton
An Hachette UK company

1

Copyright © Andrew Strauss 2009

The right of Andrew Strauss to be identified as the Author of the Work
has been asserted by him in accordance with the Copyright, Designs
and Patents Act 1988.

All rights reserved. No part of this publication may be reproduced,
stored in a retrieval system, or transmitted, in any form or by any means
without the prior written permission of the publisher, nor be otherwise
circulated in any form of binding or cover other than that in which it is
published and without a similar condition being imposed on the
subsequent purchaser.

A CIP catalogue record for this title is available from the British Library

Hardback ISBN 978 0 340 84067 2
Trade Paperback ISBN 978 1 444 70980 3

Typeset in Nexus Serif by Hewer Text UK Ltd, Edinburgh

Printed and bound in the UK by CPI Mackays, Chatham ME5 8TD

Hodder & Stoughton policy is to use papers that are natural, renewable and
recyclable products and made from wood grown in sustainable forests. The
logging and manufacturing processes are expected to conform to the
environmental regulations of the country of origin.

Hodder & Stoughton Ltd
338 Euston Road
London NW1 3BH

www.hodder.co.uk

For Ruth, Sam and Luca

CONTENTS

ACKNOWLEDGEMENTS

I sit here in the warm afterglow of victory at the Oval as England's Ashes-winning captain. Sounds pretty good, doesn't it?

Before I get too caught up with what has happened, I have to thank all the players who represented England over the last eight months that I have been in charge, but more particularly the 15 players that took part in the Ashes series. No team ever wins the Ashes without contributions from numbers one to eleven, and this series was no different. In fact, the only real reason that I can come up with for the amazing turnaround from Headingley to The Oval is that the team kept tight as a unit when it would have been tempting for many of the players to start blaming others for our performance. It says a lot about the characters in the dressing-room that they kept believing when many others doubted. Thanks also have to go to Andy Flower and the rest of the England team management for the terrific work they have done preparing the team over the last few months. They don't get the accolades that the players do, but they deserve them just as much.

Only your family really knows what a toll playing in an Ashes series takes on a player. They are the ones that have to put up with the roller-coaster of emotions, the single-tracked mind, the endless phone calls, the lack of sleep. A huge debt of gratitude has to go to Ruth, Sam and Luca, for being there for me through all these testing times, managing in their different ways to take my mind away from the stresses and strains, while at the same time reminding me of what is truly important in life. People often ask me why I wear my wedding ring around my neck when playing. The reason is that it is a constant reminder that I don't do this on my own.

I would like to thank Scyld Berry for all the hard graft that he has put into getting this book ready so soon after the series has finished. He has achieved the balance perfectly of allowing me to concentrate on the cricket, while at the same time making sure that we didn't cut corners.

Finally I would like to thank my publisher, Roddy Bloomfield of Hodder & Stoughton, for all his enthusiasm. In the first place he encouraged me to write *Testing Times* and then together with Sarah Hammond worked efficiently to see that the book progressed smoothly.

Photographic Acknowledgements

The author and publisher would like to thank the following for permission to reproduce photographs:

Hamish Blair/Getty Images, Shaun Botterill/Getty Images, Chris Brandis/AP/PA, Philip Brown, Gareth Copley/PA, Paul Ellis/AFP/Getty Images, Nigel French/Empics Sport, John Giles/PA, Paul Gilham/Getty Images, Tim Hales/AP/PA, Julian Herbert/Getty Images, Tom Hevezi/AP/PA, Mike Hewitt/Getty Images, Ian Kington/AFP/Getty Images, Andres Leighton/AP/PA, Sandra Mu/Getty Images, Indranil Mukherjee/AFP/Getty Images, Rebecca Naden/PA, Nick Potts/PA, Clive Rose/Getty Images, Tom Shaw/Getty Images, Neal Simpson/Empics Sport, Jon Super/AP/PA, Glyn Thomas/Offside, Dean Treml/AFP/Getty Images, William West/AFP/Getty Images, Kirsty Wigglesworth/AP/PA, Andrew Winning/Reuters/Action Images, Andrew Yates/AFP/Getty Images.

1
RECOVERY AND REDEMPTION

After being dropped from the England team for the tour of Sri Lanka at the end of 2007, New Zealand was not my first choice of a place to go to recuperate. I had gone 13 Test matches without scoring a hundred, in a run of bad form which had lasted six to eight months. I had wanted to go to South Africa to play four-day cricket but, for one reason and another, this possibility fell through. Then Andy Moles, the Northern Districts coach, contacted me and seemed incredibly keen for me to go and play for them in the New Year. If I was selected for the England tour of New Zealand it would be good preparation. If I wasn't, it would be useful to be out there if injuries offered me a way back into the Test side.

My visit didn't get off to an auspicious start. After a holiday in South Africa, I arrived 48 hours late in New Zealand and missed the first match. An inexperienced stair-driver at Johannesburg Airport drove the stairs into the side of the plane and broke its door. But when I did arrive in Hamilton, an hour or so's drive south of Auckland, I was immediately impressed. The players in domestic cricket in New Zealand are very young, some of them 19 to 21, because if you have not made it into the international ranks by the age of 26 or 27 you are looking for a job in the real world. There aren't the big entourages that English clubs have, and teams rely on the hunger and enthusiasm of their players. It was very instructive for me: they had a great desire to improve, really 'put in' at practice, and had an incredibly high standard of touch rugby in the warm-ups. The old codger had to be enthusiastic.

Staying with Andy Moles was, shall we say, simple yet effective. He lived on his own in a bungalow in Hamilton. When Ruth and our son came out, he very kindly vacated his house for a couple of weeks. There was a small garden which Sam appreciated by hitting balls over the fence. Northern Districts had also persuaded Toyota to lend me a 4 × 4 with my name splashed over virtually every panel. Fortunately, in the land of rugby, not many people seemed to know or care who I was.

Where this arrangement was not ideal was that I joined Northern Districts to play in the Twenty20 competition and five one-day games – and I was trying to get back into the Test side. We had some interesting journeys along the way, all to new places for me as I had never been to New Zealand before: Christchurch, Dunedin, Lincoln and Palmerston North. We stayed in Travel Lodges and motor inns, not five-star hotels, and I had to share a room, which I wasn't used to. I shared with our wicket-keeper, Pete McGlashan, whose great claim to fame – before he got into the New Zealand side for the ICC World Twenty20 – was inventing all types of cricket equipment for the twenty-first century, like a batting glove which is Velcro'd so you can rip it off between deliveries and vent your fingers.

When we went to Palmerston North, I found it fitted the archetypal description of a country town. It has one shopping mall which people come to from miles around, to the McDonald's and Subway where they could get a fix of civilisation. John Cleese once said that anybody not brave enough to commit suicide should go to Palmerston North. I was beginning to wonder whether it was all worthwhile.

I have kept a diary since going to Adelaide with the inaugural Academy intake of 2001. We were 'encouraged' to do so by the head coach Rod Marsh, the former Australian wicket-keeper – and I use inverted commas because it was semi-compulsory. By nature I am not someone who leads a structured life and likes to get all his thoughts down on paper. This was more of a cricket diary with entries about how I was batting, and what I was working on; about what it was like to be away from home, and what issues were surrounding the team. And since starting to play for England, it has been quite liberating to put my thoughts down on paper, because it has helped to give me the head-space to work out how to score runs for England.

This is my diary entry for 12 February 2008:

Here I am in Palmerston North, the middle of nowhere, following my dream of playing for England. The last few months have passed, and suddenly it feels like groundhog day again. Spending time in a hotel, waiting for a cricket match to be played, hoping that tomorrow will bring me some much needed form, continuing on a long journey to where?

The truth is that I have enjoyed coming to New Zealand and meeting new people. In a way it has been a new challenge for me and, to a degree, I have passed the challenge. I have settled in well with the boys, I have handed out advice like a senior player should, but I haven't really scored any runs, which is what I have been brought here to do.

With the England tour just around the corner, I am a little concerned about my form, that much is for sure, but what I am more worried about right at the moment is my lack of desire. Being dropped for Sri Lanka opened my eyes a little. I desperately needed some time with Ruth and Sam to reconnect and also realise what is important in life. It was three months of monotony back at home with not all that much to do apart from the odd gym session, but I loved it. I got bored but there was something really satisfying about being a family, something that I had been unable to do for so long.

The strange thing about cricket is that it toys with you. When you aren't scoring runs, you wonder why you play the game, especially at this stage of my career. On the other hand, when things are going well your ego gets massaged and suddenly you feel invincible and that the game was made for you. I suppose the real question is how long are you willing to put up with the constant ups and downs, especially when it involves being away from home and loved ones for such a long time. Is it worth it?

I don't really think that I can answer that question right now. I am not playing well, which is probably affecting my mood, I am away from Ruth and Sam, and am in a foreign country with team-mates I don't know that well. I think that after this tour, I will be in a better place to decide what the road ahead entails.

The key to it all though is: what is the motivation for playing? All players question whether they are doing the right thing at times, especially when not in form. Are we all totally motivated by money? Will we genuinely miss the adrenalin rushes, the highs, the lows? Or are we just trying to avoid, for as long as possible, the humiliation of watching someone take your place? All I can say on the matter is that I have watched someone take my place and felt the horrible feeling of rejection, but did I miss being there?

Anyway, these are questions that are swirling around in my mind. They may or not be answered in the coming weeks, but I think that if I am to give myself the best chance of performing over the tour, I have to be focused, not on whether I should be here or not, but on the present, which is my next innings or match.

Cricket-wise, I am in a difficult mental state. I have done some good work with Toby Radford [the Middlesex coach] getting further across, moving early and making sure that I don't get my front foot too far across. In my first innings here, it felt pretty good, but then the Twenty20 campaign meant that it was into slogging mode . . . going at the ball and getting my front leg out the way. I had some success but nothing like enough. Coming back into one-day cricket, I got caught down the legside for 0 in the first game, and then laboured for 10 runs on a difficult pitch in the second. Not the sort of scores that you expect from an overseas pro, and pretty frustrating. I will continue to do the right things, train hard, and hopefully things will come right. What I have to do more than anything though is back myself. Rather than think of pressures, I have to go out and enjoy the challenge and back myself to come through it. There is no reason why I shouldn't score runs. I should be in my prime and, with my experience, if I can get into some decent form, then there is no reason why I shouldn't go on a golden run of form. That has got to be the plan. Let's see how it all goes.

A few days later I played my last innings for Northern Districts, still without much to show for the time and money they had invested. I went to pull my second ball and it lobbed to mid-on – the easiest catch I have ever seen in my life (I am not going to count the one I dropped during the Stanford tournament in Antigua because the lights were so poor). And the mid-on fielder dropped it. It was such an easy catch that my partner just stood there in the middle of the pitch as he watched incredulously, and he was run out. But I went on to make a hundred. It was in a losing cause, admittedly, but this innings set me on the road to recovery and redemption.

My next two entries were not long delayed, and much more purposeful and optimistic.

24 February 2008

Twelve days since my last entry, and it may as well be 12 months because everything feels completely different. Twelve days ago, I was playing for Northern Districts struggling to get some form, wondering if everything is worth the trouble. Now I am back with the England side, something that seems so familiar, and have also come in having scored a hundred in my last innings for NDs.

It was the perfect way to finish, and I really felt as though I owed them something after the way they treated me. It took some early luck, but in the end people only remember the runs you score, and time in the middle was completely invaluable. It is always hard to look back at an innings and learn lessons from it, because generally it feels so easy when you get runs. You do what is natural, and you score runs. It is only when you get out that you start analysing where you went wrong. I suppose the lesson to be learned from the hundred was not to think about technique when you play. The first 30 runs were scrappy because I was constantly thinking about where my weight was etc., rather than the game situation and the areas that I needed to hit the ball. By the end of the innings, I was playing the ball later and on merit, which we all know is the way to go. Unfortunately it is always much easier to do that when you have a hundred to your name than nought.

I arrived in Christchurch with a slight spring in my step. I didn't have to pretend that my game was in order while being secretly very worried about it, and I rightly felt quite positive about what is to come. All in all it is good to be back. It seems as though the players are happy that I am here, and there is definitely a feeling of coming back to the family. I suppose I knew it was going to be a bit like this ... not missing it when you are away but settling straight back in again when you are back.

As is always the case with tours, they start slowly without much intensity. There were only five Test specialists together [Strauss, Steve Harmison, Matthew Hoggard, Vaughan and Monty Panesar], and although we trained pretty hard, the practice sessions were not particularly challenging. As is also the case with tours, the intensity picks up very sharply and dramatically, and if you are not aware, you can end up not getting your levels up in time for the First Test. We have now joined up with the rest of the squad and we play the first practice game tomorrow. I am looking forward to it, although I feel a little nervous but, all in all, I know that I need a good couple of performances over the next few days to get into the Test side. I am sure that they want to put me in, but if I struggle and Owais [Shah] gets runs, then the decision may be difficult to make.

27 February 2008

The two-day practice match didn't really go to plan. I got four off quite a few balls, and then hit my stumps trying to deflect the ball from hitting them. I felt pretty gutted, especially as most of the rest of the guys did get runs, especially Owais. Thankfully they have picked me for the warm-up game tomorrow, and I will get one or two more chances to show that I deserve to be in the side, although I am batting three, not opening.

I'm not really sure how I feel about this. On the one hand it is great to get in the side at any position, and the fact that they have included me shows that they have plenty of confidence in my abilities. Batting at three is slightly different, but not overly so, especially if we lose an early wicket. All in all, it will be a different challenge, and one that I should be capable of overcoming, although I have to make sure that I prepare myself mentally. The thing is to be switched on enough when waiting to bat to know how the bowlers are trying to take their wickets, without expending too much energy doing so. Above all though, it is important to be excited about it rather than worrying about what may happen.

I think the stuff I talked about the other day is incredibly important, especially at three. As it is a different position, the opposition will be looking for signs of hesitancy, and I have to make sure more than ever that I portray that I am in control of events. Good body language, stomach for a fight and sheer willpower will ensure success, but you have got to want it. Do not shy away from the challenge, and push all negative thoughts to the back of your mind.

Before the First Test we had a first-class warm-up match in Dunedin against a New Zealand Major Association XI, effectively their A team. In accordance with our habit of making a slow start on tours we were dismissed for 131 in our first innings, to which I contributed 5 runs. But we reacted strongly – another of England's habits during my time – and we drew the game comfortably, and I did contribute on this occasion:

2 March 2008

My birthday today, although in truth my present came yesterday with a second-innings century when I really needed it. I am not very good at putting down my feelings when I score runs because it generally seems easy. You see the ball, make the right decisions and score runs. There is none of the mental anguish that comes with low scores, no soul-searching to see if you are mentally hungry enough, no questioning desire. All it is is a feeling of peace and tranquillity. God, it feels good.

There were, however, a couple of things that came out of the innings that should be important, both for this series and beyond. The first was a feeling of inner calm. It is hard to describe really because it isn't tangible, but I didn't feel any pressure to score runs quickly. In fact I was more than happy to play out maiden after maiden if necessary. There were no hopeful shots, just reacting to the ball that was coming down at me. I could have continued batting all day. The only times that I got a little hasty against the spinner were the times that I came close to getting out. It was just watch the ball, get still and react.

Linked to this, but not quite the same, was a willingness to keep all the percentages in my favour. If I look back at the innings that I have played over the last 18 months there has been a general intent to be aggressive, to take the game to the bowler, and in doing so I have lowered my percentages of staying in. When I play my best, I may score quickly, but I do so by picking off balls, and letting them come rather than going at them. Mentally it was like going back to a familiar playground, one whose location you have forgotten. When you arrive there it is very familiar, comforting and exciting, but the real joy is in the rediscovery.

I am feeling really good about the Test match now, because I have remembered how to score runs. It doesn't guarantee anything, but it makes life a hell of a lot easier. Here's to a good practice week, a memorable Test match, and the best present of all, seeing Ruth and Sam at the end.

4 March 2008

I can't say how excited I am about the game tomorrow. Everything just feels right. I feel in good form, I feel confident, I am excited to be back, I can't wait to play Test cricket again, and I know that at the end of the week I am seeing my family again. Life is pretty good at the moment.

The practice over the last couple of days has been excellent. I have continued in practice what I was doing in the match the other day. When batting in the net, it has all been about switching on, getting trigger movements out the way, keep still and react to the ball. I have hit the ball straight, and feel well balanced.

Over the last few days I have read a couple of books that have been really interesting. Firstly Justin Langer's book came up with some ideas about form, making the most of it, getting out of bad form etc., as well as some good quotes and stories.

Today, though, I read a very thought-provoking book called *The Secret*. It explains that the law of attraction governs everything, and if you can get it working for you, you can achieve anything. If you think about the concept too hard, then you can get caught up in why and how it should work, but everything that I have experienced in life backs it up.

The theory is that what you think about happens. If you think positive thoughts, then those positive thoughts will come about. For example, in a game of cards, the person who believes he is going to win usually does. It may be the most experienced player, or the one with the most money etc., but he thinks he is going to win and, more importantly, he believes he is going to win. At the other end of the scale, the gambler with one chip left, who has lost repeatedly on the night, is more often than not going to lose.

Why most people don't achieve as much as they should do is because they don't really know what they want in life, what their goals are, and as a result they don't focus all their energy on believing that they can be achieved.

Think about cricket. Who are the most successful players . . . the ones with the most belief. Okay, some get that belief from being extremely talented, but more often than not they are positive people who believe that they are in control of their destiny.

Why do we score runs when we are in good form? Simple. We believe that we are going to, and so it happens.

Why do we not score runs when we are out of form? Simple. In our minds are thousands of negative thoughts. We are worried about technical problems, about our place in the side, about being humiliated and, sure enough, it comes to pass.

How then do we get back into form? I haven't tried it but it sounds reasonably simple. Firstly, we have to get ourselves believing in positive thoughts, rather than negative. So, whenever a negative thought comes into our mind, we have to push it right back and, instead, think about something positive in our life. It could be family, bank balance, golf swing, whatever is making you happy. Probably best to have a range of things to think about whenever those negative thoughts arrive.

Secondly, you have to adopt a winning frame of mind. Wake up in the morning, and be grateful for everything you have and everything that is going to happen to you that day. Also give something to someone or do something for someone. It will make you feel better about yourself and start thinking positive thoughts.

Thirdly, you have to have a clear goal that you are trying to achieve . . . i.e. score runs that day. Draw it on your hand, or put up a sign, so that every time you see it you remember what that goal is and you believe that you are going to achieve it.

Fourthly, visualise doing it. Maybe, on the day before the match, imagine the scoreboard with a hundred on it, see the bowler running in, see yourself playing the shot to score that hundredth run. Hear the applause, feel yourself raising your bat to the crowd. Look at the weather, smell the smell. Feel it in every pore in your body.

I suppose this is the sort of stuff that sports psychologists talk about when they say 'reconnect with past success' when they talk to you. Having spent plenty of time in the last 12 months searching desperately for form, there are worse things to do than be positive, be grateful for having the chance to play for England, and savour the idea of scoring a century.

As it turned out, Hamilton was a classic example of the First Test jinx which has started to pursue us. In 2004, starting with the First Test in the West Indies, England won four opening Tests in a row, before losing the first against Australia at Lord's. Starting then, we haven't won the opener and have lost half of them.

Hamilton ended up being a complete disaster because we batted like idiots on the final day and handed victory to New Zealand. Going into the second innings of that Test, when we were set 300 to win off 81 overs, there was a feeling of people being under pressure. We knew we should draw it, and we had everything to lose, with only an outside chance of a win. Then in the space of an hour and a half, after competing pretty well for the first four days, a match which most people had pencilled in as a draw was turned round by Kyle Mills in an excellent spell of swing and seam bowling. We might have underestimated him before the series: I got a pretty good ball that left me and I edged it. We were 25 for three and worse followed. We were all out for 110 and New Zealand won with 26 overs to spare.

I haven't been in many dressing-rooms lower than England's that night: very quiet and disconsolate. A side we had expected to beat had outfought us on a slow attritional wicket. Everyone was reconnecting with the feelings of defeat in Sri Lanka, and most guys realised we had to change. The two main casualties were Matthew Hoggard and Steve Harmison who had struggled to get anything out of the slow wicket. These were two big decisions because they had been two very influential bowlers for England in the 2005 Ashes series, not to mention before and afterwards. Those two bowlers being dropped brought it to the front of everyone's mind that the 2005 era was over and we had to move on.

On the batting front, I couldn't believe how relaxed I was when batting. I was at peace with myself, especially in the first innings, where I got stuck in for a session, scoring 43 before maybe getting a little ahead of myself against Daniel Vettori and getting the only ball that turned in the game just after lunch. In the second innings, although I couldn't have done too much with that ball from Mills, I probably wasn't as switched on as I could have been. I wasn't in my zone where I move early, keep still and let the ball come, and maybe I paid the price.

As with all England teams though, we were incredibly motivated to respond to this setback, and so often a team which has those thoughts performs well. We won the Second Test largely thanks to the new-ball bowling of Jimmy Anderson who took five wickets in New Zealand's first innings, and of Ryan Sidebottom who took five in their second. When conditions allow him to swing the ball for a long time, Anderson is as threatening as anyone in world cricket. If he wasn't quite so effective in his second innings, it was because he was the recipient of a football-induced ankle injury. Our medical staff had just relented about letting us play football – and when Anderson tripped over, with nobody within ten yards of him, you could see the shock-waves go through the medical team. But they strapped up his ankle, and Anderson bowled through it, just like the bowlers of old say they used to do.

Tim Ambrose's hundred in our first innings was another factor in our win. He had taken over from Matt Prior after the tour of Sri Lanka and right from the start I enjoyed fielding at first slip next to him. He has a refreshingly old-fashioned attitude: instead of electrolyte drinks and Caesar salads, it's cups of coffee and rolled-up cigarettes. But he impressed everyone on that trip with the softness of his hands when keeping and his aggression when he shared the match-winning partnership with Paul Collingwood in the Second Test.

When I batted though, I felt nervous in my first innings, and struggled to get in that calm place that I have been in lately, and in the end perished playing a shot I shouldn't have and getting out softly. I was so pissed off with myself it was unreal. That feeling of utter frustration and feeling sorry for yourself is so debilitating.

Thankfully, the second day in Wellington was far better and I took a couple of catches in helping us get a useful 140–run lead. In my diary entry for 14 March, I wrote:

> Tomorrow is an important day for me, and I have to go out there and get a score, but the only way that I will do that is by sticking to my game-plan, getting in the zone, being patient to every ball, not getting emotional or frustrated, and playing each and every ball on its merits. The other key is to keep being positive in mind. It is so easy to be thinking negative thoughts about what might happen in the future, and let a hundred things get into your mind rather than watching each and every ball like it is your last, and backing your game. That is all you can do. Remember when you wake up in the morning to be grateful for everything you have in your life, kiss Sam and Ruth goodbye, enjoy the fact that you are fortunate enough to be representing your country, doing something you love. Enjoy the fact that tomorrow may be the day that we go a long way to winning the game. Be happy that you have great mates. Be excited about the challenge, and let instinct take over.

Having spent much of the night tossing and turning, wondering what lay in store for me on the third day, I went out there and played pretty well. I wasn't hitting the ball quite as well as I would have wanted but a battling 44 was enough to get us into a position to win the game, as well as keep my place in the side. In the end, it was a really satisfying win after a long, tough, barren spell for the lads, and the series was level at one-all.

But I still had not made a hundred, and now 15 Tests had passed without one. I still hadn't made a fifty in this series. Time was running out and the Third Test in Napier was going to be the last of the series, and maybe my last for England for a long time, perhaps ever. Undoubtedly that match saw the most nerve-wracking and gut-wrenching days of my career.

In the build-up I was distracted by the need to get runs, even when I was away from the ground. When Ruth and I took Sam to a park near the hotel in Napier, she would look up to see me playing shadow shots or fiddling with my grip when I was meant to be playing with Sam on the swing. It was the only time in my life I have struggled to sleep. I knew it was do-or-die time. My team-mates knew it. The media knew it.

Your team-mates in those circumstances are not sure what to say to motivate you. But I can remember one conversation in the middle of a net practice before the game. Collingwood came down the net and said to me: 'Straussy, you're not playing your game.' I said: 'I've been working for three months to improve.' He said: 'I know your strengths are pulls and cuts and I've hardly seen you play one all tour.' In some ways those words almost underlined the point that I was in the last-chance saloon. But it was reassuring that one of my mates had taken enough interest to think about my plight and say something.

My diary entry on the eve of the Third Test was more upbeat than I actually felt.

So here we are again, set for the Final Test match of the series, a match that both sides desperately want to win in order to win the series, and for England the end of another long hard winter. For me, I need a score, both for myself and our chances of winning the series. I feel in reasonable nick, but the key is to be in the right mindset from ball one. Remember what works for you. Get the trigger in early, keep still and play the ball on its merits. Have a clear mind and stay in your bubble, whether you are scoring quickly or not. Now is not the time to be thinking about technique or anything other than watching the ball like a hawk . . . it is too important a game for that. Remember to enjoy the occasion, Strauss, and come out fighting. These are the sort of games that people remember, the sort of games that winners come to the table, these are the sort of occasions that get your blood flowing, and now is the time to show everyone your class. Enjoy the five days, and remember that your beautiful family are right there with you. Be thankful.

Not surprisingly, given the stresses and lack of sleep, I felt tired on the first morning of the Final Test in Napier and before I had woken up properly I was back in the dressing-room, out for nought, caught in the gully off the debutant swing bowler Tim Southee. In the dressing-room I was absolutely distraught – the claps on the shoulder and the 'bad lucks' did not register at all. All I could do was stare at my bat and think it was coming to an end.

That night I had a dinner with my wife that was in complete contrast to the dinner I had enjoyed with her after scoring my hundred on debut for England. Then I was thinking about heading into a world I knew nothing about. This time I was seriously contemplating that the journey might well be over and I would have to come to terms with life back in the county system.

For some reason, by the time I started my second innings, all that stress and pressure of feeling that I had to perform had left my body. With only one innings left I felt it was too much to expect to pull it out of the bag, so I was just going to enjoy my last innings for England. What was meant to be was meant to be, and worrying about it was not going to help.

As I went out to bat, my first priority was not to bag a pair. I wasn't nervous, and my ninth or tenth ball was a juicy half-volley on my legs from Chris Martin, and I was up and running. I was helped by the fact that I had to bat for only one session that evening, so once I got to 20 or so I had the goal of getting through to close of play, by when I had reached 42. That night I felt that it could have been all over by now – but I was still fighting and had still got a chance. Realistically, though, it was going to take a hundred, not a fifty, to keep my England career going.

Walking out the next day with 42 to my name, I felt a mixture of hope and excitement, two feelings I hadn't experienced much in the recent past. I flashed at a wide ball early on, and it went past gully, exactly where I had been caught in the first innings, and I remember thinking this might be my day. I pushed Martin down the ground to reach 50 and I was focusing on what the New Zealand bowlers were trying to do, and for the first time in a long time I felt in control of my destiny.

As I hadn't made a hundred for 15 Tests, and for 19 months, the last thing I was going to do was give it away. They had two spinners in Daniel Vettori and Jeetan Patel, and an old ball, but I was not going to take any sort of risk. I was not going to make the same mistake as against India at Lord's the previous summer when I tried to force the pace to reach my century and was out for 96. So I had to endure a couple of very spicy overs with the second new ball from Martin when 97, and I played and missed two or three times. Then came a wide delivery which I drove off the front foot through the covers. Now I think about it, for the first time since, it was the same shot which had brought up my hundred on my Test debut at Lord's.

I finished that day – only the third day of the game as the first innings were over so quickly – on 173 not out. I felt as proud as I have ever done. When you dig really deep, sometimes it is for your team, sometimes for yourself. In the dressing-room everyone said pretty much the same thing: that it had taken a lot of guts and my character had come through. More than anything, performing in those circumstances made me think that when the going gets tough, that is what motivates and brings out the best in me. And, when you are armed with that knowledge, it gives you huge confidence for difficult times in the future.

When I got back to the hotel that evening I felt a warm glow at the back of my neck, stiffness in my limbs, an ache in my lower back from bending over all day, tingling legs from the mandatory ice-bath up to my waist, and such total mental fatigue that even constructing a sentence was hard work. All those wonderful by-products of scoring a Test hundred. We had some room service and I'm not sure whether Ruth tucked Sam or me up in bed first. I think I was asleep by 8.30 or 9 o'clock.

As always after a big innings, you wake up during the night and replay your favourite shots in a mental highlights package. The way the bowlers were bowling; the shot to reach my hundred, hitting Daniel Vettori – by some irony, the captain of Northern Districts, whenever his New Zealand duties allowed – over mid-wicket to reach 150; and that flash wide of gully when I was 43. This time the recollection did not make me sit bolt upright or bring on a cold sweat, only a pleasant smile.

England v New Zealand
Third Test, Napier, 22-26 March 2008

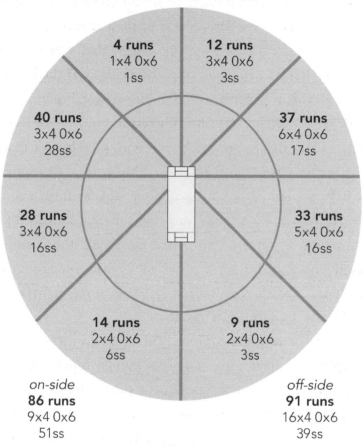

4 runs
1x4 0x6
1ss

12 runs
3x4 0x6
3ss

40 runs
3x4 0x6
28ss

37 runs
6x4 0x6
17ss

28 runs
3x4 0x6
16ss

33 runs
5x4 0x6
16ss

14 runs
2x4 0x6
6ss

9 runs
2x4 0x6
3ss

on-side
86 runs
9x4 0x6
51ss

off-side
91 runs
16x4 0x6
39ss

AJ Strauss
2nd Innings 177

Runs	177	Scoring shots (ss)		Non-scoring shots	
Balls faced	343	**1s**	53	**0s**	253
Strike rate	51.60	**2s**	12		
Scoring shots	90	**4s**	25		

2
UNDERCURRENT

It is amazing how one innings can completely alter your mindset, rescue your career, and change public perceptions. My hundred in Napier had – if only temporarily – taken my name off the England-batsmen-in-danger list. Suddenly I was back in favour, with the press and the public, for coming through the toughest of times. In a lot of ways the pressure was now off, but I knew that I had to push myself really hard in future to ensure I did not get into the same situation again. One visit to the last-chance saloon was quite enough, thank you.

The media have to have somebody on that England-batsmen-in-danger list, however, and when the series in New Zealand was over and we had returned to England, their attention turned to the next batsman struggling for form: the captain, Michael Vaughan. He had endured three difficult Tests in New Zealand, scoring 123 runs in his six innings as opening batsman.

It is never easy when you feel your position in the side is under threat, and being captain makes the situation even harder. Vaughan had come through a couple of periods of poor form before. During the 2004–5 series in South Africa, as an example, he did not score a fifty except in the Johannesburg Test, where he made one in each innings; then he had a couple of low-scoring Tests against Australia before rebounding with his 166 in the third match at Old Trafford. If any one batting contribution turned the tables in that

Ashes series in England's favour, it was Vaughan's century, when he dominated the Australians in every way.

In New Zealand, however, it had become clear that the captaincy was weighing on his shoulders. He had always been incredibly good at making light of the burden, and continuously reinforcing positive thoughts in his players' minds. In the first book I wrote, *Coming into Play*, I tried to describe him as someone who, if surrounded by enemy soldiers and armed himself with only a toy gun, would say, 'Okay, here's how we are going to counter-attack, it's going to be a real breeze and we'll have a laugh along the way.' And it is true: he is, in general, a very optimistic person, blessed with the amazing ability to make people relax in panic-inducing situations with the odd comment here or there.

Clearly, a lot of elements or ingredients go into being the successful captain of an international cricket team: form on the pitch; tactical nous; a longer-term strategy; communication skills. But, above all, he must have the respect and the willingness of the players to play for him; and throughout his time as England captain, nobody had any trouble about playing under Vaughan. I will always feel a large amount of loyalty to him. During my run-drought in 2006 he always wanted me in his team, and I believe he was pretty instrumental in bringing me back into the England side for the Test series in New Zealand.

But towards the back end of the New Zealand tour, for the first time, he looked tired, and I suspect that must have had some-thing to do with proceedings behind the scenes, specifically his relationship with Peter Moores and the ECB. His second innings swish in the Third Test at Napier – the cue for the start of my career-saving 177 – was the sign of a tired mind, which I recognised.

In some ways I found it quite surprising that Vaughan and Moores found conflict in their relationship as England's captain and coach. On the surface they are both people who are passionate about the England cricket team. They are both eager to communicate, and talk honestly and openly.

I had first encountered Moores when Middlesex played the Sussex team of whom he was coach, and we generally lost to them, which irked me hugely. Partly it was because Sussex were local rivals, and partly because they seemed to be a team without natural match winners except for their Pakistani legspinner Mushtaq Ahmed. But Sussex always seemed to be very well drilled, and a tight unit. Normally in county cricket the away team arrive at a ground in the mornings before the home side, but every time we turned up in the mornings at Hove we would find Moores already in the nets, giving somebody throw-downs. As Middlesex then were in a slightly shambolic state, this highlighted how far behind the leading county teams we were.

When Moores moved to the Academy and became coach of the England A tours to the West Indies and Bangladesh, all the items of news, talk and gossip that we heard added up to a very positive feedback. The other players in the England team and I realised that he was a man who knew the way the game should be played, while his communication skills were in contrast to his predecessor, Duncan Fletcher, who was taciturn by nature and never wasted a word. The players on the fringes of the England team must have appreciated Moores' style and methods, which enabled them to know where they stood.

The best things about Moores during his time as England's coach were his energy and enthusiasm. He had one of those batteries which never runs down. He was so passionate about the game that he could never stop thinking about it. I can remember about two months into his reign, which began in April 2007, some players remarking on the sheer enormity of his energy and wondering how long he would be able to sustain it. But he did sustain it, at least until almost the end of his reign.

As someone who played under Fletcher and Moores, I do not think that what we did at training sessions varied much from one to the other. It was not so much what Moores did but how he did it. On the training ground he was a constant presence. He would check up on the slip-practice session, then the next minute he would go over to the group working on catching skiers, and the next minute he would be watching Monty Panesar bowl walk-throughs and offering some worthwhile tips. It was all good advice; but I suppose the sheer volume of the information passed on meant that over time its effect became diluted.

For myself, I had a pretty good relationship with Moores. He was always very supportive about my getting back into the side after I had been dropped for the tour of Sri Lanka in late 2007, and at the start of the tour of New Zealand he had come up with valuable advice about how I should practise more purposefully. He always believed in training hard and, given that I had just had three months off when I was out of the England side, I was more inclined to do it than those who had done an energy-sapping tour of Sri Lanka and then gone to New Zealand for two Twenty20 internationals, which we won, and five one-day internationals, which we lost 3–1 with a tie in Napier. I was happy simply to be back in the fold and had no qualms about the constant demands.

To be fair to Moores and Vaughan, the players knew very little of their uneasy relationship. The pair kept their thoughts to themselves and in the team environment they supported each other one hundred per cent. But by the end of our tour of New Zealand, if not before, there was an undercurrent that the England team was not a happy place.

With the benefit of hindsight, we can see that the role of the England coach changed when Fletcher resigned, just before he was pushed, and Moores took over. It is fair to say that Moores' job description was in effect that of England team director. Part of this new job was to challenge the players in such a way that they moved forwards, to get them out of their comfort zones, and all of this was a very worthy goal. But Vaughan had come out of a different relationship with Fletcher. As England's coach from 1999 until 2007, Fletcher had fought many battles behind the scenes with the ECB. He had had a major input into all the planning off the field, but as soon as the team went on to the field the captain – firstly Nasser Hussain, then Vaughan from 2003 – had his say.

I can only assume that the cause of the conflict between Moores and Vaughan was that each one wanted to be in control.

My diary was full of the joys of spring in April 2008. Reading it through again I can almost hear the birds singing in the trees and see bunny rabbits playing in the fields:

16 April 2008

Here we are, it is the morning of the first championship match of the season, and generally I feel pretty excited about the season. It has been a relaxing few weeks, basking in my century, which is pretty unique. Usually any satisfaction from an innings only lasts until the next one begins, but on this occasion I have had the best part of a month with only the sweet feeling of being in form, and images of me raising my bat going through my head.

I suppose the danger is that I can take things for granted a little going back to county cricket, and just expect things to happen. What I have to make sure of is that I apply myself as much as during a Test match. If it's nipping around or hard to score, I have to be prepared to take my medicine and do the hard yards, and if that is the case, then I have to enjoy the fact that I am pissing the opposition off. If I get the method right, then I will get runs, and the method is dependent on my mindset. I feel really positive about this season. Family life is good, I feel in good form, let's hope for a cracker of a year. 2008 is my year!

A month later, the birds were still singing in the trees, if not quite with the same gusto. Middlesex were in the second division of the county championship, and promotion was to remain elusive, but we were to make some forward strides in limited-overs cricket during the season, especially the Twenty20 competition which we won. Although I didn't play much part in that achievement, I helped to set the ball rolling in our 50–over cricket by scoring 163 in our Friends Provident game at The Oval. I was pleased to hear it was Middlesex's highest innings in one-day cricket, although I have to add that the boundary was quite short on one side, and one of Surrey's bowlers was 40 years old. The former England allrounder Chris Lewis, who hadn't played county cricket for eight years, had been brought out of retirement.

14 May 2008

It has been an entertaining month, with some notable success (163 v Surrey) mixed in with some average scores (plenty of 20s and 30s). I have been really happy with the way I have been hitting the ball, but I suppose I am a little disappointed about not going on when I feel as though I have done quite a lot of work avoiding getting out for those sorts of scores. Mostly though, I have got out to decent balls, and haven't given it away too often, so can't be too upset with myself.

The First Test versus New Zealand starts tomorrow, and I am feeling pretty relaxed, quite excited about what is to come, and generally grateful that I am still involved in the set-up. For the first time in a long time, I am not particularly worried about justifying my place in the side, and I go into the match feeling really upbeat. The danger of course with that is that I don't apply myself quite as much as I should, get a little easy on myself, and end up putting more pressure on by not performing well enough. The reality though is that to look at things that way is pretty negative and not particularly helpful. My mantra this season is to look on the bright side of everything, not dwell on negatives, and be grateful. I do have to put pressure on myself, but that can come from match situations, and hunger to make the most of decent form rather than clutching for my place.

I feel that I know the New Zealand bowlers pretty well now, and there aren't going to be too many surprises, but as we found out in NZ, they have the ability to wear opponents down, and I can't fall into that trap. Remember your game plan, Strauss, play straight or legside, be patient and there is a big score waiting for you this week. Remember what happened four years ago as well, great time for a repeat.

For those of us who had played with Vaughan for a long time, and found him an inspiring captain and close friend, it was very satisfying to see him make a hundred in the First Test against New Zealand at Lord's, knowing that all was not right with him. But the match turned out to be a bit of a damp squib with neither side able to spend enough time on the pitch in one go to really grab the game by the scruff of the neck. Given the conditions though, batting was pretty tricky, and the continual rain interruptions didn't exactly help matters. Generally I was really happy with the way I played. I was extremely patient, only scoring my fifty off 150 balls, which is as slow as it comes for me. The great thing, though, is that I knew by now that if I limited the areas in which I looked to score, then I would get runs. Occasionally I might get a decent ball but, by and large, I had reached a stage when I would only get myself out when I was looking to play shots that I did not need to: for example, hitting through extra-cover.

The Second Test at Old Trafford will go down as England's fifth highest run-chase: a pretty special achievement, regardless of the opposition. We celebrated that night but at the back of our minds, as we sipped our beers, we knew we should never have had to chase as many as 294 in the fourth innings. Although the pitch was quick and bouncy, we struggled to bowl New Zealand out in their first innings, with Ross Taylor scoring a magnificent 154. We were then bundled out for 200 by Daniel Vettori on a wicket that was beginning to take spin. In spite of the fact that New Zealand had no out-and-out quick bowlers or attacking threats, we could not take the initiative in our first innings and up the tempo against their very disciplined medium-pacers. All our batsmen found it very frustrating to block out maidens when everyone felt we should be pushing on.

Before the game I had reasoned it would be a free-scoring affair because of the pitch. I had told myself – or, at any rate, my diary – that it would be sensible to play the percentages and hang in for when the wicket flattened out. The last thing I wanted to do was go easy on myself. I was in decent nick and had to do everything I could to stay in it. I even told myself to remember how hard it can be to score runs at times and to be grateful that life was a little easier now. My last sentence before the Test was: 'A hundred this week, please.'

But I was out for 60 and it was only thanks to some late hitting from Stuart Broad that we passed the follow-on figure of 182, and were all out for 202. I think we were guilty of being disrespectful to their bowling attack. Jacob Oram, I believe at that time, had the second best economy-rate in Test cricket. Martin, Mills and Iain O'Brien drew on their domestic experience of strong and freezing winds to maintain their accuracy. Ultimately our frustration gave way to poor shots and a sub-standard total, 179 behind New Zealand on first innings.

For saving the situation we owed a lot to Vaughan and the tactical nous which is part of the make-up of a successful captain. Some nervy New Zealand batting helped: they were not used to being in a position to dictate terms. Monty Panesar exploited this nerviness, bowling downwind even more effectively than Vettori had done and taking his best Test figures of six for 37, including his hundredth wicket for England.

From the moment we walked out on the field to chase 294 we

knew that positive cricket would get us over the line. By the close of play on the third evening we had taken the score to 76 for one. On the fourth and final morning the captain continually pushed me to run hard and put the New Zealand fielders under pressure. The wind was howling from the Warwick Road end towards the Brian Statham end: so when any fielder threw from the Brian Statham end, we could take an extra run on his arm. Vaughan scored 48, and his tactical contribution should not be underestimated.

My hundred was one of the more satisfying of my career although, looking back, my first innings was almost as important as the hundred because the wicket was at its most difficult then. What constantly surprises me about scoring runs is how easy it feels. You are in control of events, you have no worries about your technique, you have no fear of failure. It is like riding a perfect wave, or hitting a perfect golf shot. It feels effortless and rhythmical without you having to put any thought into it.

Since Napier I had felt completely comfortable about my game. It had been like returning to the house where you grew up. You had forgotten it, but immediately you return you remember the place where you had fought as kids, or the toy car you had left under the bed. When I made my hundred at Old Trafford it was as though I was on autopilot. My prayer was answered.

For this reason, when I wrote up my diary, I knew the entry about my hundred at Old Trafford would not be much use in the future. I might look to find a secret there, a little gem that would kick-start me back into form. But I don't think entries like that hold the answers. The bits which are worth looking back on are the innings I had played in New Zealand, when I was scrapping for runs and trying to turn things around.

Collingwood and Ian Bell saw us home in the Second Test by six wickets. They had replaced Vaughan and me as numbers one and two on the England-batsmen-in-danger list, even though Bell had scored a hundred in the same Napier Test as I did. They both responded in the right fashion and saw us home on the stroke of tea, and in the process they reminded me how precious form is, how hard it is to get there, and therefore how vital it is to make the most of it. I remembered my third Test against New Zealand in the series when I made my debut in 2004. Then I let little thoughts into my head about how I was due a failure at Test level, and funnily enough it happened.

I was in no mood to do that again as we went to Trent Bridge for the last of six consecutive Tests against New Zealand. I knew their bowlers, I knew how they were trying to get me out, I had a game-plan for each of them, and I was in nick. If ever there was a time to nail it, it was then. I decided that, regardless of how many runs I got, I would be seriously pissed off if I gave it away. If I was dismissed by a good ball, then 'no worries', as the Aussies say, but if I gave it away while in good form, that would be inexcusable.

The final Test against New Zealand turned out to be a one-sided affair, with their spirit having been broken by the defeat at Old Trafford. I scored 37 in quite testing conditions before giving it away in exactly the fashion I told myself not to, which took the gloss off what was a great series for me. In the end, I won the man of the series award to complete a remarkable turnaround from six months previously.

Trent Bridge offered a perfect opportunity for our swing bowlers to test the techniques of batsmen who were used to playing Kookaburra balls which do not swing for long periods. Anderson took their first six wickets, and seven for 43 in all in their first innings, and it was another of those occasions when he looked as threatening as anybody in world cricket.

Fielding at first slip can be pretty tedious at times, for example in the subcontinent and on some pitches now in the Caribbean. You feel the ball is never going to come to you, which makes it very difficult because you are not fully switched on if the ball does come. For most of the series in New Zealand, and again at Trent Bridge, it was the other way round: you felt almost every ball was going to come to you because every ball from Anderson and Ryan Sidebottom was in the area where the batsman might nick it. You were always prepared for the sight and the sound of the nick that batsmen dread and fielders anticipate.

It was fitting that Sidebottom bowled New Zealand out in their second innings to cap his twelve months back in the team. He is one of the bigger contradictions I have come across in an England shirt. Off the field he is very quiet, well-mannered and modest. On the field he turns into a raging lion. He gets so frustrated when he sees a batsman play and miss, or when a fielder misses the ball, or when an edge goes between third slip and gully, that you can almost see his blood boiling. I have felt for my safety standing at first slip when he has picked the ball up in his follow-through and hurled it back – a sign of how desperate his passion was to play for England after so long on the county treadmill.

Duncan Fletcher was always keen on bowlers who were 85 mph plus. From the outside it looked as though Sidebottom was a bit below this threshold, and when he first played for England in 2001 – against Pakistan at Lord's – he struggled to swing the ball back into right-handers. But increasingly loud reports came out of Trent Bridge after he had moved there from Yorkshire: I remember speaking to Stephen Fleming when he said that Sidebottom was swinging it and at good pace. One or two eyebrows were raised when he was brought back for the last three Tests against West Indies in 2007: calling up a 30-year-old could have been considered a step backwards. But from his first over at Headingley we realised he was different from the original Ryan Sidebottom. He had fine control over his length, and sometimes swung the ball dramatically, and the West Indians all struggled against his over-the-wicket angle. A player who had gone away to learn his game in differing conditions had come back a far more complete bowler. The sheer number of county cricketers makes it easier for the England selectors to discard players, when the objective is to find the next Ian Botham or Bob Willis. Sidebottom, and to a certain extent Matthew Hoggard, have shown the value of going back to county cricket and learning the game in a less pressurised environment.

At the end of the two consecutive series against New Zealand the England players felt we had done enough to justify a 4–1 result overall, and we took confidence from our convincing victory into the series against South Africa. But a 3–1 defeat by New Zealand in the one-day series – after England had won the first game at Chester-le-Street emphatically – reminded us that things were not rosy. There was still an undercurrent, a feeling that we were not playing well. The series against South Africa would tell us where we really were as a Test match side.

3
RESIGNATION

After the Test series against New Zealand, I was called up as a standby for Alastair Cook in the one-day internationals, not having played a 50-over game for England since the 2007 World Cup. I ended up having to go to every ground without ever playing, which was a bit of a pain, while at the same time playing Twenty20 for Middlesex. What was meant to be a quiet, relaxing time ended up being not quite so, although without having to play high-pressure cricket, I still felt quite rested.

The domestic Twenty20 did not go particularly well for me personally, although Middlesex qualified for finals day at the Rose Bowl, which was to have its consequences in the months ahead. Along the way Middlesex unearthed some talent: Dawid Malan, who had been born in London and grown up in South Africa, scored a hundred against Lancashire which prompted Andrew Flintoff to shake him by the hand. I think I went into the Twenty20 with the wrong attitude. I got pissed off when I got out, rather than just enjoying the liberation that comes from being able to break the shackles. It was not the end of the world, but the lesson was learned.

As South Africa were rivalling Australia to become the number one Test side, I was almost as excited as if it was going to be an Ashes series. Also, there is something about playing a team that you have done well against previously that makes them feel familiar and welcome, and the 2004–5 series in South Africa had been my best abroad. I was given the chance to play against them in one of their two warm-up matches, against Middlesex at Uxbridge, and I accepted. I had lost my batting rhythm after twelfth-manning for England and playing Twenty20 for my county. On paper the South African pace attack looked as fierce as anything I had seen; as an opening batsman I was going to get them at their best; and here was the opportunity to watch them, then go away and do some specific practice before the First Test.

Genuine pace always causes problems, but also provides opportunities, and I knew that as long as I was in the right frame of mind, then the pace aspect wouldn't be too much of a problem. In the Uxbridge game I only scored 29, before being dismissed off an inside edge on to my jumper which carried through to Mark Boucher, but I had the chance to play all three of their fast bowlers without their getting an advantage over me. Between them Dale Steyn, Makhaya Ntini and Morne Morkel offered swing and skiddiness at high pace; an angle going across the left-handers and bounce; and, in Morkel's case, height and pace that are similar to Steve Harmison's and few others in world cricket, but at least he was young and liable to bowl some loose stuff. These three were supported by Jacques Kallis and Paul Harris, a regulation left-arm spinner who usually bowled wider of off stump than Vettori.

As I saw the forthcoming encounter after the Middlesex game, it was bound to be aggressive, competitive cricket. But there was absolutely no reason why I shouldn't get loads of runs in the four Tests, provided I was patient, played to my game-plan, and didn't get sucked in. That had got to be my goal for the series.

On another note, Ruth was due with our second child during the Lord's Test. Fortunately her mother had arrived from Australia so she was much more relaxed. I was secretly hoping for a century and being able to attend the birth. It was a hell of a lot to ask but, as I told my diary on the eve of the match, if you don't ask . . .

I suppose one out of two was not too bad. Being there for the birth on Monday was fantastic, and Ruth's timing was absolutely first-rate. As for the century bit, who knows what might have happened if I hadn't been given out lbw to a ball that pitched miles outside leg stump. Despite being pretty disappointed with the decision, I was really happy with the way I played after we were put in on a wicket that offered a little for the bowlers. I felt right back into my bubble, with very similar feelings to how I played against New Zealand. I was patient, only scoring 8 off my first 53 balls, but didn't worry about that at all. In fact, I remember whistling a song continuously throughout the innings, which shows how relaxed I was.

Then we played some of our best cricket for a long time as Kevin Pietersen and Ian Bell batted exceptionally well, and South Africa could not respond in their first innings. Bell's 199 was the best I had seen him play. He was under pressure going into the series, but those who had been crying out for him to make a match-defining contribution got what they wanted. Bell is one of those players that punters get frustrated about because he makes the game look so easy when he is batting well, so that it is hard to comprehend when he gets out. But, in spite of being so talented, he goes through the same mental battles as everybody else. He struggles against certain bowlers, and he goes through periods of bad form, and he has difficulty in realising the high expectations that people have of him. At his best – as he was in this innings at Lord's – he is composed, in control, with good body language, and all class against fast bowling.

Sharing a large partnership with Pietersen is not easy, yet he and Bell put on 286, by far England's highest for the fourth wicket against South Africa ever. Given the way Pietersen plays, he is rightly the centre of public attention, and the opposition as well focus on him: his size and presence at the wicket, his exaggerated mannerisms, they all demand everyone's attention. At the other end you have got to decide whether to play the same game and take it to the opposition; or, to play the role of his wing-man, give him the strike, and calm him down if necessary – a role that Paul Collingwood always plays so well. In this innings, it was a huge credit to Bell that he seemed able to play both of these roles. He got Pietersen on strike by nurdling singles, yet he also played some shots that were as memorable as his partner's audacious drives and flicks. South Africa had no answer to the class of both batsmen on that wicket.

Making a team follow on is, normally, very motivating for the side which enforces it. They are in control and they only need ten more bits of good cricket to win the game. The other side of the coin is that the bowlers are tired and the opposition are doubly determined not to lose those ten wickets. And when we took the field we knew we would not be helped by the pitch. In 2006 and 2007 we had found that the Lord's Test pitches would not deteriorate: they just lost their zip and died, without giving any help to Monty Panesar or any other bowler. So we needed something to set off a chain reaction that would lead us to victory.

For South Africa, 346 behind on the first innings, Graeme Smith and Neil McKenzie illustrated the value of an opening partnership. How many Test sides have lost a series when the opening partnership has fired? A successful opening pair enable their team to get over the new ball, settle the butterflies in the dressing-room, and knock the life out of a bowling attack which was full of expectation. At no time did South Africa's batsmen look to take the game to us, both in that Test and in the series as a whole, but their very solid professional cricket wore us down.

Smith's century was a precursor for the rest of the series as he led from the front. McKenzie left the ball very well. Standing at first slip I found he had the most annoying habit of looking as though he was going to play the ball when he was actually leaving it – like England's wicket-keeper/batsman Jack Russell used to do. At first we were not sure whether it was a ruse, but by the end it was clear he had good judgment outside off stump and any interest in a slip catch had subsided by the end. South Africa's third century in their second innings, by Hashim Amla, was equally impressive. We felt he would be vulnerable to the short ball but he stood up to the barrage and played some fine shots. He was more composed than the player we had seen in South Africa in 2004–5, with a less exaggerated backlift, and he had an excellent series.

We spent three days in the field at Lord's trying to dismiss South Africa twice. In such circumstances it is not the fielding, but the expectation of further fielding, that makes you tired. When you wake up in the morning and have not taken many wickets the previous day, you are subdued. At the warm-up the bowlers are trying to conserve energy; the touch rugby is played at a sedate pace as you realise you will spend six hours in the field. As the day goes on, the levels of collective energy go up and down. If you are not taking wickets, the levels are low, and the hour after lunch is the biggest test. When you are digesting pudding and coffee, that is the danger time for fielders.

The final session, which in theory ought to be the most tiring, is often not so because there is light at the end of the tunnel. With only two hours to go, an extra spring comes into everyone's step, and often a second new ball is around the corner. Thus a day in the field goes in fits and starts. For slip fielders, the hardest part is continuously concentrating – not the physical exertion which there is for bowlers and cover fielders. We know one lapse could cost us the game. Yet if you stand in the same position for six or seven hours without the ball once coming in your direction, it is very hard to convince yourself that the next ball is going to come – and by then the ball is likely to be old, and you have to stand that much closer, and you are genuinely surprised when the ball at last comes in your direction. It is then that the best slip fielders overcome the feeling of panic, and track the ball for as long as possible before committing themselves. If you are startled, you snatch at it, and more often than not the ball lands on the deck and you end up hoping that a big hole will engulf you.

By the time I went off to see my baby delivered, it was pretty apparent that we had contracted the disease of flat-wicketitis. Nothing was happening, and even Vaughan's inventiveness was having no effect. I remember Collingwood saying at lunch-time on the final day: 'I'd get your missus to ring and say she's in labour.' An hour later, when the note came on to say that she was actually in labour, I didn't believe it because I thought Collingwood had fixed it. Ruth gave birth to our second son that afternoon as the First Test ground to a draw in my absence. We named him Luca.

So long as we were winning, against New Zealand, or drawing, against South Africa, the undercurrent in the England environment remained just that: an undercurrent. But when we lost the Second Test to South Africa, the current came to the surface, and once that happened, there was no going back.

Lord's finished on the Monday evening, and the Second Test started on the Friday a couple of hundred miles away at Headingley. After bowling and fielding for three straight days, I was worried that we would not be rested enough, and when we met up at the team hotel – I came up later than the others after spending a bit of time with Ruth and making some domestic arrangements for our new arrival – it was clear from our bowlers' faces that they had not recovered from Lord's. Sidebottom, for whom Headingley was his first home and who had swung the ball so much against West Indies the year before, was not only tired but less than fully fit. Even James Anderson, who normally has a spring in his step, was anything but energetic as we had our first practice session.

In addition, I think I was listening to Radio 5 on the motorway up to Leeds when it was announced that a Nottinghamshire bowler called Darren Pattinson was joining the England Test squad. Never having met him or played against him, one of my concerns was that I would meet him in the team hotel and mistake him for an autograph-hunter.

It was a shock that Pattinson had been selected because England, previously during my time in the team, had been keen to select from a basic squad. This selection was more left-field. Headingley does encourage swing bowlers, so there have been players called up for Test matches there on a horses-for-courses basis, like Neil Mallender, Phil Newport, Mark Ilott and Steve Watkin, to name a few in the last 20 years. But, firstly, it soon became a massive talking-point in the media that this guy was to all intents and purposes Australian, and had never expressed an interest in representing England, although he had a British passport. Secondly, nobody in the England team had heard about this new kid at Nottinghamshire, and we hadn't even heard on the grapevine about how he bowled.

All this was grossly unfair on Pattinson. He clearly felt uncomfortable because of his nationality, or to be precise his Australian upbringing, and because he had no friends in the team: Sidebottom, also from Nottinghamshire, had been passed unfit, while Pattinson and Stuart Broad had not played a championship match together at that stage. Pattinson was made the scapegoat for our ten-wicket defeat by South Africa, but he bowled okay, and it was the batsmen who did not do their job. Besides, you do not expect debutants to win you games.

There was another surprise concerning Pattinson. He had been announced as a swing bowler, ideal for Headingley, and when he pitched a full length he did outswing it a bit. But as the game and the ball wore on, it became apparent that he was more one of your Aussie hit-the-deck bowlers. The selectors did not have much evidence to go on – Pattinson had played only 11 first-class matches, and half of them were for Victoria – and they might have been influenced by Trent Bridge, his home-from-home ground, where the ball swings for everybody.

But the main reason we lost, as I said, was that we did not bat well enough in our first innings. We were not at the races on the opening day and were bowled out in 52 overs on a pretty decent wicket, some of us playing some pretty average shots. Then the South African batsmen carried on from where they had left off at Lord's and out-performed as a batting unit. We had cameos, we had starts, we had excellent hundreds, but we did not perform often enough in this series as a unit. And the South Africans played attritional cricket without the Master of Attrition, Kallis, making a big score (he topped their bowling averages but averaged only 14 with the bat). Ashwell Prince had made a century in the first innings at Lord's, and at Headingley he ground us down with 149 while A.B. de Villiers made 174. Together, with patience, they batted us out of the game, then we surrendered in our second innings when everyone was completely knackered after fielding for two more days.

I was fairly philosophical about my batting, as I battled well for 27 in the first innings before getting out to Morkel around the wicket, and then got a brute of a ball from Ntini from around the wicket in the second innings. Generally they were two good balls, although clearly those round-the-wicket back-of-a-length balls were something that I had to address.

As if there had not been controversy enough in the Headingley Test, what with Pattinson's selection and England's defeat, we had two catches that never were. They highlighted the problems of using technology in cricket and of players judging catches for themselves.

On the first day I edged a ball to de Villiers at third slip. I saw him dive for it, and I saw the ball had not gone cleanly into his hands before it was obscured by his body. Although the South Africans went off to celebrate, it became blatantly clear from the replays on the electronic screen that the ball had touched the ground; and de Villiers, one of the best fielders in the world, looked sheepish. To be fair, he came up at lunch-time and apologised and said he thought that he had caught it.

Vaughan too had some words to say at lunch-time, in his case with South Africa's captain, Smith. Then, in the last session of the opening day, the whole situation was turned on its head when Vaughan took a catch at mid-off offered by Amla. My feeling was and is that Vaughan genuinely thought he had caught it, and he did not drop the ball then scoop it up, but the television replays were inconclusive. And after what had gone on with de Villiers, the South Africans were not happy that Vaughan had claimed the catch and some tension broke out between the two teams.

In the end, it all seemed to illustrate the fact that there is often no way of deciding whether the ball has carried to a fielder or not. There is a bigger role to be played by better technology in cricket, because fielders cannot always be one hundred per cent sure when they catch balls very close to the ground. The only certainty is that you look pretty bad when you claim a catch that isn't.

After we had gone 1–0 down at Headingley, Vaughan was pretty disconsolate in the build-up to the Third Test at Edgbaston. It was not so much that we had lost, by ten wickets, but the way we had lost. We had shown little fight in being dismissed for 202 and 327 on what rolled out into a flat wicket. As always when England go behind, we felt we needed to bounce back, to show we were better than we had been at Leeds. It is frustrating that we need to lose first before playing our best, but it was like that at Edgbaston in 2005 and that series turned out all right in the end.

On the eve of the Third Test in Birmingham I reflected in my diary:

This week is a massive one for the side and me personally. We desperately need to win to keep the series alive, and I feel as though I need runs to keep my good form this summer going. I haven't thought all that much about cricket over the last week or so as I have been at home with the kids, but I really need to get the juices going this week. We are entering a stage where we have been playing for quite a long time now without a long break, and it is easy to get into a 'just another game' mode. In fact this is not just another game. It is vitally important, and I need to contribute, as much for the team as myself. What is going to be really important is for me to put myself into the match situation, rather than worrying about my own runs etc., and think about my contribution being for the team.

My practice has been excellent running into the game, with plenty of practice and focus, but now I need to get myself into the right frame of mind in order to score runs this week. Remember: get trigger out the way, wait for the ball, play the percentages, and be patient. That will work more times than it doesn't.

I really fancy a big score this week. I am imagining lifting my bat to celebrate my hundred.

South Africa, unlike Australia in 2005, did not let us back into the series at Edgbaston. It was a perfect pitch for a Test match:

runs were scored, wickets fell at regular intervals and, as so often in those circumstances, it was a tight game with a close result. Andrew Flintoff bowled similarly to the way he had three years before on this ground. Then the culmination was his dismissal of Ricky Ponting. Now it was his dismissal of Kallis with a jaffa – a reverse-away-swinging yorker at great pace that hit his off stump – as he broke the spine of the South African innings just when Kallis was, at last, looking dangerous.

Getting 20 in both innings was a complete pain in the arse. Stepping on my stumps in the first innings was even more so because there are enough ways to get out as it is, and I had worked very hard to get to that score. In the second innings I was out to the same ball I had got out to at Headingley, back-of-a-length from over the wicket. I thought squaring my stance up had helped that situation, but I had to think about leaving everything short of a length, so I would not be drawn into a shot unnecessarily. It was more a problem of playing balls that I didn't need to, rather than a massive technical fault. You could never let your guard down against this South African attack as they were good enough to bowl you a good ball at any stage.

The highlight of our second innings was an incredibly gutsy innings from Collingwood, whose head was next on the chopping block at that time. His form had reached a point similar to mine in New Zealand: the last-chance saloon, the edge of the precipice. He came out playing his shots without a hint of nerves. When I spoke to him that evening, offering my congratulations for the character he showed, he said: 'In my mind it was already over and I wanted to go down guns blazing instead of just giving up.' The same frame of mind as I had in Napier.

With the wicket offering increasing turn, we sensed a huge opportunity to bowl out South Africa for less than 280, and at 93 for four, and again at 171 for five, it looked as though the game was heading our way. But what we had not reckoned for was one of the great Test-winning innings from Smith. He bats in a way that is not necessarily pleasing on the eye: he muscles the ball around, he has a very impressive temperament, he knows his own game and he has shots all round the wicket. Although Monty Panesar hit the patches of rough which we thought would bring us victory, Smith never let him settle, mixing up sweeps with pulls and flicks. For a captain, nothing enhances his authority more than winning a game for his team. We were distraught at the end; but Smith's innings deserved to win the Test and the series, their first in England since returning to the post-apartheid fold.

The Edgbaston game was the only time in his career as captain of England that I saw Vaughan publicly doubting himself. He made a couple of jokes about his not scoring runs: he said that Jimmy Anderson was more likely to score runs than he was. This was the gallows humour that cricketers so often come out with, but not Michael Vaughan, so I knew he was struggling and unhappy with his game. None of us in the England team felt he was responsible for our defeat – 2–0 down now against South Africa – but he did.

On the Sunday morning, which should have been the fifth day of the match, I turned on my television to hear that he was going to resign at a press conference later that day. I texted him straight away, and he said it was true – he couldn't bring himself to tell us the previous night. I was absolutely amazed that he was going to relinquish his captaincy. They say most captains outstay their time, but his players were a hundred per cent behind him and thought he would get his batting back. Maybe, though, one of the most masterful strokes of Vaughan's captaincy was that he decided to go before anyone thought his time was up.

4
STANFORD

Following on the heels of another long summer was the inaugural, and perhaps the final, Stanford Twenty20 for $20 million in Antigua. I was surplus to England's requirements but had the fortune of going there with Middlesex, the domestic champions of 2008. On finals day at the Rose Bowl, they had won their semi-final and final on the back of some power-hitting by Owais Shah and Tyron Henderson. Now, as England's Twenty20 champions, we were going to play Trinidad and Tobago, the winners of Stanford's domestic tournament.

Even when the Middlesex lads were getting together at Gatwick Airport, nobody knew what to expect. It was a big step into the unknown both for Middlesex and England. There had been a long debate about the England team playing against a non-international side for what appeared to be nothing more than financial reasons. Nothing makes cricket people, or sport people, talk more than a cricket scandal; and the whole Stanford episode gave them plenty of material to discuss.

Kevin Pietersen, England's new Test and one-day captain, was perhaps under more pressure than anyone during the Stanford tournament. He had been appointed just before the Oval Test against South Africa, and by winning it England had a consolation victory to set against our two defeats. Then he had led England to a 4–0 victory in the one-day series against South Africa and everything he had touched had turned to gold. But as the mouth-piece of the side he was asked most of the difficult questions about England becoming involved with the Stanford Superstars, and some of them would have taxed the most skilled diplomat.

I had been a little surprised when, the day after Michael Vaughan's resignation speech at Loughborough (and Paul Collingwood's stepping down as one-day captain), Pietersen was announced as the next England captain, three days before the Fourth Test. Clearly, the ECB's priority was to have one captain for all forms of the game – Test, 50–over, and 20–over – and I agreed with that intention. It makes the lines of leadership and management clearer. It also gives the captain a better chance to mould the England teams in his own image.

On the other hand, Pietersen had no experience of captaining any side, whether KwaZulu Natal, Nottinghamshire or Hampshire, although he had deputised for Collingwood in a one-day interna-tional against New Zealand at Lord's earlier in the summer, and had by all accounts done a decent job, even though England lost. It was, therefore, a big ask for him to go from never having captained a side to be the full-time captain of England in all three formats. Also, his name had not been mentioned much as a future England captain, so the media and public were taken by surprise as well.

But Pietersen did have two big advantages to set against this lack of captaincy experience. Firstly, he had enormous confi-dence, both in his ability as a cricketer and in life in general, and I thought this would rub off on the England team. Secondly, he was never afraid to speak his mind. In the end, this turned out to be a double-edged sword when he talked with the ECB, and especially the managing director Hugh Morris, about replacing Peter Moores as the England coach. But, at the outset of his captaincy, Pietersen's outspokenness seemed to me a distinct asset because he was ready to have the difficult conversations which the England captain has to have with some people.

On the day that Vaughan resigned I got a phone call from Pietersen to say he had been approached to take over the captaincy, and what did I think? I replied that he would be a fool not to accept it. If you don't accept, I told him, you will regret it because the offer might never come again. However, we all knew that he and Moores had never seen eye to eye, and we knew how important the relationship between captain and coach was.

Around this time the media had talked about me doing the Test captaincy and someone else doing the one-day captaincy. But I certainly did not feel disappointed that the selectors had rung Pietersen not me. I understood their need to have one captain in all forms, and I had been having a lean series against South Africa with the bat, although I was not unhappy with the state of my game. I thought that if Pietersen could overcome his inexperience in the tactical side of the game, he had the capability to make an excellent captain of England. But I still wondered if the tensions in the relationship between him and Moores would surface when England were not performing well.

Thankfully, in his first Test match and his first five one-day internationals England played some excellent cricket. Pietersen began by showing that the captaincy would not affect his batting by scoring a hundred in his first Test innings as England captain, something which had been done only twice before (although I managed it in my second innings, against Pakistan in 2006). The South Africans may not have been entirely fired up in the Fourth and final Test, having already won their first series in England since 1965, but Pietersen could hardly have done anything more than he did. When we were set a fourth-innings target of just under 200, I helped Alastair Cook start with a century stand and we won by six wickets.

I was not involved in the one-day series that followed when Pietersen and his players knocked what was left of the stuffing out of the South Africans. Only rain in the last international at Cardiff stopped England winning 5–0. Pietersen continued to score runs in his inimitable style: 90 not out, 5, and 40 in a run-chase at Lord's that was similar to ours in Barbados a few months later under Duckworth/Lewis. (England were set 137 off 20 at Lord's, 135 off the same number of overs in Barbados.) At every press conference Pietersen handled the media well; England played aggressive cricket in the same style as he batted; and he was rapidly learning the tactics involved in Test and one-day cricket in England. It was only later, in the Stanford tournament and on our tour of India before Christmas, that the difficulties became apparent.

Being in Antigua with Middlesex I had the advantage of seeing things a bit more objectively than the other England players, although to an extent the county players were bound up with England's situation. Starting with the flight out from Gatwick, travelling with Middlesex was a less luxurious affair than with England. We were staying at the Jolly Beach hotel, a resort that would have been at its best in the mid-1970s. I began to appreciate many of the perks which I had previously taken for granted, like having your luggage looked after by the management, a special check-in at airports, and room keys waiting for you at reception. With Middlesex in Antigua, it was more like an old-time England tour, or a club tour. And it was quite refreshing that everything was up to us: we had to organise our own practices and training, but we also had more time and scope to enjoy ourselves than England ever do.

The first feeling I had about a potential spanner in England's works occurred when we arrived in Antigua about a week before the England players came to the island. (Some of them came from England while most of the bowlers had been warming up in Barbados.) From the moment Middlesex arrived, besides the heat and humidity, we noticed how very different the pitches were, not only from those in England but from those in other parts of the Caribbean. The ball would skid on and spinners were very hard to manoeuvre. In the five or six days of practice I and the rest of the Middlesex team did not really get to grips with these conditions. The England players had only half as long, and the majority opinion among the county players was that this inexperience of playing spinners on skiddy wickets might cost England when it came to the big game on Saturday 1 November, when they played the Stanford Superstars for the sum of $20 million.

Almost as soon as England had arrived in Antigua, complete with Barmy Army supporters and media, Pietersen had to deal with the whole debate about whether England should be there in the first place and, also, whether Sir Allen Stanford was the sort of person that England's cricket team should be seen to be doing business with. It certainly overshadowed events on the pitch at Stanford's ground, right next to the airport. My strong feeling was that it was wrong to criticise Stanford for putting on a show that was to all intents and purposes the same as his Stanford domestic tournament, which he had staged twice before to widespread approval. There were justifiable arguments about whether England should be playing against a non-international team, which to me were very valid, but once we were there I could not agree with the sentiment that Stanford was at fault for all this.

Another area of concern was one that I had been involved in myself at a two-day England training camp at Henley, when we had a series of chats about how to deal with Stanford from a public relations point of view. We – or rather the England players in the one-day team – did not want to be seen to be motivated by winning a million dollars each, but it was hard to justify the big game from anything other than a monetary aspect. At the end of our talks it was decided that the only way was to say the Stanford tournament was a good warm-up for the one-day series in India, which was to follow almost straight afterwards; but it did not carry much weight. You could see, even at that Henley meeting, that some players were uneasy about focusing on the money. Pride in representing our country is usually the main reason for players going on to the field to play for England.

Originally, when Stanford had landed at Lord's in his helicopter to an effusive welcome, it had been announced that the big game would be winners-take-all. But by the time we met in Henley, a more English, less American, view was prevailing among the players and boards of both sides. Out of the $20 million it was agreed that, if England won, a million dollars would go to each of the eleven players involved, another million divided among the four other players in the 15-man squad, and another million divided among all the management staff. That left $7 million, which was earmarked to help grassroots cricket in both England and the West Indies. If the money had eventually found its way into schools and clubs, it could have done a lot of good. But even so, at least for PR purposes, $7 million seemed small by comparison with the $13 million which the players (and management) were going to win.

From the outside, or at least from the Jolly Beach in Antigua, the England camp did not look to be a happy place in Stanford week. The players had to spend too much time fending off questions, which ranged from whether they should be there in the first place to whether Stanford was becoming overly friendly with wives and girlfriends after he had visited one of the stands during a warm-up game – at what was his ground – and sat Emily Prior on his lap. Most of these questions were either difficult or impossible to answer.

The standard of cricket, amid the storm of newspaper stories, was not particularly high. We were not aided by the floodlighting at Stanford's ground. Having watched the Stanford domestic tournament a couple of times on television before coming out, we had arrogantly assumed the standard of fielding was pretty low, but we – Middlesex and England players, Trinidadians and Stanford Superstars – added our names to the list of people who had dropped catches at the ground, and I missed the easiest chance of my career.

My excuse is that the floodlighting made the ball seem to be somewhere other than where it was. It was like a half-moon: half the ball was light and the other half was dark. So when you were fielding – it was fine when batting – you could focus only on the half-lit part.

Middlesex managed to lose the big game against Trinidad for $280,000 after we had looked to be in a pretty impregnable position: Trinidad were 49 for four chasing our 118. Our special signing, designed to make up for Owais Shah being required by England, was Neil Carter, who opens the batting and bowling for Warwickshire; but he got spanked by the West Indian wicket-keeper/batsman Denesh Ramdin who saw Trinidad home by five wickets with some wristy hits. It was thoroughly dispiriting for the Middlesex players who had worked so hard to win our domestic Twenty20. But we had not adapted well to the conditions – Trinidad used three spinners who skidded the ball through – and we paid the price, offset by a runners-up prize of $100,000.

Before the Stanford Twenty20 for $20 million on 1 November, Independence Day in Antigua, electricity could be detected in the air. The players of one side knew their lives would be transformed by winning a million dollars each, while the players on the other could only dream of what might have been as they saw the money slipping from their grasp. I watched from the *Test Match Special* box, doing my first stint of radio commentary, and quickly ran out of things to say. As England's wickets tumbled without a partner-ship of any sort, it was like watching a train wreck. A combination of smart bowling and fielding, and less than smart batting, saw England capitulate to 99 all out inside the 20 overs.

Right: Man of the series against New Zealand in England in 2008! And it could have been oblivion.

Below: The best captain I played under: Michael Vaughan scoring his last Test century against New Zealand at Lord's.

New chips off old blocks: Sam Strauss and Archie Vaughan look at the npower Trophy after England won it at Trent Bridge in 2008.

The South African fielders about to have their hopes disappointed after A. B. de Villiers had claimed a slip catch in the Headingley Test of 2008.

Kevin Pietersen, before his first Test as England captain, talks with Peter Moores and myself at The Oval in August 2008. Little did we know . . .

Chris Gayle and Sir Allen Stanford celebrate the win by the Stanford Superstars over England in Antigua. Gayle had the last laugh.

Kevin Pietersen and Hugh Morris before we fly to Abu Dhabi to prepare for the England tour of India.

A proud moment on becoming the first England batsman to score a century in both innings of a Test in Asia. And we still lost.

Sachin Tendulkar after scoring his forty-second Test century to take India to victory over England in Chennai.

On one of the first days that Middlesex practised at Stanford's ground, we had to wait and watch until the Superstars had finished their practice session, and we were amazed at the drills they did. A training camp of six weeks is unheard of in international cricket; by way of comparison with the Stanford Superstars, England had a training camp of three days. Under the coaching of Eldine Baptiste and Roger Harper, who had both played in the great Lloyd–Richards era of the 1980s, the Superstars looked fitter, sharper and more motivated than any West Indian side I had seen before. About the last time I had seen them at practice, in May 2007, they had done a pre-match warm-up at Headingley wearing their batting gloves because it was so cold. Now they were very impressive, and the practices they did seemed to be specific to Twenty20 cricket, not just general drills.

England's total was knocked off without the loss of any wickets and suddenly the Superstars were $13 million richer. In some ways it was a fitting end to the tournament. Some players who had come from what were reported to be 'humble beginnings' had taken the chance to lift themselves and their families. It is fair to say that we – England – underestimated the Stanford team. They had some very powerful hitters that we had never seen before: Andre Fletcher, who also kept wicket, and Kieron Pollard in particular impressed with their clean striking, both on the big day and during the week.

But Chris Gayle was always going to be the Superstars' most dangerous batsman. He is one of the great exponents of short-form cricket. His laid back manner and seeming distaste for raising his heart-beat belie the fact that he has an incredible talent and shrewd cricket brain. In many ways he is the antithesis of the

MCC coaching manual: he does not move his feet anywhere, and he uses his bat more like a baseball bat than a cricket one. When he hits, the boundary fielders do not have to move because the ball normally sails over their heads, and then he takes a single, which is smart thinking – he does not try to hit every ball.

Gayle, on the field, is a man of few words. He does not get flustered. He seems to receive huge respect from his team-mates. I think this respect stems not only from his batting powers and his captaincy on the field but also, not least, because he has taken on the West Indian board and risked his job out of his willingness to put his principles first.

The next time England came across Gayle was in his native Jamaica the following February. On the first morning of the Test series Andrew Flintoff took the new ball and Gayle struck his second ball over long-on for six, without even needing a follow-through. Gayle then was still the captain of West Indies. Pietersen, however, was no longer the captain of England.

5
AUSTRALIA

It was like going to one of those expensive spa retreats, when we spent a month in Australia after the Stanford series. Ruth and I were far removed from our normal life of travelling, media interest and me playing cricket. All the dust and dirt was washed away by the wilderness of outback Victoria.

Ruth's family lives outside Ballarat, where the sheer enormity of the continent soon becomes apparent. You can drive for hours in any direction without coming to a town. The bush is pristine, unspoilt, as undisturbed as it was before Europeans settled there. Spending quality time with my two sons was very special: on my daily walks with Sam in the early mornings we would startle kangaroos and sheep, a far cry from the soft-play areas of west London.

As is often the case in small communities, the familiarity which people have with one other leads to a genuine goodwill and interest in the affairs of others – again a contrast to London where people keep themselves to themselves. In the lone street of an outback settlement in Victoria, people stop and talk in an unimposing way. England cricketers often bemoan the lack of time off from the international schedule, and what I appreciated most in being involved only in the Test side at this juncture of my career was that I could go away, let my mind settle, reflect on our last series against South Africa, and make sure my hunger was there when I returned for the tour of India.

But even in outback Australia the game of cricket is never far away. It is on terrestrial television, so everyone is interested. The Australian equivalent of *Test Match Special* is usually the radio station which your hire car is tuned into. Cricket is an integral part of national life: in the village school playground the kids all had their white sunhats on and their suncream and their bat and ball, and the spectacle reaffirmed how important sport is as a part of their national consciousness. The odd person around Ballarat recognised a Pommie opening batsman and was not shy to tell me about our prospects for the Ashes series of 2009. You expect that in Australia, and it adds to the rivalry.

My first memories of an Ashes series were auspicious: it was the 1986–7 series in Australia which England won under a Middlesex captain, Mike Gatting. No specific incident sticks out in my mind so much as the fact that England had won, and how big such an event was. It was soon after my family had moved to the United Kingdom, from Australia. My dad had been an insurance broker in South Africa, and had moved out in 1984 when he was not happy about the country's immediate prospects and he was offered a job in Melbourne. We spent 18 months there, until 1986, when he was offered another job in London. At one level it was strange to leave behind friends and extended family, but at the age of seven or so everything like moving house is an adventure.

I played my first game of Australian Rules football in Melbourne, and my first game of mini-rugby because my dad was not happy about me turning into an Aussie Rules footballer. I can remember getting my first cricket bat in Australia, for a birthday present. In my memory we went to an enormous sports shop, which might actually seem pretty small if I went back to it now, and the bat was almost as huge. I could hardly lift it. From the start I batted left-handed, and I cannot have been too bad because I was chosen to play for my school in Melbourne at soft-ball cricket.

My first memory of real cricket was going to the Melbourne Cricket Ground to watch Australia against New Zealand. I recall Dean Jones batting, and also dropping a catch, to my dad's disgust. I absolutely loved the experience. I also remember watching Allan Border bat on television when a spinner got him out and the commentator said: 'I think that ball would've got any left-hander in the world!' And I remember wondering if the ball – which might have been an offbreak that turned and hit off stump – would have got me out. This illustrates the interest I had in the game at the age of seven, by the way, not my self-belief.

From the moment I arrived at my prep school in England, at Caldicott, it was one big sportathon. Rugby was the primary focus of the school – Chris Sheasby and Andy Harriman, who represented England, went there – but cricket was an important part of the school's life. I remember bowling my left-arm chinamen and opening the batting for the Under-8s. By the time I had been a year in England, my heroes had changed from Dean Jones and Allan Border to David Gower and Graham Gooch as I became more and more anglicised and a slight Aussie twang became less and less pronounced.

Although I did not realise it at the time, I have since: I was very fortunate to go to a school with such outstanding facilities. There was a real interest in sport, apart from it being a means of keeping the kids occupied and tiring them out and bonding them together.

And regardless of what people say about developing your cricket on the streets in Asia, having access to the best facilities at any early age is a huge advantage. The coaching was out of the MCC text-book, but the very fact of playing at a young age laid the foundation of my batting. In fact, thinking of my England team-mates, I cannot think of one who did not start playing at an early age with the possible exception of Kevin Pietersen, who did not bat so much as bowl.

My first half-century did not come until my last year at Caldicott because I was small and could not hit the ball off the square: my coach there tried to make me keep wicket because my batting was solid but I could not make the same contribution as other, bigger kids. When I moved on to Radley College I started playing in the age-group above, but I was one of those guys the media would refer to as 'talented but under-achieving', as I would make 40s and 50s then get out. I finally broke my duck and made my first hundred at 15, funnily enough against a school on tour from Melbourne. I still kept wicket at Radley, until my second to last year when I had some knee problems, and realised that keeping was hard work. I preferred the less tiring options of slip and the covers.

Other England players have been selected at Under-15 national level and for England youth sides. At 16 I was selected for Oxfordshire Under-19s, but when we played the larger counties we kept bumping into prodigies who were already representing their first-class county second elevens. Playing for a minor county, it was easy to be intimidated by the shiny tracksuits and sponsors' logos sported by the youth players of Middlesex or Sussex.

For me, at this stage, cricket was just fun, a great way to spend a summer. Playing some games for Gerrard's Cross in the holidays was the way for my mum to get me out of the house. I played rugby, golf and tennis, as well as cricket, and it seemed normal. But now I know how lucky I was to have had those opportunities.

At Durham University, whenever I wasn't reading economics (which was often), I underwent the transition from being a recreational cricketer into one who had the ambition to play the game for a living. In my first year it was a load of students playing with a hangover. In my second year the ECB set up a centre of excellence which became a breeding ground for professional cricketers. The Durham team became exceptionally strong. Five or six – Robin Martin-Jenkins, Luke Sutton, Mark Chilton, Ben Hutton, Simon Francis – soon went on to become county cricketers, and I thought if they could do it, why can't I?

This new centre of excellence at Durham was in some respects higher in standard than Middlesex second eleven. We had, for instance, a very sophisticated fitness programme, and I was forced to give up rugby to focus on my cricket fitness. We also had a psychologist who examined our personalities and what problems we would have to deal with if we were to go on from university and play professional cricket for a living.

The head of Durham's centre of excellence was the former Lancashire and England left-handed opening batsman, Graeme Fowler. Having him as my coach at Durham helped a lot because he had been there and done what I now aimed to do. I only saw him bat on tape: he went at the ball pretty hard and had a method all his own, but he was obviously an effective batsman who could take a game away, as when he set up an England Test victory in what is now Chennai, and was Madras, with a double-hundred. He was amazingly enthusiastic about cricket, and his passion rubbed off on a bunch of students. It says a lot for him that so many of that original batch went on to successful cricketing careers.

My early dealings with Middlesex were not very promising. The coach at Radley, Andy Wagner, arranged for me to have a trial at Lord's. Little realising there was a second-team dressing-room in the pavilion, I blundered into the Middlesex first-team dressing-room during a match, to be greeted by thunderous stares from such famous people as Mark Ramprakash and Angus Fraser. After being directed to my proper place, I did not do very well in the nets. In fact, I thought I had bowled – some creditable left-arm seam – as well as I had batted, which shows I must have been pretty awful. Still, Middlesex's coach Don Bennett said he wanted to watch me play a week later for Oxfordshire Under-19s against Middlesex Under-19s. And after that game I was drafted into Middlesex's second eleven and scored 60 in my first one-day trial, then 98 in my first three-day trial.

Middlesex offered me a contract as things moved quickly, perhaps too quickly. My play against spin was awful, for a start. I also had not seen any life beyond school and university. But my sheltered upbringing in academic life had one advantage: having to revise for exams on my own enabled me to work at my cricket without needing somebody standing over me. At private school I had been spoon-fed, but at university I had to be motivated and disciplined in order to pass my economics exams.

During my first two seasons in the Middlesex second team

I learnt a huge amount. It was a pretty tough environment in which Ben Hutton and I – a couple of public school buffoons – were taught about cricket and life by the wily cockney stalwarts of the team. Then my cricket education was taken to another level when I went to Australia to play grade. I arrived in Sydney with Luke Sutton, neither of us knowing what to expect or what the standard would be. We began to feel our way in this darkness but it was very soon apparent this was a take-no-prisoners environment. A Pom with a county contract had to prove himself even more than the other guys who went to club training because reputations meant nothing. Everybody had a real hunger to rise to the first grade: even in third grade at Sydney University, where I spent my first winter, there were talented stroke-makers.

The first piece of sledging that I can remember had come from an Australian, which formed some sort of preparation for playing grade in Sydney. Peter Sleep, who had played a few Tests as an allrounder in the 1980s, was coaching and playing for Lancashire second eleven against Middlesex second eleven. Sleep was bowling his leg-breaks, I could not lay bat on ball, and he shouted to his players: 'This is how shit the standard of second eleven is!' So I was not too surprised when I joined Mosman at the start of two seasons as their overseas professional. I had my flight and accommodation paid for and was offered a bonus if I scored 500 runs in the season. (I did not earn it in my first but did in the second.) We went to indoor nets at the Sydney Cricket Ground, I took my guard and was about to face my first ball when one of my new team-mates – Warwick Adlam, who played for New South Wales – walked behind the back of the net and said: 'Listen here, Pom, everyone in the club is watching you, don't screw up!'

My experience of first-class cricket in England until that time had come at the back end of the county season, after university term, when a lot of players were going through the motions, aiming for their 1,000 runs or 50 wickets for the season so their contract would be renewed. At Mosman, when there was no New South Wales game going on, I stood at third slip while the bowling was in the hands of Phil Alley, a fast left-hander who was the tallest first-class cricketer Australia has ever produced and who took 90 first-class wickets; Brett Lee, who needs no introduction, and his elder brother Shane Lee, who played 45 one-day internationals for Australia as an allrounder.

When we played Bankstown, their opening batsman did not wear a helmet, and Brett Lee was tearing in and bowling bouncers at this guy without a helmet, and he got a couple of hook shots in: Brett Lee bowling bouncers at a guy without a helmet who hooked him for four! Such intensity in Australian grade cricket was on a different scale to anything I had known before. This was not about making money but representing your state and then perhaps your country, and the only way to do that was runs and wickets for your grade club at weekends. One system judged on performance and results; in the other, English, system you were given a contract on the basis of potential, or something that a coach liked about your technique which might lead you to scoring runs.

In my two seasons for Mosman I was just an average member of the team, not outstanding except when I scored 160 against the University of New South Wales, and averaging about 35. But my time in Australia was not wasted on or off the field. One evening I went to the Bourbon and Beefsteak bar in King's Cross with a mate, Bob Easton, who had come over with the Barmy Army to watch the England tour of Australia in 1998–9. Like a good backpacker, he stayed on the floor of my flat for about six weeks. After watching a one-day international at the SCG, we had run out of establishments which served good beer, so we headed to King's Cross and a place that was always open. The Bourbon and Beefsteak was pretty empty by the time Bob and I arrived, but we saw two girls on the other side of the bar who looked bored and were about to leave. We got chatting and found they were both actresses. Bob's relationship with his actress was temporary, but the young Victorian I chatted to is now my wife.

6
CARNAGE AND CHENNAI

On 27 November 2008 I woke up in a hostel at the Bangalore cricket stadium to a number of text messages. The first was from Paul Collingwood which said that he didn't think our Test series in India was going to go ahead. Others were texts from family and friends asking for news. As I had gone to bed early the previous night and had no idea what they were talking about, I jumped out of bed and switched on one of the many 24-hour news channels on Indian television and watched dramatic events unfold in real time. The scenes were harrowing. None of the footage was edited. You saw, as if at first hand, explosions in rooms, people falling down injured or dead, commandos storming buildings, interviews with people who had just escaped being massacred.

If you were on the other side of the world, these televised scenes of the terrorist attack on Mumbai would have made a lasting impression on you. If you were in the country, they made you feel intensely sad for the Indian people that they had this suffering on their soil. For those of us who had stayed at the Taj Mahal in Mumbai, the carnage brought home very starkly how close we cricketers had come to a catastrophe. We were not the targets, but early reports of the terrorists seeking out British and American citizens made me feel very vulnerable and very far from home. At such a moment cricket pales into insignificance and your only thoughts are of getting away from such a hostile environment and back to your family. You can't help but think what you would have done in those circumstances, and quite how horrific it would have been to be involved.

Monty Panesar and I were training with the High Performance squad in Bangalore ahead of the Test series. The England one-day players had first news of the Mumbai massacres on their way back from the fifth international in Cuttack to their hotel in Bhubaneshwar. The two of us and the Performance squad had an early morning gym session where the talk was about what was unfolding and how it would affect the tour. We were kept in the loop about an hour behind the England one-day team. Sajid Mahmood and Amjad Khan, members of the Performance squad in Bangalore, had been about to join them as cover for the last two internationals.

For quite a few of us, our first thoughts were of how to get home. Waiting around in India did not seem right. The country was in a state of shock. Cricket was not at the forefront of anybody's mind. The decision came from our manager Guy Jackson that we were to pull out, and I assumed the tour was completely over so I looked for a flight to Australia to get back to Ruth and the kids. But I was told to go to England and hold my horses there. It was a relief to get on a plane, a direct flight out of Bangalore to London, but it was a hollow feeling because I was not going to be reunited with my family, which was the main reason for getting out.

Once back in England, in the days following the Mumbai massacre, the dust settled reasonably quickly so far as unharmed cricketers were concerned. As I sat in my living room on my own, weighing up whether it was right to return to India so soon after the attack, I was initially annoyed at the Indian board and the ECB for saying the Test series would still go ahead while shots were being fired in Mumbai: that seemed to be disrespectful and insensitive. I also thought the England players should not be placed in the middle of a massive game of politics with the Indian cricket board. Clearly there was far more to this than merely fulfilling a fixture. The Indian cricket board desperately needed us to return to their country, and there were massive incentives for the ECB to go back to restore a fractured relationship with the Indian board. Forcing the players to choose individually was potentially damaging, as we had found out in 2004 when players were given the option of touring Zimbabwe or not; and players had to consider how safe their place in the side was, which should not have been a factor but inevitably was. Finally, rushing us back to India with limited practice time meant that we were unlikely to be fully prepared to play a Test match and to perform as well as we should.

But by the time the BBC rang and I did an interview over the phone from my home, I had gone through everything in my head. The longer we spent at home – and the England one-day players had arrived home the day after the Performance squad – the more I realised that if our security experts said it was safe to go back to India, the main losers if we did not go back would be the game of cricket; and as international cricketers we had to consider the big picture. If we did not travel to India, Pakistan and Sri Lanka when security said it was safe, the game would be split. I did not think that I could realistically pull out of the tour unless we were told that it was not safe to go. Also, if I was to pull out of the tour, then I would be left very vulnerable to attack for all sorts of reasons ... as a player, you get involved in the politics at your peril. So, unless Ruth was adamant that she did not want me to return to India, and if the security report said it was safe, I decided to go.

As is always the case, time brought with it different perspectives and fresh information. As it transpired, the ECB did things pretty much right from there on, and great credit must go to the managing director Hugh Morris. We went out to Abu Dhabi to get as prepared as possible, and also await the full version of the report by England's security officer, Reg Dickason. This was undoubtedly the right thing to do, and it served the additional purpose of getting the whole squad on to the plane.

Still, boarding a plane to go on an England cricket tour to Abu Dhabi was frankly bizarre. We were trying to get our heads around the fact that we were due to start a Test match in a week's time but we were not going to India until two days before the match. Before we left London, we had not received any security report from Reg Dickason, on which our immediate futures hinged. We were to wait and practise in Abu Dhabi while he completed his inspection of Chennai, where the First Test was going to be relocated from Ahmedabad. Then he would go to inspect Mohali, where the Second Test was going to be relocated from Mumbai.

None of us had been to Abu Dhabi and none of us knew what the training facilities would be like. As it turned out, the place was ideal. It was a bit of an oasis in every sense, compared to India in that few people cared who we were. Abu Dhabi has ambitions to host more and more international cricket and, as the hospitality was first-rate in our experience, it would seem that the proximity of Dubai and Abu Dhabi to the Asian subcontinent offers a ready-made solution to the problem if teams are unable to tour one or other of the countries there.

The three days in Abu Dhabi were perfect in terms of bringing everyone back together, providing a bit of light-hearted training, and allowing us to start preparing mentally for the challenge of the two Tests. We also had the benefit of some high-intensity practice against the pace bowlers in the Performance squad who flew out with us. One of them had to replace Ryan Sidebottom owing to injury – Amjad Khan was selected in the end – so they were well motivated in the net sessions at the Sheikh Zayed stadium. All this work brought the team closer together, as had the unusual circumstances of us being a group of men caught up in a tragedy.

As I told my diary in the build-up to the Chennai Test, in a lot of ways the series was going to be about more than just the results: it was going to be about the game of cricket continuing in the face of terrorism. Having said that, we could not use our lack of preparation as an excuse for failure. I asked myself: was it going to be difficult to go into the First Test without a warm-up match in India, and the answer was yes. Was that going to lose us the series? The answer was no. We were going to lose the series if we didn't play well, regardless of the level of practice. In some ways, I concluded in my diary entry, this episode might actually show how insignificant practice is when it comes to Test cricket. Your mental state is crucial, which is helped by good practice, hindered by bad.

None of us knew what to expect in Chennai when we arrived less than a fortnight after the first shots had been fired in Mumbai. We had been told there would be commandos everywhere and the level of security would be unprecedented, but we did not know how the public would receive us. At the airport we saw machine-gun bunkers and hundreds of commandos, and interspersed among them a thousand or two ordinary Indians staring at us through the windows of our bus: if anyone had wanted to finish us off, they could have done. Security was overbearing thereafter, and we could not go out of the hotel except to the ground, but the general feeling was that it was better to be safe than sorry. And as our attention turned to cricket we forgot about security.

Whereas Abu Dhabi had been warm, Chennai was incredibly hot – and one of our practices was washed out by rain, leaving us even less time to acclimatise. Knowing that we were undercooked, however, took a bit of the pressure off us: this match had a bigger context than who won or lost. This was liberating in a way. We just had to go out and play the game we love, and show that the sport was alive and well.

I had played a Test series in India before, in early 2006 under Andrew Flintoff's captaincy, and had made a hundred in the Third Test in Mumbai. But in Abu Dhabi I had still spoken to the one-day players about what they had experienced during the five internationals in India (the last two had been abandoned). Kevin Pietersen, who had scored a hundred in the last of them, said to me: 'Straussy, I've just worked out what to do in India. You mustn't hit the ball too early – you've got to hit it into the ground.' So I tried it in the nets at Abu Dhabi and it seemed to help. I also told Pietersen that Duncan Fletcher had gone on about the same technique of hitting the ball into the ground. In my first two Tests in India on England's tour of 2005–6, I had tried to play a positive game and got myself out. I had then done a lot of work with Fletcher on playing back to the spinners and sweeping, and looking back to my diary entries for that period helped me now.

On the eve of the First Test in Chennai it seemed to me there were two sides to batting well in India. The first was to feel comfortable at the crease when not scoring quickly. The second was to play the ball late as Fletcher and Pietersen had suggested. Combined, these were two big challenges because you can get tied down, and the boundaries dry up, and the ball goes soft, and the Indians try to bowl maidens before the ball starts to reverse-swing – and the risks inherent in raising the tempo then are very high.

Another source of motivation, as I can recall saying to Paul Collingwood, was that when I had been left out of England's tour of Sri Lanka I had been told that playing spin wasn't my game and that was one of the main reasons I had been dropped. The chairman of selectors, David Graveney, had told me so. Now I wanted to prove him wrong.

Sitting in my room at the Taj hotel in Chennai the evening before the First Test, I made the following entry in my diary:

Tomorrow is the start of the series, and I am not entirely sure how I feel. I probably don't feel quite the pressure that I have in previous series. Maybe that is to do with the lack of build-up, and the circumstances. I am a little concerned that I haven't played a game out here yet, but I would rather go into this game with no form than bad form. I know from experience that a low-intensity warm-up game, where your lack of focus inevitably leads to low scores, is anything but ideal preparation for a tough Test series.

At the moment I feel at peace with my game. I feel balanced, composed, and happy with it. Much of this has to do with the way I finished the season for Middlesex with scores of 78, 38, 45, 104, 28 n.o., 174 and 75. My method is working again, and it is incredibly powerful to have that feeling. I had a chat this morning with Peter Moores, who brought it to my attention that my stats haven't been all that great over the last couple of years, and now is the time to cash in, when I am feeling good, and have learnt my lessons. I couldn't agree more. I am older, more experienced and have been through the trough, so this stage of my career should be my most productive. Where I differ with him slightly is that I am not sure that putting myself under pressure is the right way of going about it. Better to focus on what is going well, and then be absolutely ruthless in making the most of good form, because it doesn't last forever. If I do that, then everything will look after itself.

From past experiences in India, I know that there are a few fundamentals that are incredibly important to stick to out here:

1) Against the seamers, cutting is not a good idea until well set, and only then if you are absolutely sure that there isn't some degree of low bounce in the wicket.
2) Hitting through extra cover is a big no-no for me. Be patient enough to leave the wider balls. Play straight, hit straight, and be patient.
3) Patience is crucial. It may take five hours to score a hundred. Do not at any stage feel that you have to up the tempo. Bat time.
4) It is important to be busy against the spin. Singles are very important, as is the odd boundary. You can't wait there like a sitting duck. Be busy, score off the back foot, and keep them thinking, especially when it is spinning in the second innings.

The following are my diary notes on the opposition bowlers, but shorn of my top-secret plans on how to counter them!

Zaheer Khan – Watch out for the ball that comes back, and leave anything that swings away. If a good wicket, the cut is an option later on, but don't even think about it early. Be patient. He likes to try lots of variations, so he will provide scoring opportunities.

Ishant Sharma – Hits the deck with decent pace. Leave well, and pick him off when he gets too straight. He may bowl maidens if he bowls well, but he also bowls his fair share of bad balls.

Harbhajan Singh – Will probably start off bowling over the wicket. Watch the revs on the ball carefully for scrambled seam offie and doosra. Sweep an option if he comes round the wicket. Square sweep an option from over. Look for nurdle on legside and cut.

Mishra – Haven't faced him before but remember fundamentals. Slog-sweep an option, legside nurdle. Be careful when it pitches outside off stump, especially if variable turn and bounce.

Here we go on another adventure. I have good vibes, but have to commit to my game plan, and stick to it, regardless of nerves, situation etc.

The match at the Chepauk stadium began with Alastair Cook and me putting on a hundred for the first wicket for the fourth or fifth time that year. We had sometimes been told that we were too similar to have fruitful partnerships, but when he had batted at number three for England in 2006 – when I was opening with Marcus Trescothick before his illness – we had enjoyed some good partnerships for the second wicket. In 2006, when Cook and I had opened, we did not have any big partnerships because I kept getting out early. It was my fault in that I was out of form; there was nothing wrong with us as a partnership.

Cook had made his Test debut on the England tour of India less than three years before, and had made a huge impression when he flew in from the England A tour of the West Indies to Nagpur. He spoke well at team meetings; he knew his game-plan even at the age of 20; from the moment I saw him I knew he would have a long England career. So often youngsters want to be technically perfect or play eye-catching shots, but Cook was already reconciled to the fact that he was never going to be pretty to watch. Above all, at the age of 20 he already had the vital ingredient of being able to play off the back foot: he soon became one of the best hookers in the game, so the bowlers gave up bothering to bounce him, and he cut well too. I think his first scoring shot in Test cricket was a hook for four in Nagpur; then he made a hundred in the second innings of his debut Test. This brought back memories of my debut in 2004, but his was a lot more impressive because my debut had been on my home ground against New Zealand.

When we bat together, Cook and I occasionally talk about what the bowlers are trying to do, but I hate being asked what I talk about in the middle because usually it is nothing of importance. It is just bog-standard stuff about watching the ball, keep concentrating, run hard, how the wicket is playing – exchanges of information which go in one ear and out the other. One advantage of us having the same sort of technique is that we have the same weaknesses and can relate to what the other is trying to do. If, for example,

Zaheer Khan was reverse-swinging the ball, we would tell each other not to commit too early, and we would almost play French cricket with the bat in front of pad. Being similar has helped us to spot each other's difficulties more quickly.

The pivotal moment for me in Chennai came in the opening session when I had scored about 10 in 40 minutes against the new ball. I was not concerned about scoring slowly but was aware that India's spinners were about to come on. Their first over was from Amit Mishra, the legspinner, who was naturally turning most of his deliveries in to me. Mahendra Singh Dhoni set a run-saving infield, strong on the legside, with only a deep square-leg out – and I hit him twice for four in his first over with slog-sweeps along the ground in front of square. That gave me momentum and set the tone. After tea I brought up my hundred with a steer to third man off Zaheer, which was an immensely satisfying and quite emotional moment because of the tragic circumstances in Mumbai and our lack of preparation time. I was under some pressure as well for my place after the South Africa series, and we had to start well if we were going to compete in this one. By the end of the first day we had scored 229 for five – I got out just before the close, caught and bowled by Mishra – and thanks to Matt Prior's unbeaten 50 next morning we got up to 316.

We were surprised to bowl India out in their first innings for only 241. They had probably been surprised by the way we had batted after so little practice (our three-day warm-up game in Baroda had been abandoned because of the terrorist attack, as well as the sixth and seventh internationals). Our bowlers put in a fantastic effort to give us a first-innings lead of 75. Two wickets in his first over by Graeme Swann on his Test debut was the highlight: Gautam Gambhir left a ball that came straight on at him, and Rahul Dravid was hit on the back leg by an off-break. Before the Test was half over in terms of time we were batting again.

I had long had the ambition of scoring a hundred in each innings in first-class cricket but I had not come close – thanks to Nasser Hussain scuppering my second innings of 83 in my debut Test with his calling! Going in to bat a second time, I felt quite strongly that I knew the wicket and there would be nothing new beyond the ball turning a bit more, so if I got through the new ball I would get runs. Often, after a successful first innings, you can go easy on yourself and invariably you do not make runs. But Cook, Ian Bell and Pietersen all went, and at 43 for three any thoughts of coasting were taken out of my mind by our precarious position.

Slowly, Collingwood and I brought us back into the game with the sort of nudging and nurdling that probably does not bring in a lot of new supporters to the sport. By the end of day three we had taken the score up to 172 for three, a lead of 247. Using the same game-plan as for my first innings I had reached 73, while my partner was on 60. The ball was turning a lot for India's spinners but not too quickly.

For both of us to register a hundred on the fourth day was a special moment: for me because it was an ambition fulfilled and all the lonely work-outs in the gym were made to feel worthwhile. If I had been any less fit, I could not have become the first England batsman to score a hundred in each innings of a Test in Asia. The majority of my training in the last couple of years has been short-interval running, not so much weights and 40-minute runs but a schedule more suited to my role in the side. After the 2007 World Cup an overview was done of what we were doing right and what we were doing wrong in our fitness training. England's fitness levels were not bad, but Strength and Conditioning experts like Sam Bradley were brought in to make the training more specific.

Every evening of the match, when we got back to our hotel with our convoy of commandos, the highlights were being played on television channels, so I sat in my room and watched what I had achieved. Afterwards, I did not feel like dining because I had eaten at the ground, and I did not want a beer because I was so dehydrated, even after drinking a huge amount of electrolytes. But I still went down to the bar and had a beer with some of the team, including Pietersen, Collingwood and our analyst Mark Garaway. It had struck me that as an England side we were not very good at celebrating each other's success. So when I was appointed to be England's captain a few weeks after this tour of India, I introduced the practice of everyone having a beer in the dressing-room, before we went back to the hotel, to celebrate someone who had scored a century or taken five wickets in an innings. On our tour of the West Indies we seemed to share a beer at the end of every day of every Test – after the debacle in Jamaica. We only did it as a reward though, when there was something to celebrate.

In Chennai, we were very confident of winning when India set out on the fourth evening to chase 387. The wicket by now was turning and bouncing and seemed to be deteriorating – it had been prepared for the 20-over matches of the Champions League, in which Middlesex were going to be England's representatives before the Mumbai massacre forced the tournament to be cancelled. Our only nagging thought was that India's spinners had not ripped through us: it had been Zaheer who had slowed our second innings down with his reverse-swing. But then the rate at which India had to score, if they were to knock off the runs, was higher than the average run-rate in the Test to that stage, so there was no real idea of India knocking the runs off.

But in 20 mind-blowing overs on the fourth evening Virender Sehwag set up India's position so well that on the final day they had only to bat at the tempo which had prevailed on the first four. Someone who can hit the first ball of an innings for six over extra-cover has better eyesight than I have and no fear of failure. Sehwag did not actually hit the first ball of this innings for six but he did hit two of Anderson's first four balls, and two of Harmison's first four balls, to the boundary. In the game to date only one six had been hit, but Sehwag struck four of them off the 68 balls he faced. We bowled poorly but the quality of his strikes all round the ground, and his determination not to throttle back, put the pressure on us and took it off Gambhir and all the batsmen who followed.

Sehwag was dismissed shortly before the close of day four, but we had no answer to the other genius in the Indian side. Sachin Tendulkar played an innings entirely becoming a man of his class. It was utterly responsible, well paced, brilliantly thought out and a perfect example of chasing down a huge total. He did not let our spinners or seamers bowl a lot of dot-balls, he ran hard and turned ones into twos, and was very mobile for a man who had been playing Test cricket for two whole decades. With Yuvraj Singh for his partner – they came together at 224 for four – Tendulkar knocked off the runs with about an hour to spare at the same time as reaching his forty-second Test century.

Sometimes when you are beaten you have to take your hat off and simply say well played. I went to their dressing-room afterwards to get some bats signed for my benefit and Tendulkar, who is not the sort to scream and shout, had a look of pure satisfaction on his face. It was evident that he had desired a hundred to win a game for India, especially in those uniquely trying circumstances, and he had ticked off another in his long list of ambitions. He had conducted the highest ever successful run-chase in a Test in Asia.

Before the Second Test at Mohali, which Reg Dickason had checked out while we were in Chennai, I reflected in my diary:

18 December 2008
Well, I had good vibes about the game, but didn't realise that it would be that good! Undoubtedly the best match of my career, combining a first innings 123 with 108 in the second. It is amazing that I didn't get a hundred for 15 Test matches, and now I have scored two in one match . . . Funny old game all right.

Sometimes when you score runs it is hard to understand quite how you did it, or for that matter what you did differently in order for you to score those runs. Sometimes it just feels like luck is involved. Maybe you played and missed early rather than nicked one, or your edge went into a gap rather than into the slip fielder's hands. This game, however, seemed slightly different. For one, I felt completely in the zone. I didn't feel particularly nervous, I didn't feel uncomfortable about my place in the side, I just went out and administered my game-plan as set out above. It isn't rocket science, but I didn't lose concentration, and I didn't go through the gears, I just batted.

Maybe all the stuff surrounding the game, with the terrorist attack and our focus on whether we should come back or not, helped with giving me a more relaxed mindset. We hadn't had any cricket, so I didn't have any sort of baggage. The reality is though that since the end of the English season I have had a huge amount of confidence in my game once more. The last time I had this sort of confidence was in my first year in Test cricket when I could do no wrong.

I suppose the difference this time is that I appreciate this feeling so much more than previously, and intend to get as much out of it as possible. Now is definitely not the time to get easy on myself and cruise. I have one more match to go, and then can look forward to Christmas with the family, and an enjoyable break. There is absolutely no reason why I can't go on and get another hundred this week. In fact, after what went on last week, this should be the time when a hundred is at its most likely. I am in great nick, I know what the Indian bowlers are trying to do, and I have the answers. The only problem is my application and concentration, both of which I can control.

The Mohali Test did not quite work out in the way I had anticipated. International cricket seldom does. After India had scored 453 on the first two days, thanks to an enormous partnership between Gambhir and Rahul Dravid but little else, I had an overwhelming feeling when I went out to bat that I would follow my first pair of centuries in each innings with a pair of noughts. This sense of symmetry made me uncomfortable.

It was a strange light at the end of the second day when we went out to start England's first innings, only for it to be delayed until the next morning. I was not very switched on as the game seemed headed for a draw because so much playing time was being lost to fog in the mornings and bad light in the afternoons. I thought Zaheer would swing the ball away but he did not. I committed myself too early, unlike in Chennai, and was out for nought, lbw, to a ball which would have hit leg stump. In the second innings I managed an unbeaten 21 as we played out time and drew the game, before we flew home and arrived on Christmas Eve. One of England's most historic tours of modern times had lasted just over a fortnight.

7
INSTANT CAPTAINCY

The first time I thought about the England captaincy was at school. I was watching Mike Atherton on television marshalling his troops and thinking no, Phil Tufnell should be bowling or Angus Fraser should be on at the other end. In 1994, while I was the first eleven captain at Radley, I remember watching the 'dirt in pocket' affair, when Atherton was captured on camera in a Test at Lord's pulling his hand in his trouser pocket and coming out with some dirt which he then rubbed on the ball to help it to reverse-swing. What a hard job it is to be England captain, I thought, and what high standards are expected! I did not realise it then; it was only when I became England captain that I realised everyone has an opinion on whether Tufnell or Fraser should be bowling. It is one of the issues that you have to deal with. And if the bowling change you make is not a success, you will be criticised.

I had already fulfilled my schoolboy dream of captaining England in 2006, when I led in the Test series against Pakistan and five one-day internationals against Sri Lanka. As a stand-in captain, I began to appreciate some of the demands of the job but by no means all of them. In the space of three months I experienced the two extremes of success and failure. First it was a 5–0 thrashing by Sri Lanka which had me thinking: do I want this job and, if so, am I doing it the right way? Then it was a series victory against Pakistan which we won 2–0, or 3–0 if you count the forfeiture at The Oval, which ICC did count, then did not after a rethink, then eventually did so again in accordance with the laws. Pakistan had a pretty strong side, including such match winners as Inzamam, Younis Khan, Mohammed Yousuf, Danish Kaneria and Mohammed Asif. It was then that I saw the up-side of being England's captain: the satisfaction and the highs to be had from outplotting and outperforming another international team.

So when I was sitting at home in the New Year of 2009, I knew that the England captaincy was something I wanted to try again at some stage of my career. And I knew there were issues between Kevin Pietersen and Peter Moores which, like everyone else in the team, I did not know how would be played out. As managing director, Hugh Morris had spoken on the phone to me and most of the senior players shortly after Christmas, a) to find out how things were going in the team and b) how they could be made better. We – the England players – were not aware that it was make-or-break time when Morris phoned us, just that the ECB were taking steps to address what Pietersen in his first newspaper column of the New Year called an 'unhealthy situation'.

It came as a big surprise when the newspapers announced that Pietersen wanted Moores to be sacked as the England coach. From thereon everybody was in a difficult position. Pietersen was on holiday in South Africa, on safari, and probably did not realise the strength of public feeling that was being stirred up in England. The ECB was stuck in a corner: which man were they going to support out of Moores and Pietersen, if either? It added up to a messy situation in which there could be no winners, and it was sad that English cricket was in the headlines again for the wrong reasons.

A few days after the story broke about Pietersen wanting Moores sacked, I got a call from KP. He was on his way back from South Africa and he said he was resigning the England captaincy. This call came shortly after I had been contacted by Morris, who said the ECB were about to have a board meeting to consider what options they had and, if push came to shove and they needed a new captain, would I be interested in taking the job on? I thought, and replied, that there would be certain issues which had to be resolved, including the England one-day side – which I had not played in for two years – and the captaincy of it. Then came a text from Pietersen, and a phone call from Geoff Miller, who rang up to say we need you to come into Lord's. All the while there was wild speculation that Pietersen had resigned, and that Moores had resigned – everything was going off.

However, these phone calls from Morris and Miller made it clearer that my ambition to captain England again might soon be fulfilled. So I rang Pietersen to find out how he was feeling, and told him that it looked as if I might be offered the job. When he had asked my opinion about his taking on the captaincy, I had said he would be a fool not to accept. This time, I told him, I would be a fool if I did not accept. And he said: 'No problems, I will back you one hundred per cent. My problem is with the ECB and Peter Moores.'

A little over 24 hours later I was attending a press conference at Lord's as the England Test captain for the tour of the West Indies. It was one of the more daunting press conferences I have done because of the interest throughout the country, and not just from sports followers. It was on the main news on television and radio.

There had been a lack of information and a clamour to find out what was going on. I was expecting some spicy questions about Pietersen's future, and what was wrong with Moores and his coaching, and about divisions in the England side – a particularly awkward question because I had not had the chance to speak to most of them. What I saw as being of the greatest importance was that, after a devastating week for England cricket and the 16 or 17 players who represented it, the repair work had to start immediately.

Next day I met with the England selectors – Geoff Miller, Ashley Giles and James Whitaker (Moores no longer) – to discuss, among other matters, the England one-day captaincy. I felt very strongly that the captain of the England 50-over side should be worth his place, and I had to have the selectors' view on how they thought the side was evolving, and what sort of role they wanted me to play, before I would commit myself to the one-day captaincy. They, for their part, were concerned about appointing someone who had not played a one-day international for two years. But, given the upheaval of the previous few weeks, both sides felt that the main priority for England's tour of the West Indies was stability. Once we had come to this conclusion, and it had been decided that I would lead the one-day as well as the Test side, we could revisit this issue at the end of the tour.

As soon as I had finished our conversation, it dawned on me how much work had to be done before we flew to the West Indies in a fortnight. Who should take over from Moores as coach? What role exactly would he play? Who would the support staff be? (I had no say in the selection of the players as that had been done before everything blew up in the New Year.) How were we going to play the two warm-up games in St Kitts – as 11-a-side games, or 13- or 14-a-side games, as we had at the start of recent England tours? I had to discover the extent of the fall-out from what had happened. I had to ask the advice of some business people about conflict resolution. I had to decide how the tour would be run, and how to implement my general philosophy about how the England team should go forward – something which I had already thought about a lot before being appointed the captain.

Above all, though, I had to come to terms with the job of being the England captain, and the completely different lifestyle this would impose on my family. As the England captain there are always demands on your time. Even when sitting on the sofa at home with your wife or child, there is going to be a phone call from a selector, or a coach, or a player. The England captain's job is all-encompassing: it ranges from the politics of the counties to looking ahead two or three years to future tour schedules, and to what kit we are going to wear. From your family's point of view, being on call all the time is the biggest demand. From the moment I started the full-time job, my mind was always wandering back to cricket when Ruth was talking about what the kids had done today or what she would do tomorrow. The England captain has a much higher profile; there is more interest from all quarters; more people stop you in the street; more opinions are expressed about what sort of person and cricketer you are. And there is more for your family to deal with when you are away from home.

Next, my biggest priority was to find out how the players viewed what had gone on between Moores and Pietersen. The newspapers had made out there was a big division between the players, with some supporting the coach, some the captain. My impression, however, was that they did not want to be involved in this personality clash; and that the most extreme positions were taken up by Moores and Pietersen, while the players were somewhere in the middle. The first thing I did was ring up every player to find out how he felt, did he feel let down, what were we doing right as a side and what badly. And a general theme quickly became apparent: the players wanted to move on and get England back to winning.

This made life easier, but prickly subjects kept cropping up. For example, Pietersen returning to the ranks: he had been supportive on the phone but how deeply was he hurt? Or the back room staff: they had been appointed by Moores and were loyal to him, so how hurt were they? It was a great credit to everyone concerned that they acknowledged what had happened, were ready to move on, and put the interests of the England team first.

At Loughborough before the tour I sat down with the players and went through my philosophy of where the England team had to go. The primary part was that players had to be responsible for their own performances. The management, I said, were on hand to enable the players to practise in the way that best suited them. The players have to be in the best frame of mind when they go out to perform, and if they are then it follows that there are no excuses if they perform badly. My gut feeling was that there was a potential conflict between players having ownership of their game and the increasingly professional management set-up of doctors, fitness trainers, physiologists, psychologists, analysts, and batting, bowling and fielding coaches, all of whom were doing as much as they could to push the players forward. Happily, the coaches bought into my strategy and the players were keen on this new environment.

Duncan Fletcher had tried to achieve – and had achieved – something pretty similar, but there were two main differences between his regime and what I envisaged. Firstly, we did not have as many senior players in the England side as we did when he was the England coach, at least at the time when I came into the side in 2004. Then, in addition to Michael Vaughan, England had some experienced players like Marcus Trescothick, Graham Thorpe, Andrew Flintoff, Matthew Hoggard and Ashley Giles.

Secondly, under Fletcher, there was a feeling of them (management) and us (players). I wanted to break down this division so the players recognised that everything the management did was in the best interests of the team, and the management realised that if the players had problems, it was because they thought they were being prevented from doing their best.

So my aim was to bring the two sides together. But, above all, the players had to be challenged to think for themselves. You might have the best coach in the world, but he will never be out in the middle with you telling you how to bat or bowl. Out in the middle, without a coach, you have to be able to adapt to whatever is thrown at you by the opposition, the conditions or match situation. If you are not used to doing so, you can easily be fazed on big occasions.

When we flew to the West Indies towards the end of January, England did not have a full-time head coach. Andy Flower, hitherto the assistant coach with responsibility for batting, was going to take over part of Moores' job, while Phil Neale was going to deal with some of the administrative duties that Moores had undertaken, like organising the medical staff. The captain's role was going to be different from before in that I had more control than previous captains – again helping to fill the vacuum left by Moores' departure. For this tour I was the head of the management team: if issues arose involving Flower and me, or Neale and me, the ultimate responsibility was mine. But we all realised that we would need to have a bit of a suck-it-and-see approach.

At the back of my mind was the thought that if the cricket went the wrong way, the issues of the previous few weeks might resurface; and I was worried about how the players would react to having more responsibility; and about how the management would react to having more of an advisory role, rather than dictating terms as they had under Moores. Crises in cricket usually come out of nowhere, and it was more difficult than normal to predict how we were going to react to them.

In St Kitts the tour started well off the pitch. The island's government looked after us and provided excellent facilities, including the hotel. Everyone was happy to be running round in the West Indian sun, training and netting, and the first two weeks bonded us together again. On the pitch, after beating a St Kitts XI in a three-day game, things became more tricky when we were put to the sword by West Indies A: an innings of 282 by Lendl Simmons, and a century by an even younger Trinidadian, Adrian Barath, who was only 18 at the time, kept us in the field while they added 262 for the second wicket. Together the pair of them made it apparent that taking wickets would be an arduous process on slow, low pitches like those of the subcontinent. The age of balls flying through above head-height on West Indian pitches was long gone.

After our two warm-up matches in St Kitts we flew to Jamaica for the First Test. On the eve of it I sat down and made my first diary entry since the tour of India. (As is always the case, I had switched off from cricket completely as soon as the last match had finished.)

3 February 2009

Since the tour of India, the whole world of English cricket has changed and the offshoot from it all is that I sit here in my suite in the hotel this evening as captain of England. Not a standby captain, but the captain of England. It is a pretty powerful position, especially as on this tour there is no head coach, and by and large I have thoroughly enjoyed it. There have been plenty of emotions going through my head over the last few weeks, but above all is a feeling that this is the right time for me, and also that I am ready for the job. Every time the job has come up previously, the thought of it has concerned me, but not this time. The players have been very supportive, and I have really enjoyed talking about and implementing some new ideas about the way forward.

The more I think about it though, the set-up and the environment only count for so much. We need to give the players as few excuses as possible, but in the end it is about the players taking responsibility and playing for both themselves and each other. I desperately need the players to play for me, but the only way I can do that is by being honest and leading by example.

The First Test starts tomorrow, and by and large I feel quite relaxed about it. I'm not quite sure why because it is my first Test as captain and it is an important series. I suppose I am quite relaxed because I have no real worries about my game, which is still in excellent working order (scores of 0, 103 and 97 in warm-up matches), and I feel confident that the captaincy stuff will go okay.

Batting-wise this tour is a challenge, mainly due to the pace of the bowlers we are up against. Fidel Edwards is awkward, and the other two bowlers are of decent pace as well. I think I have game-plans for all of them though, and I just need to get myself in my bubble. If I do that there is no reason why my good form should not continue.

Captaincy-wise, I think that I have to remember to stay calm at all times. It is so easy to get caught up in the whole thing, and be too pumped up. My great strength is the fact that I am pretty unflappable, and I will need to remain that way if I want to be successful.

One note of caution at this stage that is important. This is a very long tour, especially with the ODIs, and it is going to be difficult to remain enthusiastic throughout everything. It is absolutely crucial though that I do remain so, especially on my first tour as captain. Results will have a huge bearing on how enjoyable the tour is, but in the end, you can only do your best, and one day I will look back on this tour with great affection. My first tour as England captain.

By the morning of the Jamaica Test, however, there were plenty of nerves around. As I saw it, in my first Test as full-time captain, everyone had to hit the ground running. The cricket was going to be tough because West Indies had been through something of a resurgence: under Chris Gayle they had won a Test match in South Africa, competed for long periods of their home series against Australia, and drawn 0–0 in New Zealand.

Besides Gayle, for batting, they had Ramnaresh Sarwan and Shiv

Chanderpaul, who had held West Indies together in the last Test series between the two sides, and a new batsman of the same style as Chanderpaul in Brendan Nash. In addition to Edwards, they had Jerome Taylor and Daren Powell to use the new ball, and a new left-arm spinner in Sulieman Benn.

For our part, after a winless winter, there was a desperation to get it right on the pitch: we had lost the one-day series 5–0 in India, and the Test series there 1–0, as well as the Stanford game in Antigua. And in the middle of the First Test in Kingston it so happened there was going to be an Indian Premier League auction which, despite our best efforts, was bound to be a distraction. Looking back, it seems as though all these events conspired together against us.

It was the second IPL auction but the first in which English players had been involved. Kevin Pietersen and Andrew Flintoff were already being touted as the most expensive IPL players ever, and several others were up for sale, although of the members of the England Test squad only Paul Collingwood and Owais Shah were bought. Even the most committed England player of all time would have found it impossible not to have kept one eye on the auction in Goa on the second night of the Jamaica Test if he had been involved. When you are talking about earning life-changing sums of money, obviously you are going to be interested. But I would not use any of this as an excuse for our defeat in the First Test. The guys involved never gave any impression they were being distracted from the game – and it is hard to turn up in the England dressing-room on the morning of a Test match and not concentrate. There was just banter in the team bus, and a shaking of hands, and the odd chirp about who was going to buy the drinks. It was a good thing that Pietersen and Flintoff were bought at the same price of $1.55 million and therefore came out with honours even, so there was no competition in that regard between them.

For the first three days, the Jamaica Test was a gruelling war of attrition. Pietersen reminded us of how important he is by scoring 97 in the first innings and in very difficult circumstances. It was a slow, stopping wicket with a slow outfield. Players like Pietersen who had the power to pierce the field were the only batsmen who could score fluently; even Flintoff found it difficult to score. As the pitch dried out, our bowlers had to toil exceptionally hard, but Stuart Broad finished with five wickets and we were satisfied with being in touching distance – a deficit of 74 – after the first innings.

Everything then went horribly pear-shaped. In 20-odd overs the game was lost. Our batsmen were humiliated. We were bowled out for 51, England's third lowest total ever. English cricket was back in the news for the wrong reasons. It looked as though we had choked. Jerome Taylor took five wickets and won the man of the match award. West Indies were celebrating an innings victory, and it was their first win against us since 2000.

Looking back, I still cannot fathom how we were bowled out for 51. Taylor bowled excellently and accurately, but after the first few overs of our second innings it was obvious that the wicket was not difficult. Perhaps the truth is that we gave away a couple of wickets, we did not handle the pressure, and it became one of those crazy sessions when everything goes in the bowling side's favour. The ball did not miss the edge of the bat, it caught the edge. Or it did not miss the stumps, it clipped the side of them, as in Paul

Collingwood's case. And the chances did not evade the fielder, they went straight to him.

Our defeat, by an innings, was a real punch in the guts for the side and me. When you lose a Test match – if it has to happen – you want to feel the opposition have worn you down over a long period, or they have done something inspirational, or the wicket has deteriorated so much that the toss was vital. But as we sat in our dressing-room at Sabina Park we could only look at ourselves and realise that we were the architects of our own downfall and, as if that wasn't bad enough, we had been bowled out for one of the lowest scores in England's Test history – in my first match as full-time captain.

When I woke up next morning, feeling disconsolate and depressed, my first thought was: how could we possibly turn round what had just happened? The players were hurt and saddened. Our confidence had taken a huge knock. And it was up to me and Andy Flower to right the ship in only four days before the Second Test began at the Sir Vivian Richards stadium in Antigua.

8
REVIVAL

12 February 2009

Think of the worst possible way to start a tour, especially as captain, and now you have it. The defeat in Jamaica last week was an absolute shocker, with us working hard to stay in contention in the game for three days before being blown away for 51 on the fourth afternoon.

It was a shocker of a game for me also, with scores of 7 and 9, so all in all things couldn't have gone much worse.

Having said all of that, it has happened, it has been and gone. Generally the captaincy went okay during the game, although at times I was a little slow to react to events, and might have been a little bolder, and more assured in what I wanted to do. I should remember at all times that it is my head on the block, so if in doubt I should do what I feel is right, rather than what others feel.

On the batting side, I got out pretty much the same way in both innings, nicking off to Taylor. I am not overly worried about my form, because I still have a fair amount of confidence there, but I just need to be absolutely certain about my game-plan and stick to it. I don't have to be particularly more aggressive, but I do have to be busy. I suppose that so much time has been taken up with the captaincy side that I may not have thought about my batting quite as much as I should have over the last few weeks. I haven't really got any worries about technique, but possibly I should have mentally prepared myself for batting a little more before last week's game.

There were two other vital cogs in the wheel of revival. The first was a team meeting which we had when we arrived in Antigua – the most honest team meeting that I have been involved in. The players said what they really felt about the team, and about each other, and where they felt let down. Andy Flower chaired this meeting and he did so in a very straight, honest and non-provocative way. I think that, to a man, we came out of that meeting feeling one hundred per cent better about ourselves and clearer in our minds about what we had to do to get back into the series. Having been our batting coach under Peter Moores, Flower was now filling in as head coach, and until that stage he felt unsure about whether he would or should apply for the full-time job. Some headhunters had been employed to carry out a worldwide search for the right person to coach England, and the interviews were going to take place in London after our tour. And I think it was hereabouts, following our defeat in Jamaica, when we had to pick ourselves off the floor, that Flower realised he could play a significant part in our revival.

One of the themes of this clear-the-air team meeting in Antigua was that it was no good sitting in meetings and just talking about being positive, or about bowling in a certain way – we had to go out there and do it. We also knew the only way to react to the completely justified criticism which we had all received after losing the First Test by an innings was to answer it on the pitch.

The second cog in the wheel was that the families all arrived in Antigua. Their presence always gives us a sense of perspective. I had my two boys playing around in the hotel, with Sam old enough to be in the swimming pool. Steve Harmison had his kids, Andrew

Flintoff his family, and all together we dragged ourselves out of the doldrums and realised that our lives were not that bad after all.

Before our arrival in Antigua we had heard that the outfield at the Sir Vivian Richards stadium could be a problem. Those of us who had been at the Stanford tournament three months before remembered there had been no grass on the outfield then. A digger had been visible at this stadium in an area of marshland a couple of miles outside St John's, and it had been sitting in a field of sand, which had been brought in to offset the marshiness. There were no other buildings within sight of the stadium: Antiguans over the years had been deterred by the swamp at North Sound, but not the Chinese engineers who had constructed the stadium for the 2007 World Cup. England had played there against Sri Lanka, and lost by 2 runs, just before I had been recalled to the side, but Australia's game against Bangladesh had been reduced substantially by overnight rain when the drains could not cope, even in tropical sunshine.

The West Indian board told us that we would not be allowed to practise at the Sir Vivian Richards stadium until one day before the game, which raised a few of our eyebrows; and when we finally arrived there we could see why. Under a light covering of grass was a sandpit. Imagine playing cricket on a beach: running after a ball is not easy for fielders, while for bowlers a consistent surface on which to run in is essential for delivery. Would this new ground be fit enough to play the Second Test on it?

Both sides adopted the attitude that we would just have to get on with it, while Hugh Morris on behalf of the ECB wrote to the

ICC before the game to say the field was not fit. But in the first over, after I had lost the toss and Chris Gayle had asked us to bat, it was apparent that there was no way the game could go on. Jerome Taylor ended up bowling round the wicket because he could not get enough of a grip for his feet when bowling over the wicket, and the ball was coming out of his hand at three-quarter pace. Once Fidel Edwards at the other end had aborted his run-up three or four times, the umpires – Daryl Harper and Tony Hill – wisely stepped in and said the ground was not fit for Test cricket. They asked my opinion and I agreed it was unfit: pace bowlers should not be forced to bowl at only 70 per cent of capacity in a Test match. If abandoning the game for the day was the best option, then it had to be done.

No rocket scientist was required, however, to realise that the outfield could not be changed overnight: to dig out some if not all of the sand and replace it with soil, then re-lay turf on top, would take weeks or months, not hours. The only viable options were either to move to the Antigua Recreation Ground, a venue with history and tradition but dilapidated in parts and possibly dangerous for spectators, or relocate to another island. The anger and disappointment on the faces of all the England supporters – who made up almost the entire crowd, as Antiguans clearly had not taken to their new out-of-town stadium in spite of its illustrious name – made me think we should try the ARG and resume proceedings as soon as possible.

Fortunately the West Indian board and the ECB, who had Giles Clarke on site to expedite the discussions, agreed with this relocation. Bringing the ARG back to its rightful place as a Test venue was then a task for the Antiguan government and the West Indian board, and from then on everyone worked hard to do so, not least the television crews who had to work through the night to transfer their lorry-loads of equipment. Electricians spread out hundreds of metres of cables, workmen sawed and banged in nails, an enormous roller levelled what had been turned into a football pitch, and the old ground – the spiritual home of such figures in cricket's folklore as Chicky, with his disco, and Gravy, with his range of colourful costumes – was brought to life again. The ARG is in the centre of St John's, and so long as cricket is played there it will be at the centre of Antiguan life.

As the engineers and electricians did not have time to install all the usual equipment – for instance a trench has to be dug from the boundary edge to the middle to lay a cable for the stump camera – the experiment in this series with referrals had to be suspended for what was now the Third Test. But the match was none the worse for that.

The pitch at this new, and old, venue made us reconsider our team. Steve Harmison had been left out of the Second Test because the slow, low nature of the Sir Vivian Richards stadium would not have suited his style. Monty Panesar had been selected, because we felt that on a pitch where spinners would not extract bounce and turn, he would do better than Graeme Swann in building up pressure. After we had netted at the ARG it was clear the wicket there would have more pace and bounce, so we went for Swann as the more attacking option, especially against the West Indians' numerous left-handed batsmen, and for Harmison instead of Ryan Sidebottom. Ian Bell, who had replaced Michael Vaughan at number three for the Jamaica Test, the two Tests in India and the Oval Test against South Africa, without getting past 25, had already been replaced by Owais Shah. On the surface it may have seemed a strange decision to change the England side after no more than ten balls, but I believed there were sound cricketing reasons.

Preparation had been far from ideal for what had suddenly become the Third Test of this series, but generally I felt good, as my entry shows:

14 February 2009

Valentine's day follows Friday 13th, and one Second Test follows another Second Test. Amazingly the game was abandoned on Friday only ten balls into the game due to a completely unacceptable outfield. It is astonishing quite how shambolic things have been in Antigua generally. In our hotel the service has been the exact opposite of 'service with a smile'. Quite how you cannot monitor an outfield to make sure that it is going to be okay for Test cricket is quite bizarre, but anything is possible out here.

Before the abandonment, I had eased my way to 6 not out, and was generally feeling very comfortable at the wicket, and quite positive. Tomorrow at the Recreation Ground, I have to have a similar mindset.

If the nets at the Rec ground are anything to go by, there may well be some pace and bounce in the wicket. This should suit us, but it should also make life quite uncomfortable for opening batsmen. If that is the case, then I have to show my mettle, get stuck in, and lead by example.

I am quite excited about tomorrow, but we need to switch on again very quickly, and also remember what happened in Jamaica, because that is motivation if ever you needed it.

All of the twenty-two players who went into the Third Test felt they had a duty to put on a good game of cricket. From England's point of view, we had even more of a duty to do so after our defeat in the Kingston Test. This was the type of language I used when speaking to the team before the start. And I felt I had to lead by example: my very first conclusion, after the private soul-searching in Jamaica, was that I had to take the lead with the bat. I had been as guilty as anyone in the First Test of not playing positive shots. I had hung around in the second innings in particular but not thrown any counter-punches. After a side is out for 51, their confidence takes a battering, and batsmen can be tentative and worry about getting out. If you are thinking like that and cannot play authoritative shots, you are almost waiting for your dismissal.

In practice at the ARG we had prepared for a genuinely quick and bouncy wicket, and we were pleasantly surprised. When Chris Gayle asked us to bat first, I thought it was going to be one of those days when the blood flowed and it would be a real battle with the bowler – him against me, rather than me against me, which is how it can be on a slow wicket. I was also conscious that we had been too defensive against the bowling of Gayle and Sulieman Benn in the Jamaica Test. In our first innings there we had scored 186 runs off 54 overs by their three quick bowlers, and 117 off 68.2 overs by their two spinners. Benn, the tallest left-armer I had seen, made some history for himself by becoming the first West Indian spinner for 35 years – since Lance Gibbs – to take eight wickets in a Test match.

So my heart and my head told me it was time to attack them after I had played myself in at the ARG and found that the pitch was not affected by the football centre circle running across it. I whacked

Benn for a couple of fours and a straight six. After getting past 50 it was fairly smooth sailing. I have been fairly good at converting fifties into hundreds, and this West Indian attack was at its best with a new ball. The nurdle to square-leg to bring up my hundred before tea was very satisfying for two extra reasons: because the week before we had been bowled out for 51, and because it was my first as England's full-time captain and you have to get your own house in order.

It was also encouraging to see Shah play with freedom in his first innings back. He played the spinners beautifully and kept the momentum going even though it was only his third Test. By the time I got out just before the close we were in a strong position, and next day an excellent hundred by Collingwood and a fifty by Kevin Pietersen meant that all our batsmen had stood up. So we turned an unimposing total into an imposing one, 566 for nine declared, and dismissed Gayle before the end of the second day.

Following his century in Jamaica, Ramnaresh Sarwan played with even more freedom and had our seamers scratching their heads: how could we stop him cutting almost anything outside off stump, however full, to cover or third man? Fortunately for us, he tried to smack a six against Graeme Swann to reach his hundred and was caught. Pietersen had tried to reach his hundred in Jamaica in similar fashion off Benn, and Collingwood was to fall on 96 when trying to hit a boundary in the next Test in Barbados. In the 90s you are well aware that a hundred is round the corner and, if a spinner is bowling, there is a definite temptation to get it over with and press on to a big score. There is somebody perched on your shoulder saying, 'Finish it off, get rid of the hassle and nervousness with one shot!'

I have found it better, on the whole, to suppress the urge ever since I ran down the wicket to Anil Kumble in the Lord's Test of 2007 and edged a catch to slip on 96. The best advice I had – Graham Gooch used to say it – was to get to a hundred in the same way that you have got to 90. Far more batsmen walk off after playing a big shot and thinking why did I do that than those who keep playing the same way. There is no reason to go for it, but such are the emotions and pressures at times that logic can go out of the window. In the Barbados Test, when I was 99, I did go to three figures with a six off Benn, but all the fielders were up to save the single so it did not feel like a risky shot, and it was one of my better decisions.

The ball after getting out Sarwan, Swann dismissed Denesh Ramdin with a full toss caught and bowled, and went on to finish with figures of 24–7–57–5. His achievement was not quite as historic as Benn's in Jamaica, but it was still ten years since an England offspinner had taken five wickets in an innings (Peter Such at Sydney). Swann had gone to India as very much our second spinner, but from the moment I joined up with the squad he seemed much more mature than when I had roomed with him at the Academy in Adelaide in 2001. With his attacking nature, he has always bowled big-turning deliveries, but in those days he could get frustrated and bowl the odd short ball and be expensive.

It was great to see the transformation in Swann. In the nets, in New Zealand as well as India, I thought he was harder to play, as well as still being Jack the Lad, cracking jokes in the dressing-room and keeping the team going with his energy in depressing moments. So it was not a risk to select him for the Third Test in Antigua: we knew he was going to take wickets at some stage of the series, we were just surprised that it was so soon. Swann offered plenty of variation; he knew how he wanted to get players out. The theory that regular offspinners cannot get Test wickets is not one I have bought into, and especially when the batsman is a left-hander, as more and more seem to be now. In Lance Gibbs's day about one or two batsmen in a side would be left-handed; now it is at least one third and sometimes half a team.

We were 281 runs ahead on first innings, and I decided to bat again. The follow-on is one of those conventions often applied as a matter of course, but I am not sure it should be. Some pitches behave their worst on day five and you do not want to have to chase a lot of runs then. The follow-on has to be applied on a case-by-case basis, and there were several individual considerations that went into this one. Harmison had gone down with food poisoning on the third day; Flintoff's hip had flared up, so badly that he was soon to fly home for treatment and missed the rest of this Test series; and if James Anderson and Stuart Broad were going to do most of the fast bowling in the West Indian second innings, in tropical heat, they needed a break before then. These were the primary reasons why we did not enforce the follow-on – and then, as if to confirm the sense of this decision, Swann's elbow flared up on the fourth morning. He tried to bowl into the coach's mitt and he could not get his arm over: it was too painful because of the pieces of bone which were floating around in his elbow and had to be removed in an operation in the United States after the Test series. This was a major concern because the game was all teed up for spinners in the fourth innings. In the end, after some rest and treatment, Swann was able to contribute 39 overs second time round.

I had ten minutes to prepare myself for our second innings after deciding against the follow-on, and it was an oversight that we did not discuss the matter of a nightwatchman properly. Nobody wants to think about losing a wicket in a short spell of play, and we had only seven overs to bat before the end of day three. There were arguments on both sides, for sending Anderson in as nightwatchman – he had done the job in our first innings – and for not sending him in. The main reason for using a night-watchman was that if Shah had come in and got out on that third evening, he would not have been around to force the pace on the fourth day, and he would have been particularly useful in getting after Benn and the other West Indian left-arm spinner, Ryan Hinds. All in all, it was something we discussed, but only briefly as there was so little time, and we would do it differently if we had our time again.

The instruction to Anderson, and to Alastair Cook, on the fourth morning was to play positively. But Anderson does not have big shots, which is why he is a nightwatchman. Cook wanted to force the pace but in this sort of situation you cannot give away wickets because that will pressurise players lower in the order. The plan has to be to keep wickets in hand so that you can force the pace towards the end of the innings, and we did that. We were only four wickets down when we reached 150 and added the next 50 runs in only eight overs – against fielders who were far more spread out than in a one-day international as there were no fielding restrictions, and in the face of a very slow over-rate.

At the start of the fourth day, when calculating when we should declare and what sort of target we should set them, we were looking at 450 in 130 overs. But with Pietersen switch-hitting and Collingwood smacking it, we accelerated so quickly that we posted a lead of 450 sooner than we had planned. We kept going, knowing that the ARG would not deteriorate: West Indies, on this ground, had made the highest successful run-chase ever in Test cricket in 2002–3, 418 for seven against Australia, and about half of their present team had played in that match. Such thoughts we had in mind as we chewed over when to declare – and, in hindsight, we know we should have declared earlier.

At tea on the fourth day West Indies were 32 without loss after 14 overs. At the close they were three down for 143, with Sarwan and Shivnarine Chanderpaul at the wicket. Our efforts to win on day five were immense. We gave everything we had, everybody chipped in. But, to lead them to safety, West Indies had two of the best players in the world at 'batting time'. Sarwan was enjoying the form of his life, and he made amends for getting out for 94 in his first innings by going to another century: when you are hot, you are hot, and he was a thorn in our side in this series until Trinidad. Chanderpaul was determined to bat all day to save his team. He reached his fifty shortly before Sarwan got to his hundred. Together they batted through until lunch and then to the afternoon drinks break and the second new ball which followed straight afterwards.

It was only when Broad dismissed the pair of them – Chanderpaul with a fine off-cutter – that we felt we had a chance.

So began a manic last session, in which we had to take their last five wickets, starting with Nash and Ramdin. In spite of his injured hip, Flintoff kept charging in, and Swann kept twirling, and wickets falling. But rain before the start had kept us down to only 19 overs in the morning session, costing us several overs. We knew it was going to be too dark by 6 p.m. because daylight goes much earlier around the equator than at home. And so when Daren Powell and Fidel Edwards came together with what turned out to be 14 overs remaining, I could not use fast bowlers all of the time. In the end, the West Indians' last pair held out, with considerable encouragement from their supporters, who must have been far more numerous than if the game had been staged at the Sir Vivian Richards stadium. After 128 overs, West Indies were 370 for nine and the Third Test was drawn.

There is a photograph of Powell and Edwards celebrating the end of the game. I have taken my helmet off, after fielding at silly point, and am holding my head with my right hand. I had no complaints about how the team had performed. It was indeed an exceptional comeback after our defeat in Jamaica. But it was deeply disappointing not to have got over the line.

25 February 2009

It is horrible to have to write this entry and say that we only drew the game in Antigua. It is horrible because we deserved so much better after five days of hard graft and sweat, in which we dominated proceedings from ball one right through to the final ball of the game.

It all started so well. I was determined to lead from the front in this game and I did just that, playing more positively than I have for years in getting 169 on day one. I was happy to go at the ball, and take some calculated risks against both spin and seam. I did have a bit of luck, to be fair, but by and large my frame of mind took me to the century. It was exactly the sort of innings that I needed to play early in my captaincy career, and it was therefore as satisfying as any I have played for England.

From there, things got a little more difficult. Fred got injured, so his bowling was curtailed. Harmison was sick, so couldn't bowl with any sort of hostility, and Swann, although he bowled brilliantly to take five wickets in the first innings, struggled seriously with his elbow after that. With this situation in mind, we couldn't seriously contemplate the follow-on, but we might have played out the second innings better than we did. I went out and tried to be too positive on the third evening and came unstuck, and we were probably too cautious with the declaration, and probably could have had another half an hour at them.

The only reason that any of these are issues is that we ended the game with them nine wickets down, and bad light finally saving the day. Early rain on the final day didn't help either, but we generally did everything right, toiled exceptionally hard, and didn't get what we deserved. It was hard to take, and has taken a while to get over.

As for tomorrow's game [the Fourth Test in Barbados], we need to show that same fight and determination that we did last week. I have to continue to look to be positive in the way I play, but also play to the conditions. I felt that in the second innings I went a little over the top, and tomorrow I have to combine intent with selection. I feel in great form, and 66 retired in the game in between the Tests confirmed how good I feel about my batting. This wicket may be quite quick and bouncy. If that is the case, my job as captain will be to stand up to the quicks, and show that I will not be intimidated. If I can set the tone, the rest will follow.

It is safe to say that the Fourth Test at Kensington Oval did not live up to the expectations of the 10,000 or so England supporters who travelled to see it. In fact, I do not think anyone wants to see the bat dominate the ball excessively, or the other way round. It is no contest if only 17 wickets fall in five days. We conceded the highest total ever made against England – 749 for nine declared – and yet we scored even more runs for even fewer wickets, 879 for eight, spread over two innings.

If you go out and score a hundred on a pitch made for batting, it feels devalued when almost everybody else does. You feel simply that you have not missed the boat. There is no real satisfaction if you have not had to dig deep to reach a hundred; there is nothing special about it if you have not rescued your side. Spectators can watch batsmen playing attractive shots on batting pitches, but bowlers have no chance of taking wickets. I scored a hundred, and so did Ravi Bopara; and Cook scored his first century after 27 Test innings without one; and Sarwan helped himself to 291; and Ramdin made his maiden Test hundred, batting fantastically to stop us winning the game; while Cook was dismissed in the 90s in his first innings, when we put together England's highest opening partnership ever against West Indies, and so was Collingwood.

Bopara came in to replace Flintoff at number six, and grabbed his chance with real flair and conviction. There were those of us sitting on the balcony who thought he was slightly mad to keep hooking Edwards as he ran in on his home ground, but Bopara backed himself and succeeded. He had just had a whirlwind journey from New Zealand, where he had been representing the England Lions, and had not much time to acclimatise: in a two-day practice game on the south coast of Barbados he had scored 60-odd for batting practice.

One of the constant themes of this series in the West Indies was how flat the pitches were, and Barbados saw the outstanding example. Looking into the future, Test cricket has to be an attractive product if it is to survive, and the state of pitches is a massive contributory factor in attracting people. There are too many dead, flat, slow pitches around the world. Batsmen have to work for their runs on them, but it is an issue of temperament not technique.

In addition to spicing up pitches, administrators have to look at the balls as well. Kookaburras, the sort we used in the West Indies, swing for about eight overs when new. Then, after 20 or so overs, the seam goes flat and the leather grows soft. You can feel the old ball coming off your bat less quickly than a new ball. If the pitch is slow as well, the carry to the keeper steadily diminishes and slip fielders go out of the game. I did not have a single slip catch come to me in the whole series in the West Indies, and one chance in the first warm-up game in St Kitts. We had about three slip catches in all over the four (and a bit) Tests.

In England we are lucky that the weather and conditions do some of this spicing up and ensure that most of our Test matches are conclusively decided. In the Caribbean I do not know if the West Indian board were determined to preserve their team's lead once they were 1–0 up. I think that since some of their pitches were dug up in preparation for the World Cup in 2007 it has been tricky on most of their grounds to get a result. On the last England tour in 2004 the ball went through in Kingston and Barbados, but perhaps in general their pitches were getting slower even before the World Cup.

The only other remarkable feature of the Barbados Test was that referrals reared their head again, after a Test without them at the Antigua Recreation Ground. I, personally, have always had problems with players being involved in the decision-making process because it can undermine umpires. Cricket is about the umpires making decisions and players living and dying by those decisions.

Technology, however, is playing an increasing part in the professional game, at domestic and international level, and we do not want people watching on their screens as big errors are made. And if you are going to use technology, the third umpire surely needs all the help he can get – like Hawkeye and Hotspot – to judge. But I do not think that players should be involved. It is for the umpires on the field to call for help if they are not a hundred per cent certain. Consultation, as the process was called, was a worthwhile experiment in the Stanford tournament from what I saw of it inside and outside the radio commentary box. The umpires worked as a team and backed each other up, not one undermining the other. I thought that at times during our series in the West Indies the on-field umpires lost confidence in their ability because they kept on being told their decisions were wrong by the third umpire; and, although I know as much about umpiring as about groundsmanship, I assume that confidence is an important part of it, as in most walks of life.

In the three previous Test series in which the ICC had experimented with referrals, each side were allowed a maximum of three unsuccessful referrals per innings. In this series, we were reduced to a maximum of two, so we had to be quite tactical. The third umpire had to believe conclusively that the original on-field decision was wrong before he could over-turn it, and sometimes the odds were loaded in your favour and sometimes not. By the end, my general impression was that it was pretty hard for us players to judge if a batsman was out or not, especially if the captain is standing at mid-wicket and the keeper is watching the ball and moving his feet and the ball pitches just on or outside leg stump. The umpires are in the best position and our respect for them, as a group, was increased.

We flew into Port-of-Spain, Trinidad, feeling that we deserved to be in a better position than 1–0 down. Turning up at Queen's Park Oval and knowing that a series win was not an option was disappointing, but at least we had one more chance not to lose it. Selection was made easier because we had to gamble. We had to pick five bowlers, even though it meant Bopara had to be dropped after making his maiden hundred, and therefore Monty Panesar came back. We also knew in advance the type of cricket we had to play on another flat wicket.

The game started off in familiar circumstances. We batted first for the fourth time, and dominated the first day's play for the third time. I got my third hundred, a deeply satisfying return in my first series as captain – and decently sized hundreds too. I felt I was batting as well as I had ever done in my life. Collingwood made another hundred, and so did Matt Prior, after going home to see his wife and new baby and missing the Barbados Test. The way that Prior batted at number six – scoring an unbeaten 131 from 198 balls, and 61 from 49 balls in the second innings when we needed quick runs – showed we could, in Flintoff's absence, play five bowlers in future.

Unfortunately, it was again a case of anything you can do, we can do too. Gayle scored a hundred, and Chanderpaul made 147 not out, and Brendan Nash his maiden hundred. It took us 178.4 overs, almost two days, to bowl West Indies out as the pitch stayed its same slow self. By the fourth evening we knew it would take something spectacular to win the game in the time remaining. We felt we had to go out and bat as attackingly as we could in our second innings, and were 80 for three off 15 overs by the close, and added another 157 off only 23.4 overs by lunch on day five. Blasting bowlers everywhere is very difficult in Test cricket because the fielders can go anywhere, without any restriction, the bowlers can bowl much wider than in one-day matches, and the over-rate can be as slow as you want it to be, without risking the match referee's wrath.

Pietersen and Prior played unbelievable innings. Pietersen always thrives when you need something special or dramatic. Fine sweeps off the spinners, switch-hitting, he went through his full repertoire of manoeuvring the ball into the one area where a boundary was possible, and his running between the wickets with Prior put West Indies under even more pressure as they tried to slow the game down and give us as little time as possible to get them out.

We had two full sessions, or 66 overs, to get them out and square the series. We set them 241 to win at 3.6 runs per over, the 'natural' rate of the game to date. We had done as much as we could have done to give ourselves time. We needed to have fielders round the bat, not out saving runs, so we could hardly have declared any earlier. While I had regrets about Antigua, I was far more comfortable with this declaration. We were constantly changing our plans about how many runs to set them in how many overs. Pietersen's hundred was not a consideration and, when lunch came, everything was settled in my mind that it was the right time to declare.

We could not quite bowl them out. They were eight down at the end, with Ramdin at one end as the local hero, and Edwards blocking at the other, as he had in Antigua. Anderson had bowled brilliantly to take three wickets, finding some reverse-swing at the last, and the spinners shared five wickets between them. On that final day we played some cricket that was amazing because of the way we batted, and because of the desire and skill of our bowlers. Therefore it was disappointing, quite apart from the result, that so much focus in the media was on the timing of the declaration.

After the Trinidad Test I met Sir Garfield Sobers. More than forty years earlier he too had made a declaration in a Test at Port-of-Spain for which he had been pilloried throughout the Caribbean because England had won the match and the series 1–0. Sobers said he (like me) had no regrets about his decision, and listed some good cricket reasons for making it. He had set England a chase of 215 in 165 minutes, or what turned out to be 54 overs: the over-rate was much faster in those days, and Sobers had no pace bowler except himself to slow it down because Charlie Griffith was injured. In hindsight it was the wrong decision, Sobers said, but it was the right one on the basis of the information available at the time: for example, the 'natural' run-rate of the game until that stage.

I had set West Indies a significantly easier target in terms of runs per over – less than four runs an over, whereas Sir Garfield had set almost exactly four. But the point is that, when you make a declaration, you are not blessed with complete information. And it is a lot easier to say that someone should declare than doing it.

9
RESURRECTION

As is always the case with modern tours, the players hardly had time to draw breath after a draining Test series before turning their attention to the shorter forms of the game. The Fifth Test in Port-of-Spain finished on a Tuesday evening, only a little before sunset. On the Saturday we played a 50-over practice game at Guaracara Park in southern Trinidad, an hour's drive into the oilfields, past the Brian Lara Stadium which had been due to open for the 2007 World Cup but still had not been completed. On the Sunday we played a Twenty20 international back at Queen's Park Oval in Port-of-Spain, then flew next morning – very early next morning – to Georgetown in Guyana, where the first of our five one-day internationals started on the Friday.

So following three very difficult, arduous and ultimately unsatisfactory Tests a few of us – like Kevin Pietersen, Paul Collingwood, James Anderson and myself – had a well-earned day off on the Saturday when England played a West Indies Players Association XI. Only 'day off' is a bit of a misnomer. After a photo-call for the ICC shortly before 8 a.m., and after a few twelfth man duties while the team slogged in 30° C heat (in the shade, that is), I did a pretty intensive training session with our masseur Mark Saxby in a field beside the Guaracara Park ground.

Our fitness guru Sam Bradley had drawn up a fitness programme which involved the following:

> sprint for 80 metres
> walk for 5 metres
> stride for 10 metres
> sprint for 40 metres
> walk for 5 metres
> jog for 10 metres

Then I had to do it all over again, for half-an-hour, on a sunny afternoon in Trinidad, which is just about on the Equator. The idea is to replicate the pattern of exercise demanded of batsmen in a 50-over game. The first sprint is the equivalent of running 4, or 3 and an overthrow; then a brief pause; then sprint a 2. Whereas fitness training in cricket used to involve long aerobic runs, now it is more cricket-specific interval training.

After this session I was more tired than the guys who had been on the pitch, who won comfortably against an assortment of mainly Trinidadian players. But there were benefits to come, as well as a hindrance. The main benefit was that I went into the one-day series feeling fitter than for a long time. The hindrance was that I slightly strained my right hamstring in the process and jeopardised my chance of taking part in the Twenty20 international at Queen's Park Oval the following day.

The Twenty20 international turned out to be a fairly humiliating experience – all too similar to the Stanford Twenty20 for $20 million match in some ways. The major difference was that we had little or no time to plan for the Twenty20 international in Port-of-Spain. Given that our tour of the West Indies consisted of four Tests (originally) and five 50-over internationals, it was natural for a one-off Twenty20 to come lower down in our list of

On the Lord's balcony after being appointed England captain on 8 January 2009.

Starting at the bottom: my first Test as full-time England captain, in Jamaica, with Chris Gayle and the ICC match referee Alan Hurst.

Rock bottom: 51 all out. Sulieman Benn is more delighted than Monty Panesar or Rudi Koertzen.

It is amazing that anybody ever thought the outfield at the Sir Vivian Richards stadium at North Sound in Antigua would be fit for Test cricket.

Right: Difficult to pick up: Fidel Edwards in front of his home crowd during the Fourth Test in Barbados.

Below left: Alastair Cook and I, with a similar perspective, both scored centuries in the Barbados Test but in different innings.

Below right: The man of our series in the West Indies: Ramnaresh Sarwan, one of the finest offside stroke-players of our time, on his way to 291 in Barbados.

By the Fifth Test in Port-of-Spain Andy Flower was enjoying the job of caretaker coach so much that he had applied for the full-time role of England team director.

Fidel Edwards blocks out the last over from Monty Panesar in Port-of-Spain. Stuart Broad gets his appeal in early.

It comes to us all: Steve Bucknor says farewell after his final international as an umpire, against England in Barbados.

My first one-day international hundred since 2005, ended in Guyana by Kieron Pollard.

Nothing personal, even though he is Australian: Reg Dickason, besides being England's chief security officer, helps in our fitness training.

Left: The attacking offspinner England had been waiting for: Graeme Swann bowling against West Indies at Lord's.

Below: Devon Smith bowled through the gate by Graeme Swann in the Lord's Test. Inspired captaincy!

A highly promising Test debut: Graham Onions bowling wicket to wicket against West Indies at Lord's.

Tim Bresnan, Graeme Swann, Paul Collingwood and myself in the slips against West Indies at Riverside.

Left: Pay-back time – after James Anderson had been given a few bouncers by Fidel Edwards in the Riverside Test.

Below: The Wisden Trophy quickly regained. Back row: Kevin Pietersen, James Anderson, Graeme Swann, Graham Onions and Stuart Broad. Front row: Paul Collingwood, Ravi Bopara, myself and Tim Bresnan. Missing: Alastair Cook and Matt Prior.

priorities. But that was still no excuse for the fairly inept way we played.

With the exception of Steve Davies, who opened the innings on his England debut and batted as impressively as he had done for Worcestershire in their Pro40 season, none of our batsmen got going. By the time I came out to bat at number six – probably not a position that I was suited to, and certainly not a position I was accustomed to – we were 82 for four, and soon afterwards 98 for six in the fifteenth over. A total of 121 on a very flat wicket was never going to challenge West Indies unduly, even without Chris Gayle who had injured himself when taking the single that brought up his hundred in the Port-of-Spain Test, and they won with two overs to spare.

It was a fairly bedraggled England squad that arrived in Guyana the next day. The guys were tired after an early morning flight and a long tour. But we were all acutely aware that England had not won a single competitive game of cricket in the course of the winter. I suppose a side that has gone a long time without winning can go in one of two ways. Either it can lie down and die or dream of home. Or else it can use the fact that it has gone a long time without winning as a motivation to pick itself up and turn things around.

Two factors were in our favour. One was the attitude of the England players: that they had put far too much time and effort into this tour to go home without anything to show for it. Secondly, we were in Guyana and had some time between games, and there was not a huge amount to do apart from practise and concentrate on the cricket.

During one of our first team meetings the squad bought into the fact that we were going to use the three weeks of the one-day series as a training camp for 50-over cricket. There was going to be a lot more fitness training than we would do in a normal one-day series, and we were going to work on our one-day skills on the days between games. Furthermore, Andy Flower and Reg Dickason were going to design 'some tests to put us under pressure when we practised'. We did not know exactly what they meant at the time, but we found out soon enough.

Another of the things we looked at was how to practise better. A normal sort of practice for a one-day international involves a bit of fielding, and a net session against pace and another against spin in which you practise your batting skills by whacking the ball into side-netting without knowing exactly the angle at which it went. In Georgetown we had some middle practice and could get more of an idea of where the ball was going. We also had time to adjust to the conditions which seem to prevail nowadays in the West Indies for one-day matches, specifically slow and low pitches. The batting powerplay, when the batting side chooses the block of five overs in which only three fielders can be outside the semi-circles, was something else we had to work on.

One of our ideas was to play a game among ourselves in preparation for the five-match series. We found a club ground only a couple of hundred yards from our hotel beside the sea-wall which saves Georgetown from the Atlantic. Andrew Flintoff had returned from his treatment back home in England but was not fully fit, while I took part but was still a bit troubled by my hamstring strain. So we decided that James Anderson and Stuart

Broad should be the captains of their respective sides: both had shown real glimpses of leadership potential and we needed them to lead our bowling attack in the one-day series. It was really interesting to see them marshalling their troops. We arrogant batsmen always assume that we should be captain, but we were amazed at how astute they both were. Broad, for example, opened the bowling with the spin of Gareth Batty and kept himself back, then he almost brought off a tactical master-stroke by bringing me on to bowl at Pietersen – he had had some trouble against the left-arm spin of Yuvraj Singh in India – and he struggled to get my filthy left-arm spinners away. I conceded only five runs from my over.

This practice game was highly beneficial for us, and not only because of our glimpse of the leadership potential of Broad and Anderson. In previous one-day series we had often gone behind before thinking deeply enough about our one-day cricket, but now all 15 members of our party were thinking clearly about it before the series started. Both sides in the pick-up practice game had repeated our usual mistakes: we had lost early wickets, hadn't built partnerships and hadn't reacted quickly enough to different conditions. We had not played well but at least we had got some of the poop out of our system, so to speak, without falling behind West Indies.

The first two of the five matches were to be staged at Providence, a stadium on the road between Georgetown and the airport which had been built for the 2007 World Cup, replacing the old atmospheric ground of Bourda in the centre of Georgetown. When you are on a losing streak, you always need something out of the ordinary to break free of it and change the mindset of feeling you are going to lose every game: a piece of individual brilliance, or the opposition grabbing defeat from the jaws of victory, or else a couple of umpiring errors sway the game your way. On this occasion it was one of the bigger coaching blunders that I have seen which got our tour up and running, making Providence very providential for us.

Our batting was almost textbook perfect up until a rain break after 37 overs when we were 190 for three. Even though Collingwood had a migraine, we were looking for 300 before the batting powerplay killed us. On that slow, low wicket we were unable to hit over the top, and the loss of wickets took the momentum out of our innings. That third powerplay, which is intended to help the batting side, brought us 17 runs from the forty-first to the forty-fifth overs, for the loss of two important wickets.

West Indies, needing 271, started slowly in reply after Gayle was out and looked well behind the rate, but they did not lose a second wicket as Lendl Simmons and Ramnaresh Sarwan rebuilt. When they took their batting powerplay after 38 overs, at 173 for three, they were behind the rate but still in touching distance. By then Chanderpaul was embarked on some unbelievable hitting. He had an answer for everything: if we tried back of a length, he pulled; if we tried yorkers, he swept them; if we bowled wide of off stump, he hit over extra-cover. Having batted against Steve Harmison a lot in the nets at Durham, Chanderpaul knew what he was going to bowl and took 26 off one of his overs in that powerplay. As all of the England bowlers and the captain were scratching their heads about where to bowl to him, and wondering where our first victory of the winter would come from, he holed out at square-leg when a couple more blows would have settled the outcome. For it was getting dark by now, as the rain break had delayed the finishing time until sunset, and for this game (although the arrangement changed for the next match) the floodlights at Providence could not be used.

Thankfully, as the umpires congregated to discuss the light, the West Indian coach tried to drag his players off the field as quickly as possible. John Dyson had a Duckworth/Lewis chart with him and seemed certain that West Indies had won the game. Meanwhile, I had my own chart and found it quite hard to decipher. But by the look of it, with two balls gone in the forty-seventh over after Broad had Denesh Ramdin lbw to take the seventh West Indian wicket, we were one run ahead. So I was little surprised to see the West Indian batsmen going off, and I wondered if I had a different chart or was reading it wrong. Then, as we headed off the field, I looked up at our dressing-room and saw our analyst Mark Garaway ushering us off straightaway. He too thought Dyson had made a mistake.

Given the wisdom of hindsight, it is easy to see how Dyson made his error. It is all too easy to forget that the chart – divided into a series of vertical columns – starts with no wickets down for the first column, then one wicket down, then two and so on. But Dyson had assumed that the first column was for one wicket down instead of none. So what he was reading as the column for six wickets down was actually for seven – and West Indies were one run behind the required rate, not one run in front. It was an understandable error (Gayle kindly said afterwards he would not kill his coach for making it), and we were extremely grateful.

Two days later at Providence we fell back down to earth. Chanderpaul – who had just had a street in Georgetown named after him, he was such a local celebrity – gave us an excellent example of how to use the batting powerplay as the way to speed up the back end of the West Indian innings. After 34 overs West Indies had scored 156 for two, and Sarwan – the other local hero – was immediately out, trying to hit over the top. But Chanderpaul accelerated: he went into the powerplay with 54 from 91 balls, and emerged from it with 80 not out from 108 balls. He reverse-swept not only Collingwood and Dimitri Mascarenhas but Broad as well, and finished with an undefeated 112. As the pitch by now was even slower and lower than the first one had been, a target of 265 seemed like a lot of runs to make.

We committed the same errors as usual, losing wickets early on and steadily thereafter, not building a partnership as Sarwan and Chanderpaul had done. Batting in one-day cricket is all about partnerships: if you don't allow a partnership to develop, there is all the more pressure on the new batsman coming in. We did just about stay in touch. I managed to score my first one-day hundred for England since 2005 and although the rate was always climbing, by the time we took our batting powerplay with six overs left, a run-rate of nine an over was not out of the question. The problem was that eight wickets had gone down so Harmison was at the other end, and although I managed to get a couple more boundaries away, a shower then intervened, and when we came back our momentum had been lost. I got out for 105 and we ended 21 runs short.

It made a disappointing end to our week in Guyana, to have let the chance to go 2–0 up slip through our fingers. For me, person-ally, it was very satisfying to have made that hundred and proved to some people who had doubted me that I was worth my place in one-day cricket. That innings was one of the most physically demanding, if not the most demanding, innings I have played. South America can be incredibly hot and humid. If the West Indians are uncomfortable playing in Chester-le-Street in May, as they were soon to do, this is their riposte.

I can remember a warm-up game on a tour of Sri Lanka: as it happened, it was my first game for England of any kind, back in November 2003, at Moratuwa. I made 80-odd and in the course of it I became so tired that I could not run between the wickets. This time, in Guyana, I felt strong right up until the finish, so I felt the fitness training which I had been doing in recent months was paying off – even though the Flower–Dickason special was yet to come. Thanks to being so fit, I had a clear head for decision-making.

The pattern of this one-day series was to play on a Friday and a Sunday in one country, then fly on Monday morning to another, and play on the Friday and Sunday there. This meant that when we arrived in Barbados we still had three days to go before the third one-dayer and I decided to avail myself of one of the island's beautiful golf courses. For the Test match the previous month we had stayed at the Hilton hotel; for the third and fourth one-day internationals we moved to the same hotel as the West Indians used a little further down the coast at Accra Beach. The newspapers reported that a strike by the West Indian players was a possibility – when we had been in Guyana, their first-class players had boycotted the first day of a round of first-class matches – but I did not hear anything from them directly.

The two games in Barbados illustrated the Jekyll and Hyde

nature of England's 50-over cricket at this stage of our develop-ment. The first – the third international of the series – was an absolute humiliation. It was embarrassing to play in and embar-rassing to have to face the television cameras and print media afterwards. If we needed a reminder after Guyana that we still had a huge amount of work to do in our one-day cricket, this was it.

One of the responsibilities of being the England captain is to get the right balance when dealing with the media between supporting your team and speaking the truth. After being defeated by eight wickets at Kensington Oval – although a better indication of the margin of the West Indies victory is that they knocked off the runs in only 14.4 overs – I had to be pretty straight: 'It wasn't a contest and we didn't play well,' I said afterwards. 'The way we batted, there wasn't enough thought in it. We didn't react well to the wicket and made the same mistakes. We are all individually angry with our performances.'

There was more that had to come. 'Losing early wickets is not the way to win one-day internationals and we've done that far too often. We must remember we are playing for our country and have an obligation to play better than that.' For the Test match Kensington Oval had been mainly packed with England supporters, whereas for the one-dayer there seemed to be a balance between the supporters of each side of about half and half. Still, it was not acceptable to be bundled out for 117 with five of us being dismissed playing the hook shot.

We knew well in advance that the pitch was going to be faster than it had been for the Test match, and a lot faster than at Providence. We had practised accordingly in the nets at Kensington Oval which were pacey too. But on the day we did not perform in accordance with our plans. The last thing you want to do as a batsman is question your method against the short ball, and there were a few of us scratching our heads as we sat in the dressing-room after the premature finish wondering how we were going to play in the next game.

To add insults to injury, Gayle blasted 80 from 43 balls with eight sixes. Flintoff, in his first game back after treatment on his hip, was the only one to contain him as he bowled five overs for 19. Having been 1–0 up, we were now 2–1 down, and with no choice but to win the final two matches.

As so often with the England teams I have played with, we bounced back after a terrible performance. After being bowled out for 51 in Jamaica, we had dominated the rest of the Test series even if we could never quite finish West Indies off. After being beaten by eight wickets in the third one-dayer in Bridgetown, we won the fourth by nine wickets there. Why? After a humiliation our confidence should in theory be at its lowest; but we have come back and played good cricket.

The fourth one-dayer was the last international game in which Steve Bucknor umpired, and after standing in five successive World Cup finals and more Test matches than anybody else he thoroughly deserved the presentation he received before the start when both teams lined up in front of the pavilion. Another little present came my way when I won the toss and was able to ask West Indies to bat on a wicket which had a little moisture in it. Gayle on this occasion hit 46 from 39 balls, blasting a few more big shots but without getting away from us, and when he was out, West Indies quickly went from 72 without loss to 83 for three in the sixteenth over. Chanderpaul, at number four, was forced to play himself in.

Earlier in the week Pietersen had given a long interview to the *Daily Mail* which had achieved substantial publicity. Among other issues, he had criticised Chanderpaul. The irony was therefore not lost on us when Pietersen came on to bowl the twenty-sixth over at Chanderpaul – the conditions had led us to leave out Batty as a specialist spinner – and could not complete it because his back went into spasm. He had to be helped up the pavilion steps to lie down, while Owais Shah finished off the over and Chanderpaul batted on.

When we got to the middle of the West Indian innings it was their turn to lose wickets consistently without making a partnership. Mascarenhas, from the pavilion end, bowled his first two overs for 11 but, before and after a break for rain, he bowled some impressively canny medium-pace on a wicket which should not in theory have suited him. In his last eight overs he took three wickets for only 15, as a result of which West Indies were struggling to reach 200. Then Dwayne Bravo used the batting powerplay well at the back end of their innings, scoring most of the 50 runs off their five overs, and got them up to 239 for nine, which still felt like a very chaseable total.

As we were setting out to start our reply, the rains came down. By the time they had finished we had the minimum amount of time allowable under one-day regulations, 20 overs, in which to score 136. There was a tricky decision to be made on our part on how to go about that chase. Andy Flower and I sat down and discussed whether we should treat it like the Twenty20 international in

Trinidad, with me slipping down the order, or as an abbreviated 50-over game. I felt I was in pretty good form and keen to open the batting, and the only adjustment we made was bringing Matthew Prior up to number three as Pietersen was still suffering from his back spasm. In the event, both Ravi Bopara and I scored quickly in the first few overs of bowling powerplay and we never let the target get above sixes throughout the innings. We just needed to hit a few boundaries before cantering home, and so we had squared the series at 2–2 after a lot of people had written us off 48 hours earlier.

One of the difficulties I have had in Twenty20 cricket is being unable to score quickly right from ball one. As a traditional Test opener I always take a few overs to get myself in and judge the pace of the wicket. In this circumstance I was helped by the fact that we had played on this wicket a couple of days earlier, and from ball one the ball seemed to hit the middle of the bat. Fidel Edwards was bowling fast from one end and I felt I had to target Lionel Baker at the other to get our innings off to a quick start. I was able to do that by scoring four consecutive boundaries: a drive over cover, a pull-shot, a square-drive and an upper-cut. That gave us the momentum we needed and I suppose it proved to others, and just as importantly to myself, that it is not impossible to adapt to any circumstances if you are in good form and confident in how you play.

We had five days in St Lucia before the series ended, which for those of us who had been away for the entire tour seemed like an eternity. Rather than sitting around the hotel drinking rum punch and sun-bathing, we all recognised that we had a great opportunity to finish the tour on a high after a very difficult few months, so we continued with the fitness training and tough practice sessions. Unfortunately, two days before the fifth international it was my turn to do the Flower–Dickason pressurisation session.

This involved nine minutes of doing boxing, press-ups and sit-ups non-stop, followed by changing straight into your pads, then going into the net, and every three or four balls Flower would shout out 'run a three' or 'run a two' or 'do ten press-ups'. Then you had to be up and ready for the next ball. The idea of the session is to put you in a state where you are physically very, very tired but still facing cricket balls, and to keep thinking clearly under that sort of exertion. Everyone who did the session really enjoyed it – afterwards. And it was good to know that even when you were that tired, and you could hardly lift the bat because your arms were so sore, you still timed the ball pretty well. The reason for that is you are not thinking too much about the ball coming down at you: you are just seeing it and hitting it. A confirmation, if ever there was one, that too much thinking in cricket certainly does not help.

Going into that final one-day game I was both very excited but also slightly concerned. High-pressure one-day internationals have not gone particularly well for England teams in the past because generally we have not reacted well to that pressure. Sometimes we have been out of the game before it has been halfway through, like our 2007 World Cup match against South Africa in Bridgetown. The effect of not performing as a team on such occasions is to make you doubt your ability to perform under pressure. So I was excited about this game as an opportunity to overcome one of these hurdles, but at the same time I was concerned that, if we were to lose this game, the knowledge that we had bottled it would probably live with us well into the summer.

The prospects for us did not look particularly good early on. The game at the Beausejours stadium was reduced to 29 overs a side after rain which fell during the night and did not drain away during the morning in spite of hot sunshine. I got out early and although Bopara and Pietersen both played very well for 40s, we looked like we might fall a little short of where we wanted to be. Thankfully Collingwood batted very well at the end and got us to 172–5, a total we thought we had a decent chance of defending.

Anderson started the West Indian reply in the best possible way by getting out Gayle in the first over, caught by Flintoff at second slip. In his five innings in the series Gayle was dismissed by our opening pair five times: three to Anderson, two to Broad. Although he hit us for 80 in Bridgetown, he made only another 67 runs in the rest of the series. West Indies hit some decent shots, but the fact they were losing wickets consistently meant they were under the greater pressure. Flintoff got two wickets in his first spell then came back to take a hat-trick during the batting powerplay to settle the game and the series. Tremendous, accurate, death bowling by Flintoff once again underlined how important he is to the side.

As we sat in the dressing-room afterwards, drinking a few beers and having a fines meeting, we shared an amazing feeling of togetherness. In spite of all the odds against us after the third one-dayer, we had accomplished something and had a trophy to show for our winter. We did not go to the West Indies with the primary intention of winning the one-day series, but we felt we had deserved our success in the end. And it put us in a positive frame of mind for another arduous summer ahead.

When I look back at this time, it is important to remember we were not the complete article. Our batting was wildly inconsistent; some of our bowling in the powerplays could have been better. But we had several big hopes for the future to take back to England. Bopara did not make any match-winning contributions but he played with a huge amount of poise and competence and just looked the part of an England one-day opening batsman. We had been dying for someone at the top of the order for a long time, since Marcus Trescothick had retired, and it looked as though we might have found him.

Anderson and Broad were hostile with the new ball, and also took wickets when they came back later in an innings. As Gayle was – and is – a genuine matchwinner, getting him out early was as important a factor as any in our success; and Anderson and Broad accounted for him five times out of five. England's last significant 50-over success abroad had been in Sri Lanka a year and a half before, in October 2007, and that too had been founded on the success of our pace attack: the same pair of Anderson and Broad, backed in this case by Ryan Sidebottom who took the new ball. In the West Indies Broad and Anderson were mainly backed by Flintoff, but he played in only the last three of the five games.

The third real positive was the standard of fielding, another source of encouragement. At last we squeezed the opposition in the way in which England batting sides had been squeezed in the past. Bopara made another important contribution by becoming our backward point, with Collingwood at extra-cover, and I fielded at mid-wicket when we had only four men in the semi-circles. We lost two wickets to run-outs in the first two games but we were equal with West Indies by the end.

Occasionally you see teams like India and Pakistan who can win one-day internationals whatever the standard of their fielding. But England need to turn on a world-class fielding display in order to win one-dayers regularly, and in the West Indies, especially in the last two games when the unforced errors were virtually eliminated, I felt we were getting close. By the end we were not worried about misfielding, we were only concerned with getting the ball in as quickly as possible, and that sort of confidence can only come from a lot of sustained hard work.

Richard Halsall deserves a lot of credit as our fielding coach. He was the first fielding coach in county cricket when Peter Moores was the coach at Sussex, and when Moores was appointed to be the England coach he brought Halsall with him. He had lived part of his early life in Zimbabwe, and had gone back there as an adult to play for a season or two, and it has been a feature of Zimbabwe's cricket that they have always put a lot of emphasis on fielding.

Halsall has pioneered the use of bowling machines in fielding practices. Most coaches whack high catches with a bat; Halsall uses a bowling machine instead, for two reasons. A bowling machine is so much more accurate, and it can send the ball higher in the air and further along the ground, and therefore take us to our limits in practice.

A good example occurred during the one-day series against West Indies in England, in late May, when rain reduced it from three matches to two. Before the game in Bristol, which happens to be where the Bola bowling machine is manufactured, we divided the squad into two teams. Halsall, meanwhile, set up two bowling machines about 40 yards away from the boundary – and about 20 yards apart, so the two teams did not get in each other's way but one could see what the other was doing. Each machine was not set up on its three legs, as it normally is for batting practice, but placed on the ground.

When Halsall gave the word of command to start the practice, a ball was fired from each machine towards the boundary, and at such a speed that the fielder had to sprint and dive to stop it going over the rope. The pursuing fielder also had to flick the ball back to his team-mate who was running just behind him and who had to throw the ball back to the coach, standing beside the bowling machine, before the other team did. It simulated exactly what happens on several occasions in every 50-over game, or 20-over for that matter: the TV and radio commentators get excited saying the ball is going for four then no it isn't, the crowd strains its neck for a better view as one fielder dives, and the third umpire and match referee check their monitor to make sure that no part of the fielder was touching the boundary rope when the ball was flicked back.

This game within the game went neck-and-neck to nine-all before one team won 10–9. As a practice, it was fast, fun, competitive and worthwhile because it replicated precisely what happens on the field. And, after Halsall had helped to set such a purposeful tone, it was no coincidence that we won the international next day by the comfortable margin of six wickets, after bowling West Indies out in only 38 and a half overs; and the third international at

Edgbaston by 58 runs. In those two matches we brought off four run-outs; and whereas there had been nothing between the sides during the one-day series in the West Indies – nothing except a miscalculation by John Dyson – the gap between them a few weeks later in England was fairly emphatic.

Halsall had calculated that over the course of England's 50-over internationals in the calendar year of 2008, we had conceded or lost six runs on average per innings in unforced fielding errors. In several of our matches against West Indies in the first half of 2009, thanks to the hard work of all concerned, not a run was lost.

10
THE AUSSIES

My first net session back with Middlesex after returning from England's tour of the West Indies was no ordinary net session. It was the first time I set eyes on Phil Hughes, Middlesex's Australian import for the first six weeks of the season, and someone surely to play a big part in the Ashes coming later in the summer.

It was a slightly awkward meeting. There had been a lot of press comment about counties signing Australian players prior to the Ashes series; and I, for one, thought that counties signing Australians for short stints before the Ashes gave the players far more benefit than the teams they were playing for.

In Middlesex's defence, they had signed Hughes before he was involved in the Australian squad at all. Angus Fraser had heard about a dashing left-handed opening batsman from the outback who was making a reputation for himself with the Sydney grade side, Western Suburbs. Hughes was a very exciting prospect, with the potential to play for Australia, but Middlesex did not have a crystal ball at the time they signed him.

There are several issues involved in this debate. One is that, since air travel became relatively cheap, English county cricketers by the dozen have flown over to Australia for the winter to make a bit of money and play some cricket at the weekends; and, provided they have been good enough to make the grade, these players have been welcomed. Of the current England Test team, I myself had benefited in this way from three seasons of playing in Sydney; Paul Collingwood had been club player of the year in one of his seasons in Melbourne; Ravi Bopara and Stuart Broad had also spent a winter in Australia, toughening up themselves and their game.

On the other side of the equation, numerous Australians have been signed by English counties since 1968, when immediate registration was allowed and 'imports' did not have to qualify by residence in England before playing county cricket. Greg Chappell was the first big name, working on his game at Somerset before going back to Australia and scoring a hundred against England in the Ashes series of 1970–1. Of the 2009 Australian Test party, every one of the six specialist batsmen – Hughes, Simon Katich, Ricky Ponting, Michael Clarke, Mike Hussey and Marcus North – had played county cricket, usually at an early, formative stage of their careers.

Australia's allrounder Shane Watson was another who had played county cricket. So had Stuart Clark: in 2005 he had been playing for Middlesex, and the Australian selectors reportedly came close to calling him up before sticking with the fast but not particularly accurate Shaun Tait. Then Kent tried to sign Clark for the start of the 2009 season, before he was prevented by not being able to get a UK visa in time, and a few weeks later Gloucestershire tried to sign him for a couple of championship matches in June, before he was prevented for the same reason.

So one of the questions that arises here is: are we comparing like with like? It is highly beneficial for a young English cricketer to go to Australia for the winter; to train and play in a different environment; to learn how to make the most of a chance when it comes along because you might get only one innings, or one spell of bowling, every two weeks. But very few Englishmen have ever played first-class cricket for an Australian state: several went to Tasmania when they were finally admitted to the Sheffield Shield in the 1970s, but Ian Botham and Graeme Hick have been the only two famous players of the last generation. They went to Queensland, who then decided they were going to rely on home-grown players to win them their first Shield.

Australians who sign for counties play far more cricket – five or six days a week – than English players who join Australian clubs. Usually it is batsmen who come, and usually they make runs by the bucket-load. Before the 2009 tour, Mike Hussey had scored over 6,000 first-class runs for his three counties, and more than 3,000 runs in limited-overs games: a thorough grounding. Simon Katich had scored over 4,000 first-class runs for his four counties, and more than 2,000 limited-overs runs. The pair put in a great deal over the seasons, but there can be no doubt that they also took a great deal from the experience. Hussey must have got into the Australian Test side partly on the strength of all his runs in English cricket. Katich too must have got into the Test side, and got back into it after some time away, for the same reason.

Unfortunately, my first net session with Hughes coincided with Middlesex's press day. So I had to combine making him feel welcome with saying that importing Australians was probably not in the best interests of English cricket. I certainly did not feel Hughes was in any way at fault personally. If I had been in his situation, I would have done exactly the same thing. In fact, I had been in very much the same situation, when I had been invited to play for Northern Districts just before England's Test tour of New Zealand.

In that net session in the Nursery at Lord's, Hughes and I batted at the same time. So any glances I had in the direction of his net were in between balls that I was facing myself, and not too many conclusions could be drawn about where his strengths and weaknesses might lie. However, I did have a better chance to look at him during my first championship game of the season, against Leicestershire at Southgate. By then Hughes had already scored his maiden hundred for Middlesex against Glamorgan at Lord's.

It was very interesting to see a young guy playing in such an unorthodox manner as we shared a second wicket stand of 244 against Leicestershire. To me, that takes a huge amount of self-belief, to play the way that you know works for you, even though as a youngster many people would have told you to bat in a different way. His technique seemed impressive, but his clarity of thought and willingness to back his technique were even more impressive attributes. Time alone was going to tell whether his unorthodox style would be successful in England and places like the subcontinent, but there was no arguing with what he had done in his career to date (and he was only 20 years and a few months old when he started the season with Middlesex): he had taken Test cricket by storm and averaged over 70 in first-class cricket.

Stereotyping though this may be, Hughes had all the character-istics you would expect of a young Aussie. He was a very confident bloke, he settled well into the Middlesex dressing-room, he gave a bit of chirp when necessary and occasionally when not; and he was immensely popular with the rest of the team. To those people who had questioned how Australia were going to live without Adam Gilchrist, Justin Langer and Matthew Hayden, the depth of Australian cricket was quickly demonstrated when they toured South Africa in early 2009 and Hughes, the left-handed replacement, scored a century in each innings of his second Test – the youngest batsman ever to do so. I saw only a few highlights of those two hundreds as I was otherwise engaged in the West Indies. But I always knew that anyone who expected a weak Australian side to come to these shores was going to be disappointed.

In Middlesex's game against Leicestershire I managed to outscore him at first but we both finished up with hundreds on a typically good Southgate wicket, and the match petered out into a draw. During our partnership it struck me that Hughes's unorthodox technique stemmed from the amount of room he gave himself in which to play his shots, in the same way that someone a little bit scared of getting hit might play, but in his case he was definitely not scared of getting hit. Giving himself room opened up a huge scoring area on the offside, which opposition captains found hard to plug.

Hughes was born and brought up in Macksville in northern New South Wales where it is hot enough to grow bananas, which his father did for a living, and he was playing against adult bowlers from the age of 12. So one might conjecture that his style evolved as an attempt to get short balls away square on the offside at an age when he naturally did not have the power to score much in front of the wicket. From Macksville he had gone to Sydney and been taken under the wing of the same man who had coached Michael

Clarke, rising through the Western Suburbs ranks and becoming the youngest player, at 19, to make a century in a Sheffield Shield (or Pura Milk Cup) final.

Just before that Middlesex game at Southgate I joked with Hughes that I was going to try my best to run him out. And, to be fair, I nearly succeeded when I hit a ball straight back at the bowler – Leicestershire's overseas player from New Zealand, Iain O'Brien – and he deflected it just wide of the stumps early in Hughes's innings. Otherwise all potential rivalries were put to one side in Middlesex's cause, and it was actually very enjoyable to bat with a young guy of so much talent, whatever the future held in store.

In many ways the Australian Test party of 2009 was unrecognisable from the teams that I had played against previously. They were shorn of their legends – and I use that term having considered it – such as Shane Warne, the greatest legspinner of all time by most accounts; Glenn McGrath (another Middlesex player!); Adam Gilchrist, again, by most accounts, the greatest wicket-keeper/ batsman of all time; and Matthew Hayden, who I happened to play against very early in my career. Before I was selected for Middlesex's first team, I was picked to open the batting for British Universities in a Benson and Hedges Cup match at Oxford, and who should stride out with a mighty chest to open the innings for Hampshire but Hayden. Needless to say, he scored a hundred and won the game for his county, but he also bowled nine overs of medium-pace because Hampshire were short of seamers. Even so, I scored only a single, before returning to Durham University and Middlesex second eleven with much to learn.

You would normally have expected a huge gap to need filling after the retirement of these four players, who might all be selected for Australia's greatest ever Test XI. And Australia's defeat at home by South Africa in 2008–9 showed that while some talented players were taking the places of these legends, their team were certainly beatable. Then Australia's revival in the subsequent Test series in South Africa showed what we all know about Aussies: that they will fight, and they will come back, and they will never give up. Before the South Africans had got out of their starting blocks after a three-week rest from their tour of Australia, Ricky Ponting's new-look team took the opening day of the First Test, and piled up 400-plus after a shaky start when Hughes was dismissed by his fourth ball on his debut. Australia went on to win the First Test, and the Second, and only faltered when Marcus North went down sick on the eve of the Third Test, and they had no reserve batsman to take his place.

As England's think-tank planned for the Ashes, we knew we were likely to face some guys we had never faced before at Test level: Mitchell Johnson, the star of Australia's 2–1 victory in South Africa; Peter Siddle; North; Hughes; Nathan Hauritz; and perhaps Ben Hilfenhaus. We knew they would all be very keen to make their mark on an Ashes series, and that Ponting would be equally keen to move on and put the retirement of those legendary players behind him.

While Australia's bowling was uncertain, we were fairly sure about Australia's batting line-up: Simon Katich was going to be Hughes's opening partner, an extremely consistent performer in domestic cricket, both in Australia and in English cricket for various counties (Durham, Derbyshire, where he had been captain, and more briefly for Hampshire and Yorkshire). Katich had developed an unusual technique, almost the exact opposite of his opening partner. Katich moves a long way across his stumps to the offside, whereas Hughes goes back outside leg stump. He played against us in the 2005 series, batting at number six and making several important contributions to their cause, notably at Lord's where he held us up with his crease-occupation as well as his run-scoring: he batted longer than anybody in Australia's first innings and second-longest in their second. A gritty customer who had been forced to fight very hard to get into the Australian side in the first place – for the Headingley Test of 2001, when Steve Waugh was injured – and then to regain his spot. Also a useful bowler of chinamen, good enough to have taken six wickets in a Test innings against Zimbabwe, but our intelligence sources suggested that a shoulder injury had prevented him bowling as much as his captain would have liked.

Ricky Ponting: Australia's best batsman, he came to England with an incredible record in Test cricket of 37 hundreds, second only to Sachin Tendulkar, and an average of 56, even higher than Tendulkar's. Ponting has long been able to take the game away from you with his aggressive intent and shot-making. One encouraging feature for us was the statistic that he had been more successful in Australia than in other countries: his Test average at home was almost 61, whereas in England he had averaged 42 in his 13 Tests, and 20 in India, where he had struggled against spin – especially the offspin of Harbhajan Singh – until he had made a hundred there on Australia's tour in late 2008. At 34 he had decided that the second IPL tournament in South Africa was not for him and a break before the Ashes would be more beneficial. He was also allowed to rest from Australia's one-day series against Pakistan in Dubai and Abu Dhabi. Refreshed, and determined to advance his reputation as the creator of a new-look Australian team, in addition to having led the old world champions, he was clearly the wicket to get.

Mike Hussey enjoyed an amazing start to his Test career, averaging 86 over his first 14 Tests, which is as close to Bradman as you can get; and he also averaged more than 100 over his first 28 one-day internationals, which not even Bradman might have done if he had been a one-day finisher. Hussey's left-handed middle-order batting was a huge cog in the 2006–7 Aussie machine that humiliated us 5–0. I had not seen much of him in county cricket but his ability to concentrate has always marked him out, whether he was playing for Western Australia or one of his three English counties, Northamptonshire, Gloucestershire and Durham, where he was credited with starting the resurgence which led them to win their first championship title in 2008. For Northamptonshire he scored three treble hundreds, which took him alongside Graeme Hick and Wally Hammond as the scorer of the most trebles in county cricket – and he played considerably less than the other two. More an accumulator than a dominator, Hussey had still been highly effective when batting between Ponting and Clarke; or at least he was until a dip in form during 2008 which lasted into 2009.

Michael Clarke: one of the youngest members of Australia's Test party and yet the third most experienced after Ponting and Lee in terms of caps, leading him to be the vice-captain. Another teenage prodigy, like Ponting and Hughes, he started his Test career in the best possible fashion with a hundred on debut: 151 against India in Bangalore, and made in pretty rapid time off 248 balls with four sixes. He suffered the inevitable dip in form, and was omitted from the Australian side soon after the 2005 series, when he scored a fine 91 in the opening Test at Lord's but added only one 50 thereafter. He came back out the other side as an increasingly consistent performer, although he has yet to surpass that 151 as his highest Test score. His quick feet enable him to play spin as well as anybody in the Australian side, as evidenced by that hundred in India. His left-arm spinners can be handy in the right conditions, and as we planned our Ashes campaign we thought it was possible that Australia would go into at least some of the Tests with four pace bowlers and leave the spin bowling to part-timers like Clarke, North and Katich. Clarke has bowled more and more as his Test career has gone on, following Warne's retirement, but half of his 18 wickets before the Ashes series came in two sensational spells: six for nine in Mumbai, in what the ICC subsequently did not consider to be 'the right conditions', and three wickets in less than a couple of overs to finish off the dramatic Test in Sydney against India.

Marcus North was someone I knew only a little about, not having played with or against him before so far as I was aware. He had replaced someone I was very aware of, Andrew Symonds, who had scored a big hundred in the Melbourne Test of 2006–7 to secure his place at number six for what looked like a long time to come. But then came some well-documented troubles, Symonds was suspended more than once for disciplinary reasons, and although he made the Australian squad for the ICC World Twenty20 he was sent home before the competition started – and, without one of their key allrounders, Australia were beaten in both of their qualifying matches. North, so we heard, was a quieter and less controversial character; a batsman who tended to walk across his wicket, like Katich, and also brought up in Perth, where straight good-length balls tend to go over the stumps rather than pin you lbw; and an increasingly useful part-time offspinner. In his two Tests in South Africa, besides hitting a hundred on his debut which spoke well of his character, he had taken a couple of wickets, before falling ill with gastro-enteritis and missing the Final Test.

A Test innings of 169 off 222 balls, with 24 fours and two sixes, scored by a wicket-keeper. It sounds like Adam Gilchrist, but it was actually Brad Haddin, playing against New Zealand in Adelaide. Haddin, as Gilchrist's successor, had enormous boots to fill but he went some of the way towards filling them in his 15 Tests before the Ashes series. Indeed, some judges thought that he was going to be more dangerous as a number seven batsman in the 2009 series than Gilchrist was in 2005 when he was nearing the end of his Test career and did not have much of an answer to Andrew Flintoff bowling from round the wicket. Haddin, we knew, was particularly strong in hitting to leg, both in the air (he often opened for Australia in one-day internationals) and along the ground; and he could be very dangerous when batting with the tail. His wicket-keeping technique – modelled on Ian Healy – was going to be tested in English conditions, where swing and the dreaded wobble after pitching can make keeping very difficult at times.

Assessing Australia's batting line-up was therefore relatively straightforward: if they did not go outside their Test party, for example by calling up Chris Rogers from Derbyshire, the only alternative was Shane Watson – and Shane Warne gave him a plug in his newspaper column, for one of the Test batting positions, at the same time that Watson had another in his series of injuries. Australia's likely bowling line-up was always going to be more difficult to predict.

For their opening four-day, 12-a-side game against Sussex, the Australians omitted Andrew McDonald, a medium-pacer who had bowled very economically in South Africa until, with the series lost, A.B. de Villiers went after him and blasted him for four consecutive sixes. It seemed fairly certain that Australia would not include an allrounder like McDonald as one of their four-man attack, but would rely on specialist bowlers.

Ben Hilfenhaus, the sharp Tasmanian outswing bowler, had filled in capably in South Africa but was likely to lose his place once his rivals were fit. So, we reasoned, Australia's attack would consist of four out of the following five, depending on the conditions: Mitchell Johnson (an absolute certainty), Brett Lee, Stuart Clark, Peter Siddle and the offspinner Nathan Hauritz. Hauritz was trying to fill Warne's unfillable boots, but he was not to be underestimated, and I thought he would be hard work. Against right-handers he would bowl quite an attacking line outside off stump, but would seek to contain in the first half of a Test, allowing the seamers to attack from the other end.

I had played alongside Lee at Mosman, and against Clark when he was representing Sutherland in Sydney grade. I had faced

Johnson in the one-day internationals of the Commonwealth Bank series which England had won in 2006–7. But Siddle was an unknown quantity to all of us in the extended England squad that was selected for a training camp before our three-day game against Warwickshire, which was prefaced by a visit to Flanders. In his two series against South Africa Siddle had clearly impressed Ponting as a strong, hit-the-deck type of bowler with good pace, stamina and aggressive intent.

Johnson was Australia's form bowler, even more than Siddle. The footage on our laptops showed him swinging the new ball into South Africa's right-handers in the Johannesburg and Durban Tests, by standing taller in the crease and getting his wrist behind the ball, as well as reversing the old ball away from right-handers (and into left-handers) as he used to do. He had come of age in South Africa and bowled brilliantly.

Lee, meanwhile, was rehabilitating after an ankle injury he had suffered during the Melbourne Test: he had recovered enough to play in the IPL in South Africa, then joined Australia's 50-over squad in Abu Dhabi and Dubai, before coming to England for the ICC World Twenty20. With age (he was now 32), Lee had added control. I had always thought him to be at his most dangerous when he was swinging the new ball or reversing the old.

Clark, like Lee, was coming back from injury and needed some bowling to regain his rhythm. As I remembered from grade cricket and his time at Middlesex, he liked to get in close to the stumps and bowl a tight line, resulting in a lot of 'bowleds' and 'lbws'. Similar in height and pace to McGrath, Clark hit the seam, which made him all the more formidable in English conditions.

In the event, neither Kent nor Gloucestershire were able to give Clark the bowling he wanted to find his rhythm before the Australians' tour started. Visa procedures stopped Clark arriving in time, so he had to make do with the Australians' two warm-up matches at Hove and Worcester. The relationship between the counties and the ECB is a complicated one. Both sides feel at times that their best interests are not being looked after, yet it is vital that their relationship is honest, healthy and co-operative. And we all have to be mindful of where the majority of the money comes from, and the principle that the man who pays the piper calls the tune, and not concentrate too much on short-term gain.

11
COUNTDOWN

The first step in England's build-up to the Ashes series of 2009 had nothing to do with playing cricket on the park. Instead, in April, the England and Wales Cricket Board had to appoint what they called the England team director, or, in more old-fashioned terminology, the coach of the national team.

After settling into the job of caretaker coach so well and helping us to win the one-day series in the West Indies, Andy Flower was the overwhelming favourite to get the permanent job. Certainly, having worked with him, I was very keen for him to get it but I was not involved in any way in the process of selecting the coach and did not even know who the other candidates were.

That Flower was appointed to be the full-time England coach was a great testament to the work he had done in the West Indies. He had taken over in difficult circumstances following Peter Moores' dismissal, and had been fiercely loyal to him. He had to deal with the fall-out from Kevin Pietersen's resignation from the captaincy and return to the ranks. Yet Flower had still brought the team together after this very messy period, put all the bygones behind him, and done what was in the best interests of the England Test and one-day teams. This was a fantastic start for a caretaker coach, and he quickly gained the respect of all the players.

We also saw a very different side to Flower from what we had experienced previously when he had been England's batting coach and Moores' assistant. He has got very clear views about how the game should be played, and we saw much more of them once he was the man in charge. He is a hugely respected figure in world cricket for his exploits on the field as a wicket-keeper/batsman (he became number one in the ICC's world Test batting rankings, and finished with an average over 50); for the stand that he and Henry Olonga made against Robert Mugabe in the 2003 World Cup by wearing black armbands during a match in Harare to symbolise the death of democracy in Zimbabwe; and for the quiet and methodical way he goes about speaking to people. What the players really appreciated about Flower was the fact that, while he was not afraid to ask difficult questions and challenge players, he was above all incredibly honest and told them what he thought; and if you are going to communicate with people, this is probably the best way to go.

What may well have been the turning-point in Flower's decision to go for the job full-time was our team meeting in Antigua after England's 51 all out in Jamaica. He had taken the caretaker role hesitantly out of loyalty to Moores as much as anything and, looking back, that meeting was significant because of the feedback he got. I think everyone was surprised by how well he went about chairing it. Before that time, when I asked him if he was going to apply for the full-time job, Flower would say he was going to take a gauge from the rest of the players during the second half of the tour. So I think this meeting was quite an important step in whetting his appetite for becoming the permanent England coach, or team director.

I had watched him a lot when he was playing for Zimbabwe. I

enjoyed the way he batted and seemed to have an answer for all the questions the bowlers threw at him. To me, that was evidence of very clear and logical thinking. I had also played against him a couple of times for Middlesex against Essex and had marvelled at his sweeping and reverse-sweeping of spinners – something which, ironically perhaps, he has not tried to force on the England players at all. If you want to list the ingredients of what makes up a good international coach, I would say respect for what you have achieved is high on the list, along with a very good cricket brain, and the ability to articulate your thoughts.

There was a real feeling in the West Indies that we were coming together as a team again, and Flower's permanent appointment meant that we all met up for the Lord's Test match in a very positive frame of mind. But there was another issue, apart from the coaching, which we had to deal with at the start of the 2009 summer. There was the messy scenario of four players in the First Test squad – Paul Collingwood, Kevin Pietersen, Andrew Flintoff and Ravi Bopara – coming back from the Indian Premier League in South Africa shortly before the Lord's Test began against the West Indies: they had to be back on 1 May, before it started on 6 May. Flintoff, unfortunately, came back earlier than scheduled after injuring his right knee.

We were all pretty conscious that when our IPL players turned up they had to have their minds switched on to the Test match we were about to play. Great credit goes to the three guys who played in that Test for coming back so energised after their time over there. They clearly loved the razzamatazz of the tournament; they clearly loved being involved with the best players in the world and learning from them; and they also enjoyed getting away from the travelling circus that accompanies the England team wherever we go, and the pressure of representing your country. Collingwood had been contracted with the Delhi Daredevils, along with Owais Shah, even though neither of them played; Pietersen had played for (and captained) Bangalore Royal Challengers, Bopara for King's XI Punjab, and Flintoff for Chennai Super Kings.

In the Trinidad Test we had opted to play five bowlers rather than the safety first option of an extra batsman instead of Flintoff, and with Matthew Prior looking every inch a quality international batsman we felt strongly that five bowlers was the way to go again at Lord's. The trouble was that, of the bowlers who had represented us in the West Indies, Steve Harmison appeared to need some time away from the set-up to regain rhythm; Ryan Sidebottom had some trouble with an Achilles heel, and Amjad Khan was injured as well.

The two bowlers who had started the season most promisingly were Graham Onions and Tim Bresnan. Onions, who had gone on a couple of England 'A tours, played in the opening game of the season for Durham, the 2008 county champions, against MCC (so keen were Ian Bell and Adil Rashid to get a game after the tour of the West Indies that they went virtually straight from St Lucia to Lord's). In his first championship match of the season for Durham Onions had taken five for 56 off 28 overs in one innings against Yorkshire, and eight wickets in the match. In his second, against Somerset, he bowled unchanged to take six for 31 and dismiss the home side for 69, even if they made a draw of it in their second innings. Bresnan, meanwhile, took a couple of wickets for MCC against Durham and three for Yorkshire against Durham, not to mention his effective lower-order hitting.

It is fantastic to see new guys coming into the squad. Obviously this is not something you want to do all the time, because that would tend to mean you are clutching at straws, but when players who have not played for England before come into the squad they make you realise quite how special it is to represent your country. These two guys who were in line to make their Test debut were like cats that had just got all the cream. The energy that Onions and Bresnan displayed in practice, the contribution they made in team meetings, the enthusiasm that rubbed off on the rest of the players prior to that First Test match: it was a great credit to the pair of them that they were not overawed when they had their chance and were determined to appreciate it.

Onions in particular enjoyed his first outing for England, taking five wickets in the West Indians' first innings, after another newcomer to the side, Bopara, had justified his inclusion at number three with a brilliant innings of 143. It was actually his second hundred for England in succession because after hitting – in large part hooking – his maiden Test century in Barbados, he had been replaced by an extra bowler in Port-of-Spain, before returning to the team at Lord's, where he was promoted from number six to three.

The number three position has proved to be more difficult for England than for most countries in this decade. Starting in 2000 these are the figures for the number three batsman in Test cricket, country by country. In other words, Ricky Ponting, Kumar Sangakkara and Rahul Dravid have been pivotal in their side, whereas England have got a century once every ten Test innings from their number three (myself included in New Zealand):

	M	I	NO	Runs	HS	Avge	100	50
Australia	106	186	22	9960	257	60.73	34	37
Sri Lanka	88	147	10	7173	287	52.35	18	33
India	100	175	17	8192	281	51.84	20	38
South Africa	106	183	17	7418	222*	44.68	18	39
Pakistan	76	134	8	5379	313	42.69	15	17
New Zealand	75	133	9	5049	274*	40.71	11	21
West Indies	103	182	4	7022	400*	39.44	21	27
England	122	219	12	8000	221	38.64	21	38
Zimbabwe	44	85	7	2252	148*	28.87	5	10
Bangladesh	59	116	1	3202	113	27.84	3	23

Table: by Philip Bailey

Bopara had endured a tough introduction to Test cricket, having played brilliantly in the World Cup of 2007 when his fifty in Antigua took England within a stroke of beating Sri Lanka, who were eventually the losing finalists. His experience amounted to only a single one-day international before the World Cup, against Australia in Sydney. He then had a couple of games against Ireland and Canada, before his partnership with Paul Nixon at the Sir Vivian Richards stadium (pre-sandpit) almost saw England home. At the end of the tournament Bopara was promoted from number seven to number three, in what turned out to be our last game under Duncan Fletcher, and he scored a neat 26 from 43 balls against West Indies before being run out. Then he had slipped down again to number seven, and sometimes eight, in England's one-day side when Peter Moores took over.

In his first three Test matches, all in Sri Lanka, Bopara had begun with a very promising 30-odd in Kandy before ending the series with three consecutive ducks, one of them a run-out. He was banished back to Essex for twelve months or so. Nevertheless, I had been very impressed with the way he had played in that World Cup under pressure: he had shown a real calmness, and an ability to think clearly, and I knew he would be back for England sooner rather than later.

As it was, Bopara had got his chance to return to the Test side in Barbados because Flintoff was injured in Antigua. He had come in and taken it with both hands by scoring that maiden hundred and, although he was dropped for the Final Test, he was knocking on the door increasingly loudly after some good performances as an opening batsman in the one-dayers. There were a few other options for the number three spot at Lord's: Ian Bell had started the season very well for Warwickshire with a big hundred against Somerset at Taunton; Michael Vaughan was very keen to come back, having been refreshed after the trials and tribulations of the summer before, and after making a hundred against Surrey in a pre-season tournament in Abu Dhabi; and Owais Shah had played the final three Tests in the West Indies. All four of these guys had real cases for occupying the number three spot.

The feeling of both Andy and myself, and of the England selectors, was that Bopara ticked all the boxes. He had a calm head under pressure; technically he was excellent, although he came back from the IPL in South Africa set in one-day mode, looking to clear his back foot out of the way (he had played the one IPL innings of real note by an England player, 84 for King's XI Punjab); he had that little bit of star quality which you could imagine being needed in an Ashes series; and he was incredibly hungry to make the number three spot his own. The position had proved difficult for England in the past, but I could see no particular reason why it should have been.

Having failed to win the opening Test for the last 14 series, our team meetings before the First Test at Lord's were all about putting that record straight. We had to put ourselves under a bit of pressure: we had played West Indies four times in a row over there, and now we had two home Tests in which to build some momentum before the Ashes series. The fact that we had not won the opening Test for such a long time – since Bangladesh at Lord's in 2005 – made a good little tester for us. We identified this as a problem, and we decided we had to come out of the blocks quickly, and with purpose, and execute our plans properly. That the Test match lasted little more than three days suggested we did this pretty well. Bopara hoisted us up to a total of 377, and some excellent seam bowling from Onions, James Anderson and Stuart Broad, backed by Graeme Swann, allowed us to bowl them out for 152 and 256, giving us a simple target of 32 which was knocked off without undue difficulty. We had broken our opening-match hoodoo and set ourselves along the way.

One of my decisions which attracted a lot of attention during the Lord's Test was opening the bowling with Swann in West Indies' first innings. There were all sorts of wildly differing opinions on whether it was the right thing to do or not. There were a number of reasons why we did do it. The first was that the West Indians' left-handed opener Devon Smith had seemed very competent against our seam bowlers in the Caribbean but had really struggled against spin in general and Swann in particular: in each of the three Tests which Swann had played (the last three) he had dismissed Smith, either bowled or leg-before. During the tourists' warm-up game at Chelmsford, Smith had got out – caught at short-leg – in the first over which Essex's offspinner James Middlebrook bowled: Alastair Cook, who had played in that game, had come back with this information. So there was certainly a chance that we would pick up a wicket in the first couple of overs, which is always crucial in gaining momentum early in an innings. The other reasoning was that, having watched the West Indians bowl first, the ball had not swung much in the first ten overs of our innings and it made sense for Anderson, our primary swing bowler, to bowl when the ball was swinging, not when it wasn't swinging. So, by giving Swann a couple of overs at the start, this plan allowed Anderson to be perfectly into his stride by the time the ball swung.

Sometimes in cricket it is very easy to conform to stereotypes and do what people have always done. I think in international cricket in particular, if you ask different questions of batsmen, it is always interesting to see how they handle them. The best players are able to adapt to anything, but batsmen around the world know that when you come up against something new it may be a challenge you are not capable of overcoming. There was also a psychological effect on Devon Smith: he now knew that we knew that he had trouble with spin, and it was no surprise whatsoever that he got out in the first over of Swann's second spell – to his first ball indeed, bowled through the gate. (Shivnarine Chanderpaul was caught at slip next ball so Swann was on a hat-trick.) In the subsequent Test at Chester-le-Street, Smith was dismissed by Swann again in his second innings, lbw on this occasion. It was like India trying Yuvraj Singh's slow left-arm against Pietersen at the start of his innings in the Mohali Test, but rather more successful.

Having travelled up to Durham we were determined to regain the Wisden Trophy which had been in West Indian hands for the last couple of months. More importantly though we had to build on what we had done at Lord's. The start of the game was over-shadowed by some comments from Chris Gayle on the future of Test cricket in which he intimated that he far preferred the 20-over format. The media loved it. Gayle was fending off more tricky deliveries from the press box than from his practice bowlers in the lead-up to the game. It had also been reported that I had criticised him for turning up in England only two days before the Lord's Test match as he had been engaged in South Africa, playing for Kolkata Knight Riders. If it was a criticism, it was an indirect one, when I said that I would not have wanted our players to turn up two days before a Test.

My view is that Test cricket has been, is, and will remain the ultimate form of the game because it is the only format that tests your courage, your skill, your temperament and your technique. Although Twenty20 cricket is a fantastic spectacle and is breathing new life into the sport as we speak, from a player's point of view there are not many who think that at the end of their career they will be judged by their strike-rate in Twenty20 rather than their batting average in Test matches. It is relevant that when we were in Trinidad for the Test and Twenty20 international there, a comment had been made during the awards ceremony held by the West Indies Players Assocation: Kieron Pollard, a member of the Stanford team which had hammered England as well as of the West Indian one-day side, stated upon receiving his award as one-day player of the year that his ultimate ambition was to play Test cricket for West Indies.

That said, I think it would be very dangerous for Test cricket to compete with Twenty20 cricket. Twenty20 is a far greater spectacle for non-cricket-lovers. There is music and excitement, there are shots going out of the ground, there is superb skill in the way bowlers deliver their yorkers and slower balls: it is a great advertisement for the game. The two forms can co-exist, with Twenty20 attracting people to cricket who then, one hopes, develop a love for the longer form. Where we are at the moment, with Twenty20 tournaments being arranged like the IPL and the Champions League and plenty more besides, is that an already busy international schedule is being squeezed to such an extent that Test matches and Twenty20 are either directly or indirectly competing with each other. I think this is dangerous for the future.

My other belief is that it would be wrong for administrators not to address the problems that exist with Test cricket. It seems there are too many largely meaningless games played; the marketing of the Test match game could be better; and there is room for innovation in the longer form, like day/night Test cricket. I am not too bothered about over-rates, which all teams seem to struggle with, whether it is because sightscreens constantly need moving or for other reasons. Test cricket is the form of the game where you want to plot the opposition's downfall, and from this stems the fascination for everyone concerned. If people are prepared to watch six hours of cricket in a day, are they that much bothered if they watch six and a half hours instead because the over-rate is a bit slower?

Looking forward, there is a case for limiting the first innings of a Test to 120 overs or so. That would lead to more positive cricket, and as a consequence more definite results. In any event, it would be wrong for us to sit around and arrogantly assume that, because Test cricket has been around for the last century and more, then it will always be around. I think if we adopt that attitude the longer form could be under real threat.

As it was, it was disappointing to see so few people at the Chester-le-Street Test so soon after Gayle's comments. The paying public appeared to be backing up his thoughts. On the field, we started where we had finished off at Lord's. The Essex team-mates Alastair Cook and Bopara both batted brilliantly to make hundreds and allow us to declare at 559 for six. For Cook, who had failed to score a century for 16 Tests before Barbados, it was his second in four Tests. Bopara seemed to settle the number three position for the Ashes once and for all with his century: it was his third in three successive Test innings, taking him into the company of some of England's all-time greats, Herbert Sutcliffe, Denis Compton, Geoffrey Boycott and Graham Gooch, Bopara's mentor at Essex from an early age.

West Indies put up a spirited resistance in their first innings as Ramnaresh Sarwan made another hundred, but Anderson swung the ball to tremendous effect, using as much skill as I have seen from any swing bowler. In their first innings he took five wickets, then he obliterated their second innings with four for 38. Bresnan, who had not been able to get much of a bowl because wickets were falling regularly to the other seamers, took three for 45 and showed he had plenty to offer at this level. In all, the 2–0 victory was satisfying because we had been given the opportunity to gain our revenge for what happened in the West Indies, and we had taken it with both hands and performed in a clinical manner. The environment behind closed doors felt tight and cohesive; there was a real excitement about what the second half of the summer was going to bring. The younger guys were starting to take more responsibility: Anderson, Broad and Cook in particular were bridging that gap between promising youngsters and experienced campaigners. In some ways it was like seeing their graduation.

With Bopara settling in at three, the side had a much more solid feel, and with Matt Prior scoring runs so consistently as a wicket-keeper, we thought we had most bases covered. You never know your vulnerable points until they are tested but certainly in these two Test matches we had answers for everything the West Indians threw at us. There are dangers inherent in playing the same opposition for months on end: in the first half of 2008 we had met New Zealand away then at home, just as we faced West Indies away then at home in the first half of 2009. I think one of the reasons why the attendance at Chester-le-Street was so low was that people had already seen so much of us playing against West Indies.

Also, what happened in 2008 was that when one team got on top it was very hard for the other to come back with such a short gap between series, and our upper hand carried over from our 2–1 victory in New Zealand to our 2–0 win in England. Against West Indies we had obviously lost the series there but had performed increasingly strongly as it went on and we had the platform to win in England. But, as much as possible, you want Test series that really fire the imagination and playing back-to-back series might not be the best way to go. Bear in mind, though, that England were originally scheduled to meet Zimbabwe in the first home series of 2009 and, when the British government put a stop to that idea, Sri Lanka were enlisted to replace them – before their IPL players refused to tour. If the ECB had not roped in West Indies, England might not have been able to cut their teeth against anybody before the Ashes.

I decided not to put myself forward for the England squad for the ICC World Twenty20. So, after the Test and one-day series against West Indies – the first international was rained off at Headingley, and we won the second and third by relatively comfortable margins at Bristol and Edgbaston – I had a break, but not most of the other guys. England went into the World Twenty20 with another captain in Paul Collingwood, who had led in the first World Twenty20 in South Africa in September 2007.

When I had taken over the captaincy for the tour of the West Indies, the fact that I was not playing one-day cricket for England had been an issue which I had to discuss with the selectors. It had been decided then by the selectors and myself that in the short term, after the Moores and Pietersen saga, there had to be stable leadership in both the 50-over and Test forms, so I had agreed to do the joint captaincy with the proviso that we looked at it again after the tour was over. Thankfully, I had got some runs in that one-day series (player of the series indeed!) and it seemed right that I should continue as 50-over captain as well. But when it came down to Twenty20 cricket, I felt pretty strongly – having played that format quite a lot for Middlesex and a little bit for England – that I was not in the top six batsmen in the country; and while in the Twenty20 format the captain can have quite a large effect upon a game, he has to be worth his place in the side in his primary function. And I did not think that was the case with me, so I spoke to the selectors and they were happy with that, and Collingwood was appointed in my stead.

England went into the ICC World Twenty20 not widely favoured by forecasters. Our international 20-over cricket has been pretty consistent in the four years that we have played it, and been pretty consistently poor. Much has been made of a lack of big hitters in the England team, but I think this to an extent is a symptom of the way we play cricket in England. Having practised at a club ground in the West Indies with an outfield of incredibly long grass, where there was not much value in playing shots along the ground, I could understand why young players in other parts of the world learn to hit the ball in the air. In England, on beautifully manicured turf in club cricket, you get far better value out of keeping the ball on the ground; and on seaming wickets it is a far riskier option to try whacking the ball over the bowler's head. As a result, the majority of young batsmen in England are technically correct but possibly do not have the flair and the wristiness of some of their counterparts overseas.

I do not believe this means we are unable to play 20-over cricket as well as other countries, but we have to adapt our games to find ways of hitting boundaries. There are plenty of ways of hitting boundaries in Twenty20: we have seen the reverse-sweeps and the switch-hits and the flicks over the wicket-keeper's head. Anything that is possible is being attempted at the moment in Twenty20 batting, and as a side we have to be ready to experiment, and willingly. If occasionally someone plays a shot in a Twenty20 game that does not come off and looks horrible, the stick that he will get for it is something we will have to put up with if it makes England a better side. But for us to sit back and say that we cannot play shots that opposition sides do would be a dangerous and unconstructive way for us to move forward in Twenty20 cricket.

I watched pretty well all of England's Twenty20 games. When England met the Netherlands and Pakistan in the qualifying round, I was in Chelmsford playing for Middlesex in a championship match against Essex. (Whenever I play an away game for Middlesex we always seem to play at Bristol or Chelmsford.) Obviously the defeat at Lord's by the Netherlands in the opening game of the tournament did not go too well: the lack of boundary-hitting was a feature here as the Dutch batsmen mowed merrily across the line and scored 72 runs in boundaries (fours and sixes combined) to 56 by England's batsmen.

But, based on the competition as a whole, I thought England were a little maligned. They played very well against Pakistan, beating the eventual champions handsomely to qualify for the Super Eights. Then – after a second low which came against South Africa, who made all the early running – Collingwood's team rallied excellently to beat India in a must-win game for both sides at Lord's, knocking out the winners of the first Twenty20 tournament. By then I was down in Padstow in Cornwall with Ruth and our two boys, drinking coffee in pavement cafes and taking one last break before preparation for the Ashes began in real earnest.

England went out of the competition after the Duckworth/Lewis calculation for the target that West Indies had to chase after a rain break at The Oval was 80 from nine overs. Overall, our bowling was up there with any country's: Anderson and Broad again, this time with Sidebottom who bowled a fine last over to deny India by 3 runs, exploited a certain hesitancy by some of India's and Pakistan's batsmen against the short ball. Adil Rashid did not seem overawed when he got his first chance in international cricket, and with Swann made the first really effective pair of spinners that England have had in Twenty20 internationals. Before the tournament, spinners had been rotated with the same frequency as England's Twenty20 wicket-keepers.

As a top order, Bopara, Luke Wright and Pietersen batted as effectively as any top three in the World Twenty20. The middle overs were the period where we needed to work on hitting boundaries, especially fours, and to this end the ECB soon announced that England's one-day tour of South Africa in the forthcoming autumn was going to be extended by six days to allow for extra training.

The batsman who scored most runs in the World Twenty20, Tillekeratne Dilshan, propelled Sri Lanka into the final against Pakistan and was chosen as player of the tournament. Off the 219 balls he faced, the Sri Lankan opener hit only three sixes but 46 fours – in other words Dilshan almost managed to hit every fourth ball to the boundary – and scored 317 runs in all; Jacques Kallis came second in the list of boundary-hitters with 28 fours and four sixes from 188 balls. Ruth and I, meanwhile, loaded up the car in Cornwall and headed home. In three weeks' time the Ashes were to commence.

Little more than one week before the First Test, Michael Vaughan announced his retirement from all forms of cricket with immediate effect. His right knee had prevented him from getting through a full day of championship cricket up until the end of June, and if Yorkshire's opponents were ready to allow a substitute fielder when he went off for treatment, it was doubtful whether Australia would have been so indulgent. Subs are not allowed for an injury which you take into a match.

It was a sad moment when Vaughan announced his retirement at a press conference at Edgbaston an hour before I had to give one. Watching him on television, as he wore his England blazer, I liked one line in particular: he said that he knew his time had come when his three-year-old son, Archie, had bowled him off stump in the garden after the ball had hit a weed. I knew how very keen he had been to get himself ready during the winter for one more go at Australia, and news had filtered through to Guyana – on the day we played that practice game amongst ourselves – of a hundred he had made on a pre-season tour of Abu Dhabi against Surrey. But that was the last one he had scored: he had made a couple of fifties in one-day games for Yorkshire but the runs in championship cricket refused to flow in sufficient quantity.

Once the two-Test home series against West Indies had passed, and England's training squad of 17 for the Ashes had been announced without his name in it, the will to keep going while standing at mid-off for long days for Yorkshire ebbed away. Vaughan, like Pietersen, was a player for the big occasion: it was typical that his last competitive hundred – aside from that pre-season one – had been for England at Lord's, little more than a year before. He had followed up with his clever batting and tactical thinking against New Zealand at Old Trafford, taking the game away from them with his running between wickets; and now he had gone from cricket forever.

Vaughan was the best captain I played under, and he along with Duncan Fletcher created the best environment that I had played in. Naturally enough, although we were different personalities, I tried to incorporate some of the fundamentals of his style. Taking pressure off the players, not putting even more on them, was one characteristic of Vaughan's captaincy. A second was the sense that a player was able to go out and express himself without being torn to pieces if he failed in the attempt. A third was player responsibility, which I tried to take a stage further: to make players make decisions for themselves.

We talked for an hour on the phone before England's three-day game against Warwickshire, our final warm-up before the Ashes. He gave me the benefit of his advice, and insights into the techniques of Australian players he had been watching on television through the winter. He helpfully suggested I should win the toss – because if England bowled second and fourth, Graeme Swann, and Monty Panesar if he was selected, would play more of a part than if England bowled first and third. Vaughan was as full of hopeful confidence as ever, but not in his own game any more, just in England's. And while it was sad to see him go, he seemed happy in his decision: his egg-timer, as he called it, had run out, and he could no longer face the mental strains involved in performing every day in public.

The press conference which I had to give at Edgbaston straight after Vaughan's was one of the less enjoyable in my career. The previous Friday morning we had assembled at St Pancras station to catch the Eurostar train to Lille. We were headed for the First World War battlefields in Flanders and a ceremony to commemorate the English cricketers who had died there. We had four active soldiers from the Ministry of Defence, and a war historian, to accompany us. The party consisted of the 17 players selected for the Ashes training squad, and the management staff of Andy Flower, Ottis Gibson, Richard Halsall, the physio Kirk Russell and the masseur Mark Saxby, and two press officers.

It was a very emotional and very humbling occasion to see where so many men had been killed in Flanders less than a hundred years before. We were told about Siegfried Sassoon – a club cricketer among all his other achievements, literary and military who survived the war – and about Colin Blythe who did not, whose name I had heard before without knowing the details of his brilliant career for Kent and his country as a left-arm spinner. Blythe had taken 100 Test wickets for England before joining up and being shot down. Stuart Broad was chosen to lay a tribute to Blythe at his memorial: a stone cricket ball.

Many other English cricketers had given their lives during the Great War. There was another England bowler in Major Booth of Yorkshire; Percy Jeeves, who played for Worcestershire and gave P.G. Wodehouse the idea for naming his famous fictional butler;

and many, many others. It was a thoughtful group of players who returned to a hotel in Ypres that evening, our horizons broadened.

Unfortunately, Andrew Flintoff overslept the next morning and missed the team bus for another visit to the battlefields, before we took the train back to England. On the day of Vaughan's retirement – the day before our game against Warwickshire – the story came out in the newspapers. Instead of talking up our prospects in the forthcoming series, Hugh Morris and I had to contend with questions not specifically related to cricket. I had to say that Flintoff, who had apologised to the whole team, had 'stuffed up'; and that he had generally learned when to drink and when not to drink.

In our game against Warwickshire Flintoff bowled something close to his best. None of the home batsmen made a score of note in either innings before the game was drawn, while Alastair Cook and Ravi Bopara each made a hundred and Paul Collingwood, who wanted a first-class innings, 79 not out. Most of the Australian players had not played against England in 2005 but they must have seen tape of Flintoff bowling then, and known that Australia's batsmen had no answer to him in that series. During my time in the England team no pace bowler in the world has been harder to score off than Flintoff at his best.

The day after our Edgbaston warm-up, a Saturday, I drove to Worcester to meet Andy Flower and the other England selectors. We announced a party of 13, with Ian Bell as the reserve batsman in case of an injury on the morning of the match, and the last bowling place to go to Panesar or Graham Onions. For the Lions Onions had taken some top-order wickets against the Australians, while Steve Harmison had bounced out Phil Hughes twice and shaped the ball away from their right-handers – the sign that he is in rhythm.

I liked the wide range of bowling options we had in our 13-man squad as a result of opting for a five-man attack: conventional swing, reverse-swing, hit-the-deck, back-of-a-length, bouncers (even in Harmison's absence), and left-arm and right-arm spin. Although Australia were widely acknowledged to be favourites, at least up until a week before the series, I was not displeased to hear Australia's former captain Ian Chappell saying publicly that he favoured the team that had a stronger attack to win the series, and that was England.

No less importantly, I liked the characters we had in our side. As I said in yet another press conference shortly before the series, I did not think any of them would be open to 'exploitation' by the Australians. Our visit to Flanders had emphasised the importance of being a bonded team without a weak link. The series was going to boil down to how each side handled the pressure and whether one side could nail the other when it succumbed. For my lingering memory of 2005 was how difficult it had been to finish off the Australians, even when they were down – or especially when they were down. And so to Cardiff . . .

12
NOT NAILED!

'Heads!'

As the visiting captain, it was Ricky Ponting's call.

For the first ever Test at Cardiff, the world's hundredth Test ground, a commemorative medal had been issued. On one side of the medal a batsman was pictured, and Ponting and I had agreed to call this side 'heads'. On the reverse was the name of the sponsors of the Test series, npower: this was 'tails'.

After tossing it up, I watched as the coin came down on the side of the sponsors, to my great relief. Having picked two spinners, we were even keener than we would have otherwise been to have first use of what looked like a very flat wicket that would turn as the match went on. On a warm breezy morning everything pointed to it being a really good day to bat.

The trouble was that with so much emotion around, and so many nerves, we did not bat well. You cannot have a build-up over several months and not feel different when the big day comes round. Some of our players had probably not slept too well. As an opening batsman you wonder what the first ball of the game and the series is going to be like – a bouncer? A yorker? We were nervous even though we did not admit it. We were aware that Australia started Ashes series so strongly that they had won the opening Tests of the last five series; our Lord's win against West Indies in May was all we had by comparison.

The surroundings were unfamiliar too. I had played a first-class game at Sophia Gardens, and made a hundred for Middlesex in a high-scoring game, but that had been seven years ago, long before the massive investment had turned it into a Test match venue. The Welsh national anthem followed the toss, then the Australian anthem, then 'God Save The Queen', after which I had to present the team to Rhodri Morgan, the first minister of Wales, with most of my batting kit on except for pads and gloves. The atmosphere was inspiring, as the Welsh love their singing as much as their sport. But calmness is the greatest asset on the first morning of a major series, and this is where we came unstuck.

Mitchell Johnson, Ben Hilfenhaus, Peter Siddle and Nathan Hauritz – many acres of newsprint and many laptop screens had been covered in guessing the Australian attack for the opening Test, but nobody as far as I can remember nominated these four bowlers. No Brett Lee, in other words, and no Stuart Clark. Neither of their two most experienced bowlers played, leaving their attack in the hands of four who had never played a Test in England between them.

Two days before the series began on a Wednesday, rumours circulated among the media that Lee was struggling with a low-grade abdominal tear. He had missed Australia's training at Sophia Gardens on the Monday to go to London to see a specialist, and he was ruled out of the first two Tests at least. After warming up in Hove, he had moved up another gear in their second match at Worcester to force his way back into the Test side, and pretty impressive he had been too. As the Lions game had been televised on Sky, there was a man of the match, and he was Lee.

Over ten years before I had been standing at third slip for Mosman as Lee tore in, and he was still tearing in at the age of 32 – until the end of the Worcester game. The highlights of it so far as the tourists had been concerned were the big hundreds by Mike Hussey and Marcus North, and Lee's spell of reverse-swing in the Lions' first innings. Although Lee had not had much success against England overall – he had been averaging 40 – he had still produced spells when he had gone bang, bang, bang: at Edgbaston and Trent Bridge in 2005 his pace had combined with his control and swing to take a burst of quick wickets. At Worcester the Lions' opening pair had been cruising along until Lee took five wickets in a single spell of fast, late reverse-swing: Joe Denly, Ian Bell, Vikram Solanki and Eoin Morgan were either bowled or leg-before, and Stephen Moore was caught hooking after scoring a hundred. In the Lions' second innings Lee had bowled again, but apparently he finished the match clutching his left side: in trying to regain his place after missing Australia's last four Tests, he had overstretched.

Here was both a surprise and a distraction. Our batsmen had been getting their heads around an Australian opening attack of Johnson and Lee, and now I was a little concerned in my own head that as a batting unit we would breathe a sigh of relief, and not be switched on enough to tackle Lee's replacement. It turned out to be Ben Hilfenhaus, who bowled his outswing very well and took five wickets in the match, more than any other bowler except his opening partner, Johnson, who also took five.

The square at Sophia Gardens was far greener than at New Road, and the outfield too. If Lee had played, it is doubtful whether he could have found as much reverse-swing as he had against the

Lions, because none of the balls scuffed up. But Lee would still have offered Ponting an option when the ball was old: his fast straight yorkers would have been very difficult for our tailenders to keep out in the final session. And Clark, with his wicket-to-wicket accuracy, might have been able to keep the game tight on the first evening. But the Australian selectors had gone for Hilfenhaus and his new-ball swing as their attacking option, to supplement Johnson and Siddle. It was a rational decision, although Hilfenhaus had played only in the warm-up at Hove: the Dukes balls of 2009 had been swinging and preserving their hardness much more than the batch of 2008 (for the last two Tests of that summer they had to be replaced by Dukes balls made in 2007). Playing for Middlesex in the second division of the championship before the Ashes, we had been using the new Tiflex balls, but I had heard from first division players that the Dukes had been swinging; and of course we had played with them in our two home Tests against West Indies.

Although Johnson took some getting used to, I was soon feeling very comfortable at the crease. We had our plans for playing Johnson but it is only when you are facing a bowler that you can really work out how he bowls and where your scoring areas should be. Left-arm new-ball bowlers usually swing the ball away from left-handers like me but Johnson, almost from ball one, was like a left-arm reverse-swing bowler as he made the ball angle in; and he mixed in a slower cutter, which also came into the left-hander, from the start.

The wicket reminded me of several pitches I had played on recently, but none in England: it was perhaps most like Port-of-Spain in Trinidad, where we had played the Test in March, because it was incredibly flat for the first three or four days. In normal circumstances I would not have thought about hooking Johnson, but because this pitch was so slow the hook became an option. When Johnson, bowling from the River Taff end, pitched one short, I shaped to play the shot but then pulled out, and the ball did not get up as much as I had expected. I ended up gloving it to slip, the first time in my career that I had been out like that, although I can remember a similar sort of dismissal by Lee.

When Bopara was caught off a cutter from Johnson shortly before lunch, we were 90 for three and sorely in need of a partnership from our last pair of specialist batsmen. Happily, Pietersen and Collingwood know each other's games so well that they soon revived memories of their stand of more than 300 in the Adelaide Test of 2006–7. Collingwood was alert to the 'Red Bull singles' that Pietersen likes at the start of his innings. Soon after lunch Ponting brought on Hauritz for the first time, for the thirty-second over, and Pietersen and Collingwood proceeded to give a superb demonstration of how to manipulate an offspinner around without taking any risks.

They began by sweeping Hauritz, as there was no fielder saving a single behind square-leg, so even if Pietersen or Collingwood had got a top-edge there was nobody to catch it: only two men out deep. When Ponting brought a man in on the 45° to save the single, along with the two men out deep, Pietersen and Collingwood turned their attention to the offside where there were now only four fielders and therefore huge gaps. If Ponting had a sweeper on the cover boundary, they steered and nudged the offspinner square on the offside for singles; if he did not have a sweeper, they square-cut Hauritz for four. It was not spectacular – they scored at between three and four runs an over off him – but it was masterly manipulation because it was so risk-free. And although Pietersen got out to Hauritz, trying to sweep a ball about two feet outside off stump, his patience before then should not be underestimated. He hit only four fours off his 141 balls, and even when allowing for some stiffness in his calf he felt during the partnership, this was real self-restraint in the team's cause. Seldom lost for a word, he also had a ready retort when the media asked him about his fatal sweep. 'I was unfortunate to have hit the ball into my helmet,' he said. 'If that hadn't happened, the ball would have gone to fine-leg and I would have got away with it.'

Next morning some newspapers reminded us of just how good a partnership Pietersen and Collingwood, playing in his partner's shadow but scoring just as quickly, had become. They were already, before the game, England's most prolific fourth wicket pair against all countries, ahead of Nasser Hussain and Graham Thorpe; and their stand of 138 here took their total to a record of 638 runs in their five partnerships against Australia, ahead of Ken Barrington and Colin Cowdrey. It was no surprise to me that Pietersen had got out cheaply in both innings of our warm-up against Warwickshire, or that he fired when it mattered here.

Ponting tried spin at both ends before tea, but as Michael Clarke's five overs were worked around as expertly as Hauritz's spell was, Pietersen and Collingwood were still together at the interval: 194 for three. If the first session had been Australia's, the second was England's. The third session had something for every-body as England scored 142 runs off 30 overs for the loss of four more wickets. It was reminiscent of the first day at Edgbaston in 2005 when we had scored over 400 all out in less than 80 overs and every ball seemed to bring a boundary or a wicket. The Cardiff crowd started to get behind us as Flintoff went in to bat and the beer flowed. In the first couple of sessions the spectators had been fairly silent, a bit uncertain like the players, but the trumpeter in a group of Barmy Army supporters – on the other side of the ground from where we were sitting – got the crowd going a couple of times in the afternoon, and by the last session everyone seemed to be singing 'Why, why, why, Delilah?'

Just as the partnership between Pietersen and Collingwood had gained its impetus when Australia's spinners were on, so did the stand between Flintoff and Matt Prior: Hauritz and Simon Katich bowled the last four overs before the second new ball, and Prior and Flintoff scored 22 off them. Flintoff has been criticised for the way he has played spinners, but during our tour of India before Christmas he had worked them around as well as blocking them or blasting them. So when Australia took the new ball at 288 for five, both batsmen were well set and the runs flowed even faster. At one stage Prior and Flintoff scored off eight consecutive balls. A throw-in by Hauritz on the cover boundary was pushed over the bar by Haddin and resulted in an overthrow which the crowd enjoyed; earlier, Phil Hughes had misfielded in front of the Barmy Army stand and allowed a four, which gained him some notoriety. We had hoped in advance that the Cardiff crowd would get on the Australians' backs but knew that we would have to play well first for that to happen; and now we were, they responded.

Unfortunately, just as we felt we were getting on top of the

Australians, they hit back – as they usually do – with two quick wickets before the close. Flintoff dragged on and Prior, after scoring at almost a run a ball, was bowled off an inside edge when driving at Siddle. I felt quite strongly that James Anderson should go in as nightwatchman. Stuart Broad and Graeme Swann had the potential to make some significant runs as attacking players, so it made sense for Anderson to go in ahead of them and take the second new ball. He did a great job in fending off Australia's quicker bowlers and batted through to the close.

The second morning – a cloudier, cooler day all through – was an extraordinary session as the two sides scored 138 runs, even though two overs had to be deducted for the change of innings. We scored 99 of them, and might have been helped by the stiffness of the Australian pace bowlers after the first day. Johnson, Hilfenhaus and Siddle had all been given just the one warm-up game, whereas the injured Lee and unselected Clark had played in both. Johnson, since the end of Australia's tour of South Africa, had bowled less than six competitive overs in the ICC World Twenty20 before Australia had been knocked out, and then had the Worcester warm-up. Fast bowlers always say there is nothing like match-play for getting their legs and back into shape. In any event Johnson, Australia's strike bowler, began with a spell of only three overs; and the absence of bouncers was, I am sure, welcomed by Anderson and Swann.

Broad was a bit unlucky to be bowled behind and off his legs, but he had already driven Siddle for a couple of fours. Swann steered Johnson to third man and drove him through the covers with his brand of cheery optimism and then, being Swann, decided to take on Hauritz. The offspinner's first ball of the day, after pitching straight, bounced and turned so much that it went for four byes. The whole over cost 16 runs in all as Swann went down the pitch to Hauritz and carted him for a four which Siddle, also looking a bit stiff, failed to stop, and a second four that was driven straight which Siddle might have failed to see against the trees at the Taff end. Swann finished by reverse-sweeping his fellow offspinner, an idea which appealed to Anderson who soon did the same, although only for a single.

We had talked privately and publicly about the 2009 Australians as a team to be respected but not feared. England's tailenders were fearless as they took our scoring-rate above four runs an over, while the rest of us had a few smiles on the team balcony. But underneath those smiles we batsmen knew we had made a mistake in not going on to a hundred. In our first innings we had a hand in our own dismissals, rather than Australia getting us out with magic deliveries.

The good news, when we bowled, was that the new ball swung. The bad news was that it was the second ball on the third morning which swung, not the first new ball on the second morning. The temperature was also colder on the second day, which may have stopped the ball swinging. And Anderson and Broad took a while to adjust to the completely contrasting styles of Australia's opening batsmen, Katich walking across to off stump, while Hughes stayed legside, which must have been as confusing as bowling at a right-hander and a left-hander.

Hughes's innings was brief but as eventful as he had led us to believe it would be. Before lunch, off 30 balls, he scored 28 – which removed from Katich the need to score and allowed him to settle.

Broad's first two or three balls were wide, and Hughes's footwork made them wider still. Since, when playing for Middlesex, Hughes had been relatively tied down by offspin, I gave Swann the last couple of overs before lunch from the Cathedral Road end, but ten of his twelve balls were at Katich.

After lunch we started with Flintoff from the Taff end. He gave Hughes some short-pitched balls from round the wicket and tied him down, then switched to over the wicket and cramped him so much that his bat was at 45° when he was caught off a bottom/inside edge. Flintoff generated some real pace and excitement in the crowd, and almost dismissed Katich with a low caught-and-bowled to his right. But creating an atmosphere of hostility when there were eight rows of seating behind the bowler was harder than when there was the packed Oval pavilion behind Flintoff during his epic spell in 2005. He reminded us of it when we got back to the dressing-room on the second evening, when Australia were 249 for one, saying it had only taken one spell to go through the Australians then, and we could do the same again on the third day.

Katich, as we were in the process of discovering, had turned into a consistent performer since 2005. He had scored runs in both of the warm-up games, and in almost every Test since converting into an opening batsman. He played straighter in defence than he had in 2005, but still accumulated a lot of runs off his hip behind square: two-thirds of his runs came legside (whereas only three of Hughes's 38 runs did). Katich was 6 not out at lunch, 53 at tea, and 104 – his first Ashes hundred – at the close. The lack of pace in the wicket meant we could not bounce him or get him caught in the gully as we had planned.

The two most important centuries in Australia's innings were Katich's and Ponting's because we had a lot of momentum after our innings and the dismissal of Hughes, but these two hundreds stopped us putting any pressure on Australia. Ponting's befitted one of the greatest batsmen of modern times: from his first ball he was in complete control, in accordance with his terrific record in starting a Test series. He got a huge stride in when he played forward and made sure he was right over the top of the ball before driving it; and if the ball was short, he was as quick as ever to swivel and pull. Swann kept him quiet when he bowled five consecutive maidens from the Cathedral Road end on the second afternoon, but Ponting gradually caught up with his partner until he reached the verge of his thirty-eighth Test century shortly before the close. He started the last over of the day on 99, so I brought the whole field in except fine-leg, and for the one time in his innings he showed some sign of nerves before scampering home. Before then Ponting had become the fourth batsman to 11,000 Test runs, and he had a higher average than Brian Lara, Sachin Tendulkar or Allan Border.

The only time on the second day the pace bowlers found any sideways movement was when Anderson tried the Cathedral Road end just before the close and found a hint of reverse-swing. But at least we had only nine overs to bowl on the third morning before the second new ball, which dismissed Katich in one of the ways we had planned, trapped as he walked across his wicket by a yorker which swung into him. The one drawback was that it was nearly a day later than we had wanted. In the same spell Anderson drew Mike Hussey into a drive and had him caught behind, and we had a third wicket in the session when Monty Panesar, in a tight spell, finally had Ponting bottom-edging a cut: Australia 331 for four. However, to set against those three wickets in the session, a ball from Broad to Katich had gone through the top, and a big Australian lead on first innings would see us batting for survival on a wearing pitch.

The rest of Australia's innings was all too reminiscent of our recent Tests against West Indies – the away Tests, not the home ones. A slow wicket, a long way from English conditions. No swing, except for the second new ball. No seam. No chance of the ball carrying to slip off the seamers. Batsmen for whom the challenge was not to get themselves out. No mystery spinner or bowler of unbelievable pace. Defensive fields and damage limitation.

In retrospect, what was strange about Australia's innings – their fourth highest total, we were not overjoyed to learn – was not so much that we didn't take many wickets but that we didn't create many chances. You always felt the spinners were in the game, with the odd ball turning a long way, but this did not lead to chances. There was a case for saying that Collingwood should have bowled more. When he came on with his off-cutters, he made two in a row bite and turn past North and Prior for four byes, and older Glamorgan supporters talked about Steve Barwick with his 'Basils' and Don Shepherd.

Apart from that, the only time our bowlers sniffed a chance was when we played under floodlights for the first time in a Test in England. The respective Boards had agreed before the series to use the floodlights at Cardiff, Lord's and the Oval: and I could understand that in this day and age, with so much pressure on Test cricket, you couldn't reasonably come off for bad light on grounds that had floodlights. A spell of six overs under lights started at 6.15 on the third evening. Suddenly we all had four shadows around us. A throw-in from Panesar at long-leg came out of a floodlight and Matt Prior could not pick it up: in one-day cricket, if you are fielding with a floodlight behind you, you have to throw in one bounce. We could have gone on until 7.30 but Aleem Dar and Billy Doctrove thought the combination of natural and artificial light became unplayable: they had to make their minds up without using light meters.

The ball seemed to come off the pitch a bit quicker, under lights, and nipped around. Maybe it was illusion or maybe the pitch had been freshened under the covers by a couple of hours of rain. Broad gloved Michael Clarke with a bouncer, which had Australia reeling at 474 for five. When we had to bat under floodlights the next evening, I found that the light shines off the ball and you do not see it quite so well. But if you had to bat against a red ball under lights as a matter of course, you would get used to it, as with a white ball in one-day cricket.

Next morning it was back to the previous routine. We had seen lots of footage of Marcus North, and to me he had been a bit of a dasher with a lot of shots, but here he was very disciplined against our spinners. He had made 191 at Worcester in the last of his four warm-up innings and been particularly strong in driving the pace bowlers down the ground and slog-sweeping the spinners. Here he did not straight-drive so much because of the pitch's slowness but he was very solid and composed in making his second hundred in only his third Test. Inexperienced in Test terms, he had been around the traps and the counties so much that he had scored a double-hundred for Durham on this ground.

Haddin was the dangerous customer we knew he would be when the ball was old. He played himself in on the third evening and the fourth morning and, after we had taken the third new ball, he reached fifty at lunch. Afterwards North, who already had his hundred, gave Haddin the strike so he could make the fourth century of Australia's innings by the declaration. Haddin had often opened Australia's one-day innings and his range of shots was that of a one-day opener as he took three fours in succession off Anderson and hit both spinners for six: one off Panesar, a straight-drive, came when he was bowling over the wicket and into the rough. The Australian batsmen were really aggressive only at the back end of their innings. Otherwise they were models of application and patience.

The forecast for the fourth day had been rain about 4 o'clock. We were pretty sure that Australia wanted to have a go at our second innings before play was called off, and it transpired that we had half-an-hour to get through after Ponting's declaration. As the rain was imminent, the floodlights were switched on and again the wicket became spicier than it had been in natural daylight. In those seven overs we lost two wickets, both to lbw decisions. It could have been three wickets lost to lbws but Hilfenhaus no-balled when he swung the new ball into my legs. The widespread feeling among commentators was that Bopara was unlucky as he had been hit above the knee-roll on the front foot.

I woke up on the final morning feeling a mixture of the disappointment that was still lingering from the day before, a measure of hope that we could still pull something out of the bag, and a tingling of excitement in that I possibly had a role to play in saving the game. I think all of us in the England team knew it would be difficult to bat out the last day because the ball had spun increasingly on day four and the Australians would have men round the bat. What we held on to was the fact that the wicket was still very slow and the Australian seamers would be relatively ineffective.

In our meeting before the start we talked about how important days like this would be in the team's development. It was a great chance to grab some momentum in this series, to show some fight, and to blot out some of the memories of Australia's dominance on days two, three and four. We also mentioned the necessity of doing it yourself and not relying on anyone else to see England through to safety.

By lunchtime all my feelings of excitement had gone. Most of my feelings of hope had gone too, and the disappointment was overwhelming. At 70 for five, well before lunch on the final day, after losing three wickets in little more than an hour, it looked like our race had been run. Pietersen had taken a barrage of criticism for getting out in his first innings: his reaction was to concentrate on defence and not playing the ball. He expected an outswinger from Hilfenhaus but the ball did not swing and hit his off stump.

Hauritz came on early at the river end, for the fifteenth over of our innings, the eighth of the day, with a breeze to help his drift. At the start of his over Hauritz had two men around the bat for Collingwood, and by the end of it he had four: this was the pattern for the rest of the day. That left some gaps, and to escape we needed runs: if we could score at about three runs an over with fielders around the bat, we could knock off the deficit not long after teatime. I square-cut a short ball from Hauritz for four and tried to do the same to the next but it took something out of the wicket, bounced a bit higher, and I top-edged to Haddin.

Collingwood decided to play Hauritz almost entirely off the back foot after he had been nearly caught on the front foot: he squeezed an offbreak off glove and front pad to bat-pad's right hand, but Katich is left-handed and could not quite hold on as he hit the ground. In the same over, when he was still on 11, Collingwood had to kick away an offbreak that spun between his legs. Thereafter it was a master-class in how to defend against an offspinner on a turning pitch with soft hands and infallible concentration.

Prior kept him company for ten overs before he gloved an off-break – which turned out of the rough made by Johnson – to slip while trying to cut. Flintoff kept Collingwood company for 23 overs either side of lunch. He showed again how much his defence against spin had improved in India, and his back-foot force for four off Hauritz's last ball before the interval raised our hundred and the crowd's hopes. Such situations are very difficult for attacking batsmen like Pietersen, Flintoff and to an extent Swann, whereas someone like Collingwood can play naturally.

I sat on the team balcony during the afternoon and in time-honoured cricketer's fashion refused to move as each partnership grew. I got up once to put on a jumper when Swann was batting but was back in my seat before the next over started. As we had to make up time on the final day, the afternoon session was divided into three 50–minute sessions with drinks in between. Collingwood, scoring only a single, batted through the first of them with Flintoff.

But Flintoff was out to the first ball he played after the mini-break, edging Johnson from round the wicket very low to second slip – so low that Flintoff checked with Ponting that the edge had carried.

Broad was nearly lbw to his first ball but Billy Doctrove must have thought the ball was reversing down the legside. He was nearly out to his first ball from Hauritz too, edging past Clarke's left hand at slip. When he was out, about 20 minutes before tea, it looked as though the game had gone. Collingwood and Swann were left, with Anderson and Panesar to come, and Swann was repeatedly hit by Siddle. In one over before tea Swann was hit once on each glove and on the left elbow.

At teatime we had some discussion about tactics, primarily about how much of the strike Collingwood would take. As Swann was happy to take the short balls, we decided that Collingwood would bat as normal for the time being, but would farm the strike more when Anderson and Panesar came in. It was a long shot. After tea the ball was getting older and there was no reverse-swing in the absence of Lee, and in such situations there is always hope until the last ball is bowled. Against that, Hauritz was still getting a little bite, and the second new ball was due in eight overs' time.

Collingwood, meanwhile, epitomised what we had talked about in the team meeting by not leaving the job to anybody else. After his difficult moments at the start he had not looked like getting out and was like a dog with a bone that would not let go. The position was a bit similar to the last afternoon of the Adelaide Test when Collingwood had hung on but it had been impossible to score as the ball was reversing and Shane Warne was bowling. As this afternoon wore on I became increasingly confident he would last the distance as he played the situation perfectly. Such circumstances bring out the best in him – his fight and his grittiness. He does not think about how he looks or how fast he is scoring. He is simply tenacious.

Then just as I thought we had a chance, Swann's attacking instincts took over and he was lbw to a pull shot: although it was the second new ball, it did not bounce. The match was back in Australia's hands, and when Collingwood sliced a drive to gully seven overs later, the game was up. I had talked to Andy Flower earlier about how many balls we could expect Panesar to keep out. We thought twelve balls would be too many, and now he had 69 left to survive with Anderson. Collingwood came back to the dressing-room distraught, absolutely distraught. It is worse to lose when you get so close to saving a game, and he felt it was the end. The rest of us, too, thought it was game, set and match – if not series – to Australia.

I was very concerned about Johnson bowling to our last pair of left-handers and getting one of them lbw, but Anderson just about kept him out. With seven overs remaining, Anderson steered a couple of fours to third man off Siddle and we passed their score. The crowd roared the place down: we felt it was a reconnection with 2005 as they got behind the team. Going in front ensured that two overs, plus the over being bowled, would be lost in the change-over between innings.

The Australians became more frantic to get their overs in – more than the 98 scheduled for the day – and brought on North as a part-time offspinner. I thought this was a blessing in disguise

189

because he would turn and beat the left-handers' bat rather than bring the stumps into play. Clarke, or Katich's googly, would have been more dangerous.

But we had forgotten something in the excitement. With five overs left Phil Neale suddenly came on to the balcony and said he had been speaking to the match officials and another 15 minutes were left – time for the Australians to bowl more than five overs. All sorts of toing and froing started in the dressing-room. I began wondering how long we could take to bowl one over if Australia needed a dozen or so to win. I started thinking about what tactics we would employ if they did need 12 off one over, and who would bowl it. The thought of Flintoff went through my mind but I did not speak to the players about it because that would have been tempting fate. But, above all, I felt powerless. This session of cricket gave us an understanding of what our friends and families go through every time we perform.

In the end, Anderson and Panesar looked as though they were never going to get out. It was an incredible effort by two players not known for their batting prowess to fight as hard as they did, concentrating and doing the job which we batsmen at the top of the order should have been doing.

One aspect of the match that was picked up by both the press and Ponting was the two visits on to the field near the close by our 12th man, Bilal Shafayat, and our physio Steve McCaig. Ponting felt that we were trying to waste time so that Australia wouldn't be able to take advantage of the extra time they had gained by bowling their overs so quickly in the final hour. The truth, however, is far less cunning, and I have to say far less organised. When we needed to relay the information to the players about possible extra overs, Shafayat was sent out to tell them what the situation was. While he was out there, talking through the situation, and giving the players a drink, he spilt water on Anderson's glove. Anderson called for new gloves during the next over, and in the confusion we weren't sure if he was calling for gloves or the physio, hence McCaig ran out with Shafayat the second time around. All in all it was a messy, clumsy moment that didn't look particularly good, but it came about more from a lack of attention to detail than anything else. Hopefully we won't make the same mistake again.

As the players came off the field there were no celebrations in the England dressing-room. We knew we had been the second best side in the match. But there was a huge feeling of relief. We had managed a great escape and the series was still nil-all, not 1–0 to Australia, as it usually was after the opening Test. We had rained on Australia's parade, and in a curious way momentum is so important in a Test series, and hopefully we had reversed it. We had talked so much about nailing them when we were on top, and although the Australians had been on top for most of the game we had avoided being nailed ourselves, if only by a few runs and minutes.

13
HISTORIC TRIUMPH

The Lord's Test of 2009 was the biggest, the most important, match of my captaincy and therefore of my cricket career. It had everything, and more besides. In case bowlers think they are overlooked, let me say it contained England's best performance as a bowling unit since 2005. It contained my best hundred since taking over the captaincy. It contained not only a meeting with the Queen but my introducing her to the players. And it ended, after five of the most gut-wrenching days imaginable, in England's first victory against Australia at Lord's since 1934.

All of this seemed very far away when I drove back from Cardiff on the evening that the First Test ended. As in my first Test as England's full-time captain in Jamaica, there had been so much going on that I had not been able to give my own game full attention, resulting in scores of 30 and 17. The difference between the opening Test of the series in the West Indies and the opening Ashes Test was that we had escaped, however closely or undeservedly, with a draw in Cardiff. And as we met up at the team hotel in Cardiff Bay for a quick bite and a beer before going home, there was a feeling that we had got the worst out of our system and the Australians could live to regret their failure to nail us at the first opportunity.

Three days between Test matches is not a long time. Three days between Ashes Tests at home seems shorter still. While I drove back along the M4 to west London on that Sunday evening, getting home about 11 p.m., I realised that I had to clear everything out of my head by Wednesday evening so that I could concentrate entirely on my own game if we batted first on Thursday morning. As in the Antigua Test, after we had been bowled out for 51, I knew I had to lead from the front.

There was also a bit of history hanging over us. For no obvious reason England had a bad record against Australia at Lord's – so bad that of the previous 27 Tests stretching back to 1899 England had won only once, and that had been as long ago as 1934. Some people say the Australians have been inspired by Lord's over the years: certainly Glenn McGrath was as he had run amok from the Pavilion end in his three Tests there. But I would say that England players in my time have been inspired too. We have been made to feel most welcome as MCC have tried to make the Lord's experience as special as possible: little touches like giving every player a towel embossed with his name and the MCC logo for him to keep, and a framed scorecard of the match for those who did well in it.

Luckily, I have always been able to sleep properly. I drink about five or six cups of coffee a day – preferably a latte, with no sugar – but our nutritionist says coffee is good for you and it does not keep me awake. On that Sunday evening, after a few final images of James Anderson and Monty Panesar blocking out successfully had passed through my head, I slept well and woke next morning to play with my two boys. As another taste of the sanity of home life, later that morning Ruth and I went to see a school where we thought we might send Sam. We even found time to have lunch together. In the afternoon there was a sponsor's do, and so my attention began to shift to the Second Test and all the related issues, although I managed to get home for the boys' bedtime and had another good night's sleep.

One of these issues was that Andrew Flintoff had decided, after more medical attention on the Monday, that he wanted to announce he was going to retire from Test cricket after the Ashes series in order to concentrate on 50– and 20–over matches. Recent precedent suggested this was not an ideal arrangement. Alec Stewart, in 2003, had announced he was going to retire after the Test series against South Africa, and while keeping wicket as well as ever he had averaged 22 with the bat. The following winter Steve Waugh had announced he was going to retire after one last home series against India, and it had turned into one long farewell pageant. India, while Australia's attention was elsewhere, had nipped in to square the series at 1–1 – a very rare exception to the rule of Australia's dominance at home.

A consideration on this occasion was that Flintoff, as a bowler, would not be distracted in the same way that Stewart and Waugh had been as batsmen. Indeed he might be spurred on even more than normal by the crowd as they asked him for a final flourish to remember him by. We had a team meeting and practice session on the Tuesday morning at Lord's when the timing of the announcement was discussed, and it was decided that Flintoff would release the news to the media the next day during practice. On the Tuesday afternoon most of us had another sponsor's do at a clothes store in Oxford Street.

Some light relief came on Tuesday evening when I had a benefit dinner in the pavilion at Lord's and the occasion was enlivened by a speech by Stephen Fry. A year or two earlier he had given a speech at a MCC dinner which had been very well received for its wit and wisdom. This one received equally high marks from a grateful beneficiary, being so topical in its allusions to the Cardiff Test.

Thank you ladies and gentlemen, thank you very much indeed. It is an honour to stand before so many cricketing heroes from England and from Australia and at this, my favourite time of year. The time when that magical summer sound comes to our ears and gladdens our old hearts, the welcome sound of leather on Graham Swann.

I have been asked to say a few words – well, more than a few. 'You've twenty minutes to fill,' I was firmly told by the organisers. Twenty minutes. Not sure how I'll use all that time up. Perhaps in about ten minutes or so Andrew Strauss would be kind enough to send on a physio, that should kill a bit of time.

Now, many of you will be wondering by what right I presume to stand and speak in front of this assembly of all that is high and fine and grand and noble and talented in the world of cricket, and to speak too in this very temple of all that is historic, majestic and ever so slightly preposterous and silly in that world. I certainly can't lay claim to any great cricketing achievements. I can't bat, I can't field, I bowl off the wrong foot. That sounds like a euphemism for something else, doesn't it? 'They say he bowls off the wrong foot, know what I mean? He enters stage left. Let me put it this way, he poles from the Cambridge end of the punt.' Actually as a matter of fact, although it is true in every sense that I have always bowled off the wrong foot, I have decided, since Sunday, to go into the heterosexual breeding business. My first three sons will be called Collingwood Fry, Anderson Fry and Monty Fry. That's if their mother can ever get them out, of course.

On Wednesday morning, following the dinner and Fry's speech, there was the expected media frenzy at Lord's, which the rest of us escaped by going to practise unmolested in the Nursery. In front of rows of cameras behind the pavilion Flintoff told the world that his body had taken enough of a pounding, and the time he had spent in rehabilitating his knees and ankles had taken its mental toll. If Flintoff had announced that he was going to retire with immediate effect, the psychological benefits for the Australians would no doubt have been enormous. Their senior players had seen him at his best in 2005, when none of them had got on top of his bowling in the whole series, and I am sure the junior Australian players must have seen videos of Flintoff then. Such were his pace, control and reverse-swing that he must have left an impression on all of their team one way or another.

In spite of his long-term prognosis Flintoff was going to play at Lord's, and one of the decisions we came to in the team meetings was that he would open the bowling. The sight of him pounding in for one last series would hopefully get the crowd behind us from the start of an innings, and his accuracy would stop Phil Hughes getting away to a flier as he had done at Cardiff. Our other major decision was that Graham Onions – rather than Steve Harmison – would come in as fourth seamer, having done so well in the Lord's Test against West Indies. Onions was going to take the place of Panesar, even though he had lent his name to the third of Stephen's sons.

By Wednesday afternoon the time to think about my own batting and getting my head straight was running out. I went home to see the boys and put them to bed, but I did not enjoy the occasion as much as I usually do. I returned to the team hotel near Regent's Park and finally found some time for myself. I ordered room service – I eat anything – and watched a video of myself batting in previous Tests against Australia. It may sound narcissistic but it is the quickest way to reconnect with the right mindset. I texted Ruth to say sorry for being grumpy earlier that evening, and she rang back to say some typically kind and considerate words.

Next morning went exactly according to plan. We won the toss and had a gloriously sunny morning and a dry, evenly grassed pitch to bat on – the same one as in the 2005 Lord's Test against Australia. We knew how significant it was in the opening session to build on whatever momentum we had taken away from Cardiff, and at lunch we were 126 without loss. Alastair Cook, who had not really got into the series until now, had scored 67. I had made the running in reaching 28 off only 33 balls but then he overtook me with his pulls and cover-drives. We had the luck that opening batsmen need in the first hour. Cook steered a ball from Ben Hilfenhaus past gully, whereas at Cardiff it had gone to gully. It was the same as when I had my reprieve in Napier.

While Hilfenhaus bowled a fine opening spell from the Nursery end, we soon sensed that Mitchell Johnson was struggling at the Pavilion end. His first ball was a leg stump half-volley which Cook clipped for four, and his first four overs cost 26 runs. In my experience it usually takes a bowler a game or two at Lord's before he can decide which end is better for him. The slope can make you bowl too straight at one end and too wide of off stump at the other. This problem was summed up more expertly by Simon Hughes on the basis of his experience of bowling there for Middlesex. As 'The Analyst' he wrote in the *Daily Telegraph*: 'If you're on your game, the unique properties of Lord's enhance it. But if you're off it, it can be a total hindrance . . . A bowler's confidence is at the mercy of minute factors that the Lord's slope only amplifies. The tilt of the ground can make you lean over in delivery and cause you to feel off balance. You're thinking about everything except where to put the ball.'

Once you sense a bowler is struggling, as Johnson was with the slope and perhaps his mind, you have to take full toll of every loose ball: this is the dog-eats-dog nature of Test cricket. As the outfield at Lord's is so well drained and manicured, it is a fast-scoring ground and if a bowler is having an off day there he is going to 'go'. In his first spell Johnson bowled a short and very wide ball which I cut for four, then he overcompensated next ball and I clipped another four off leg stump. When Johnson tried switching to the Nursery end, Cook cut his first two balls for four. The first eight overs by Australia's strike bowler cost 53 runs. Every one of Australia's four main bowlers was playing his first game at Lord's, and while Hilfenhaus seemed to have his game enhanced by bowling from the Nursery end, Johnson had a bit of a nightmare – and he was supposed to be Australia's senior bowler. Given their collective inexperience, there must have been a case for Australia selecting Stuart Clark, who knew the slope from his time at Middlesex.

Australia's fast bowlers were not alone in taking time to adjust to the special properties of Lord's. Brad Haddin conceded two lots of four byes as the ball dipped and swung after pitching in the peculiar way that it does in England. Then he dropped me off

At the Oxford Road Cemetery near Ypres in Belgium, Stuart Broad on behalf of the England Ashes squad lays a memorial to Colin Blythe.

Nearly ready: Katherine Jenkins sings at the opening ceremony before the First Ashes Test in Cardiff.

The scene of our great escape: the First Test venue in Cardiff. The changing-rooms are to the right of where the camera was.

Far left: Kevin Pietersen during his 69 at Cardiff, his only fifty of the series, unfortunately.

Left: In *Blackadder* they called it 'mindless optimism': Graeme Swann picks up during his first innings at Cardiff and cheerfully propels us to 425.

Below left: The first of many fine contributions: Matt Prior after scoring 56 in Cardiff.

Right: Try this for your opposite number: Ricky Ponting during his thirty-eighth Test century, his 150 in Cardiff.

Below: The pain of bowling fast with a painful right knee combines with that of saving the First Test.

Four centuries in one innings! Brad Haddin, after hitting Paul Collingwood to the boundary, becomes the fourth.

Marcus North dives for the crease and becomes the third of the four Australian century-makers at Cardiff.

Life-saver: Paul Collingwood keeps us afloat in the series with his 74 on the last day in Cardiff.

What a relief: James Anderson and Monty Panesar after blocking out for a draw in Cardiff after everyone had expected us to go 1–0 down.

Far left: Ben Hilfenhaus at Lord's: the unheralded Tasmanian who kept Australia in the series.

Left: My most important hundred, or at least right up there: 161 against Australia at Lord's.

Below left: After 'going upstairs' to the television umpire, Rudi Koertzen gives Ricky Ponting out c Strauss b Anderson. It could have been lbw.

Right: When introducing the England team to Her Majesty at Lord's, my biggest fear was that I would forget the name of one of our squad. I just managed to dredge up the name of one of our press officers, James Avery.

Below: Stuart Broad catches Simon Katich off his pull at Lord's.

Above left: Andrew Flintoff bowling at Lord's on the fourth day. On the fifth morning he told me was going to bowl un the Australians were out, and he did.

Above right: The softening up process: Michael Clarke is giv a bouncer at Lord's shortly before clippir James Anderson to short mid-wicket.

Left: Even Clarke, the form batsman of the series, cannot face Andrew Flintoff duri his great spell on the fifth morning at Lord's.

a low chance away to his left hand when I edged a no-ball from Hilfenhaus, who had been switched to the Pavilion end. Another lot of four byes came later when a ball from Marcus North went through Haddin's legs. Before North, Nathan Hauritz had tried the Nursery end and I was determined not to let him settle, sweeping him square and fine for fours.

North bowled quite a lot because of an accident to Hauritz. Cook kept scoring fluently after lunch, while I had to play myself in again and did not score for 20 minutes during a tight spell from Hilfenhaus. After adding only four more runs to my lunch score of 48, while Cook was racing ahead, I decided to break out by going down the wicket to Hauritz: if you are trying to set a lead you cannot scratch around against a spinner for too long. I well and truly middled the ball, so much so that after dislocating the top of the middle finger of the bowler's right hand it went for three runs. This was good luck for me and bad luck for Hauritz, who immediately left the field and did not bowl again for the rest of our first innings, although he bravely came back to field next morning.

Without the steadiness of their specialist spinner, Australia were in an even trickier situation. North bowled wide of our off stump with a sweeper on the cover boundary who limited us to singles, but we kept going at four runs an over, echoing the transformation in England's approach between the First and Second Tests of 2005. We had already posted a hundred opening stand for the seventh time. When we passed 182, it became England's highest opening partnership against Australia at Lord's, beating the illustrious pair of Hobbs and Sutcliffe in 1926. Only 182: a reason perhaps for England's poor Ashes record at Lord's.

When Cook was out, rather taken by surprise when Johnson bowled a straight one, Ravi Bopara kept up the pressure by clipping and cover-driving a couple of fours off Johnson and taking 10 from an over. Before I reached my hundred, Bopara was also out lbw, when Hilfenhaus followed up a sequence of stock outswingers with one that nipped back. I was on 90 when Pietersen came in, and was nearly run out soon afterwards by Ponting, who had moved himself from mid-wicket to mid-on to await the Red Bull single. Pietersen this time decided not to go through for the run and if Ponting's throw had hit the stumps at the bowler's end, instead of going for four overthrows, I would probably have gone.

Pietersen had been given an injection in his Achilles heel after the Cardiff Test and the injury seemed to prey on his mind in this game, although more so in his second innings. The over before tea, by Hilfenhaus, was one mad over. Pietersen nearly handled the ball twice in one delivery when it bounced up and down in front of him and he was tempted to brush the ball away from the wicket with his hand. Hilfenhaus then surprised him with the bouncer that he used sparingly, and Pietersen was lucky the ball lobbed short on the legside behind square and far enough from Haddin. But Pietersen showed what a team man he is, in contrast to some public perceptions, when in the same over I cut to wide third man on 97. The fielder at deep cover was Australia's substitute, Andrew McDonald, who was on for Hauritz and, being so tall, was not the nimblest of fielders. He dived to his right on the third man boundary and could not stop the ball cleanly. Sensing a third run, Pietersen ran to the danger end at full stretch, without a thought for his Achilles, and so completed my eighteenth Test century.

I should have said before that one great advantage I took into this game, which offset all the demands of captaincy, was that I had played so often at Lord's before, and not only for Middlesex. This was actually my twelfth Test at Lord's, a rate of two per year since my debut in 2004. And the first Test I had ever watched in England had been at Lord's in 1990, when my father took me, and we saw Graham Gooch score the first half of his 333. He looked so confident and unflappable and dominant as England's captain and opening batsman that he must have made some impression.

When I had scored 11 in this innings, I had reached 1,000 Test runs at Lord's. The hundred was my fourth at the ground, my favourite as well as my most familiar one. My total of Test runs – I reached 5,000 at the end of this innings – made it look as though I was barely out of nappies by comparison with Ponting and his 11,000 plus; but to have the Second Test (usually a crucial one in a series) at Lord's was a really helpful factor. The best ground in world cricket, 'the home of cricket', and a full house with everybody cheering England on: moments are seldom more special.

Australia's seamers bowled straighter and fuller after tea and thereby made batting more difficult. After reaching 196 for no wicket, we were 364 for six by the close, but I was not too unhappy with the comparison to our first-day score in Cardiff because wicket-taking opportunities were so much more plentiful here. Paul Collingwood, who could well have been suffering the after-effects of his epic in Cardiff, was the one soft dismissal here when he tried to clear mid-on. The others were bowled out: Matt Prior, like Cook, was surprised by a straight one from Johnson that actually swung and came down the slope.

I had to set an example by going on for a big hundred, as Ponting had in the opening Test. We had talked so much about giving an innings away after reaching fifty, and I was intent on not doing so after reaching my hundred. Again, as always, a bit of luck was required: a cut off Peter Siddle went to Mike Hussey at gully just above his head, but I had middled it and the chance went through his hands. During the first day at least, and perhaps the second and third as well, Australia seemed to be a bit overawed by Lord's, just as we had been overawed by the occasion in the opening Test.

On the next morning we aimed to bat through the second new ball and reach 450. I had gone home and slept in my own bed instead of the team hotel, but it made no difference. I left the first ball from Hilfenhaus, back again at the Nursery end, and I left the second, only it swung in and hit my off stump. Two more wickets followed in the next two overs, and suddenly we were 378 for nine, and Australia were back in the game. The ball was swinging under cloud. Our momentum could have been lost.

Just as Cook and I had set a first-wicket record for England against Australia at Lord's, Anderson and Onions chose the perfect moment to set a tenth-wicket record. Onions did a commendable impersonation of Hughes by giving himself room outside leg stump to explore the areas behind point. Anderson's batting had come on in leaps and bounds and, starting with his first innings in Cardiff, he had shown the same sort of spikey attitude with the bat that Simon Jones had in 2005: not just over-my-dead-body determination, but the willingness to attack. Anderson also had to maintain and extend his personal world record of most Test innings before making a duck. A total of 425 was not quite what we had wanted, but we had scored them at four runs an over, which gave us plenty of time. I was also reminded of some advice that Vaughan had offered in our conversations together: he had said that England, without Shane Warne to face in 2009, should be able to score as many runs in their second innings as their first

The Queen arrived for the start of Australia's first innings, although we waited until the lunch interval before I had the privilege of introducing the England players to her. Afterwards we took a couple of wickets before Her Majesty had other business to attend to. The pitch had quickened a little now it had thoroughly dried out. Flintoff rose to the occasion by cutting off Australia's run-supply from the Pavilion end while Anderson took two wickets in his opening spell. Hughes feathered a catch down the legside off his glove. Ponting's dismissal was controversial: Anderson's ball was heading for leg stump when Ponting tried to clip it legside. It was then deflected off his pad to my left at first slip, and I caught it low down. Rudi Koertzen thought Ponting had nicked the ball on to his pad first. He referred to the third umpire Nigel Llong as to whether the ball had carried, then raised his finger.

It was a stop-start afternoon as bad light and rain caused several brief interruptions. We could not take a third wicket before Her Majesty departed: Simon Katich and Hussey called on all their experience of English conditions gained in county cricket to see Australia up to the 100 mark. After tea came one of the most enjoyable sessions: in 20 overs before bad light brought an early close we took six wickets for 69 runs, reducing Australia to 156 for eight. In addition to Hughes, four other Australian batsmen were out to cross-bat shots. Katich scooped a short ball to fine-leg as he had done in the warm-up at Worcester; North, after being tied down, reacted with instincts that had been conditioned at the WACA in Perth, tried to pull and dragged on; Haddin and Johnson connected with their pulls and were caught off Broad.

We talked before the start of the third day about whether we would enforce the follow-on if we had the option, and we decided to leave the decision as long as possible. Whereas Friday had been a bowling day, Saturday from the outset was a batting day. Australia had only once been made to follow on in recent years – by Vaughan at Trent Bridge in 2005. They had also given up the practice of enforcing the follow-on themselves after a bad experience by Mark Taylor in Rawalpindi. The Australian habit was to bat again and expose the opposition to batting against Warne in the fourth innings on a wearing wicket, with nothing to play for except a draw.

The ball did not swing for us on the third morning. It took a couple of loose shots against Onions for us to dismiss Hauritz and Siddle. After I had gone off for an over, I made up my mind that we ought to bat again. Another consideration was that our pace bowlers had various aches and niggles: not only Flintoff's right knee but Anderson's left ankle. The year before at Lord's, when we had enforced the follow-on and bowled for three consecutive days against South Africa, Ryan Sidebottom had broken down. At Trent Bridge in 2005 Simon Jones had broken down when Australia had followed on, terminally as far as England were concerned. In a five-Test series you cannot play all your cards at once, as you would in a one-off match or three-Test series.

What we had to do, if we batted again, was bat so positively that we did not allow the Australians to recover breath. There were 82 overs scheduled to be bowled during the rest of the third day, and if we scored at four an over we would be 500 ahead by the close, leaving two days to dismiss Australia a second time.

Our second innings went according to plan overall, to the extent that we were more than 500 ahead when bad light stopped play with 11 overs left. Cook and I made brisk thirties before getting out to Hauritz, who did not seem to be troubled by his dislocation after a day's rest. Australia dragged the rate back when Bopara and Pietersen were limited to 25 runs in the last 15 overs before tea: Pietersen was hobbling at times, which stopped Bopara taking quick singles and rotating the strike, and Hilfenhaus bowled excellently, this time from the Pavilion end. Neither batsman went into the game in prime form and the middle of an Ashes Test was not the place where they could find it. But Bopara did have a slice of luck when he edged Siddle at no higher than knee height to second slip and Ponting, with his fingers pointing upwards, put it down. When catching Flintoff in England's first innings Ponting had got away with his Australian-style method.

This true batting pitch, with a bit more wear and tear on a spinner's length than in previous years, was one of Mick Hunt's finest creations. Collingwood and Prior in particular enjoyed it before the declaration. To Prior went most of the credit for our acceleration as he played a shot a ball from the moment he went in, but it has to be said he benefited from the groundwork done by Bopara and Pietersen. Ponting had taken Hauritz out of the attack as soon as Pietersen had hit him for one boundary, but Hauritz had to be brought back after Hilfenhaus had finally tired. Prior swept Hauritz to various parts of the legside, and scored faster than a run a ball in a brilliant 61. But in laying the foundation for him there was an element of teamwork which was easily missed.

On the Saturday night it rained, and again on the Sunday morning, as forecast. The first half of the fourth day was therefore a bowling day, at least until the ball aged and a squally wind blew over Lord's. I declared first thing, before play started at 11.15. Some commentators thought we should bat on a bit longer but the conditions were right for bowling; and captaincy is a matter of learning on the job. If my declaration in Antigua had been 20 or 30 minutes late, and in Trinidad perhaps five minutes late, I like to think this one was spot on.

The bowlers, as in Australia's first innings, applied unrelenting pressure from the first over and when the ball was new – either the first or second ball – something had to give. The crowd were right behind us on the fourth morning, sensing that history could be made or at least updated. They were so keyed up that individual deliveries were applauded, which is something you tend to hear more on northern grounds, but it seems only fair if batsmen are applauded for individual strokes.

Flintoff, bowling as always in this match from the Pavilion end, took the first two wickets but not without some controversy. As the pitch had more pace in it than Cardiff, we planned two gullies and a backward point for Katich in the hope that he would slice his drive in the wristy way he has, and it worked. The only trouble was that replays subsequently showed that Flintoff's front foot was over the line and Koertzen, standing in his hundredth Test, and the second umpire to that landmark after Steve Bucknor, had missed a no-ball.

The dismissal of Hughes was even more controversial. For certain he opened the face and steered a catch towards me, and I dived forwards from first slip and came up with the ball. I was sure I had caught it, and told Hughes as much when he turned to ask me. For several days afterwards I had a bruise at the tips of my fingers where the ball had landed on them. Then Ponting, at the non-striker's end, told him to stay his ground. At this point Koertzen turned to Billy Doctrove at square-leg and asked him if the ball had carried cleanly to me. Doctrove said yes, and therefore the incident was not referred to the third umpire.

Given the parameters of recent referrals, I would say in hindsight that it could have gone 'upstairs'. Similar catches, and non-catches, in the Headingley Test against South Africa in 2008 had been referred. So had a chance which Bopara had hit to Hauritz at mid-on in our second innings. Koertzen, standing close by, had referred that one – and Bopara had been given the benefit of the doubt which seems to exist on these occasions.

In Hughes' case Doctrove, at least 20 yards away at square-leg, decided he had seen the ball clearly enough not to refer it to the third umpire and told Koertzen accordingly. I suppose there was some inconsistency in the approach of the two umpires, and as players what we ask is consistency. At Cardiff Aleem Dar had a superb game, consistent and correct in every decision, but he was rested for Lord's, and came back at Edgbaston. It was noticeable that all five of the umpires who were listed to stand in this series were given two matches each. Consistency, of a kind.

A third injustice, from an Australian point of view, was done when Mike Hussey was given out caught at slip after an off-break turned out of the rough. It looked a carbon copy of my second innings dismissal: but no, the replays indicated that the ball had missed Hussey's bat completely, and leapt out of the footmarks, and Hot Spot revealed that any noise came from the bottom of Hussey's bat hitting the ground. At least there was no question about Ponting's dismissal. In the course of Broad's best spell of the series to date, from the Pavilion end and fuller than first time round, Ponting dragged on a ball too close to cut. Like Sachin Tendulkar, Ponting seemed destined never to get on the honours board at Lord's. In his three Tests there he has not made a fifty. Mind you, he has scored five more Test centuries at the Sydney Cricket Ground than I have.

When Swann followed up by whisking a quicker ball through North's high backlift, Australia were 128 for five. It was the way he had dismissed several West Indian left-handers, notably Devon Smith. And, of course, we should all have known better. Just when you think you have the measure of Australia, that is the most dangerous period because that is when they start to come back at you. Michael Clarke set off like a train in pursuit of a win, hitting three fours in an Anderson over, two of them immaculate cover-drives. Haddin, a big mate of his, also started to counter-attack. The ball was 40 overs old: it was going to be a productive partnership if we had to wait another 40 overs for the second new ball and another wicket.

We knew the Australians would produce one partnership, or even two, but not such a long one, and a record one for Australia's sixth wicket on this ground. As it turned out, Clarke and Haddin added 185 in 47 overs together before bad light brought a close. They became more and more assured as the ball aged, and the one period

in the five days when we did not control the game was this partnership. In the run-up to the second ball Collingwood had a bowl from
the Pavilion end but could not separate the pair, and we slightly
went off the boil in the field, although no chances were missed.
When the time came, I called the players together for a huddle and
told them we had to nail Australia in this Test, and show that streak
of ruthlessness which we recently had against West Indies. Nothing
Churchillian: basically, make the most of the second new ball.

The early close on the fourth evening turned out to be an advantage
to us: the second ball was only six overs old when we went off, whereas
it would have been 18 overs old if we had played out the day. There
would be plenty of life in it on the fifth morning, we told ourselves:
only five wickets left to take, and still 209 more runs for Australia
to score for a victory that would have broken all Test and first-class
records for a run-chase. Nevertheless, I have to admit, I did not sleep
well. Seventy-five years since England had last won an Ashes Test at
Lord's. Only one victory there in 27 Tests spread over 113 years! When
I have bad dreams, I think they always stem from when I went into
my finals at Durham without having done much revision. But this
current exam was more about history than economics.

On the final morning Flintoff immediately banished the night-
mares: at Chennai India had pulled off the highest successful
run-chase in Asia but Australia were not going to do anything
similar here. 'Fred' simply rose to the occasion of his last Test at
Lord's. Whereas others might have been intimidated by having a
pavilion full of MCC members urging him on, he was inspired by it
and in turn inspired the team. Anderson set the tone with a terrific
first over at Clarke, then Flintoff relieved the tension considerably

by dismissing Haddin in his first over with a ball that held its line and had him fending to Collingwood's right at second slip.

One of the best spells of fast bowling I have ever seen followed – the best since Flintoff's own spell at the Oval on the penultimate morning in September 2005. He broke Clarke's bat with a yorker, then almost broke one of his hands with a bouncer. Some England players of considerable note have under-performed against Australia but Flintoff, like Ian Botham, has raised both aspects of his game against them. He bowled for the rest of the innings and there was no point in my asking whether he would like to take a break.

Haddin was out at 313, without addition to Australia's overnight score. No chance of them winning now, except Mitchell Johnson somehow saw off Flintoff's bouncers and started driving boundaries, and Australia brought the target down to 166 with Clarke and Johnson going well, and it was exam time all over again.

Swann had been pestering for a bowl, and although Clarke is a masterful player of spin – he can play forward and back to the same ball, so quick are his feet – he was worth a go. In the warm-up at Worcester, and in the ICC Twenty20, Johnson had shown his strength in slog-sweeping over mid-wicket and if he tried it against Swann it would be against the spin.

To Swann's first ball Clarke came down the wicket as usual, and he almost yorked himself, stabbing it out to me at extra-cover. To Swann's second ball he again came down the wicket but it drifted just enough to go past Clarke's outside edge, pitched, and turned enough to hit off stump. Dismissing batsmen when well set on flat pitches: England have seldom had an offspinner like that since pitches were covered.

England v Australia
Second Test, Lord's, 16-20 August 2009

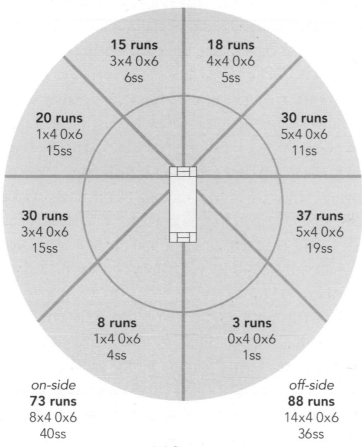

15 runs
3x4 0x6
6ss

18 runs
4x4 0x6
5ss

20 runs
1x4 0x6
15ss

30 runs
5x4 0x6
11ss

30 runs
3x4 0x6
15ss

37 runs
5x4 0x6
19ss

8 runs
1x4 0x6
4ss

3 runs
0x4 0x6
1ss

on-side
73 runs
8x4 0x6
40ss

off-side
88 runs
14x4 0x6
36ss

AJ Strauss
1st Innings 161

		Scoring shots (ss)		Non-scoring shots	
Runs	161				
Balls faced	268	1s	39	0s	192
Strike rate	60.07	2s	11		
Scoring shots	76	3s	4		
		4s	22		

We could almost relax and enjoy the final minutes. Flintoff, still going after an hour and a half without any let-up, bowled Hauritz as he tried to let one go. In Australia's first innings he had been a tad too short and the batsmen had been able to leave his stock ball on height, but he and Ottis Gibson had talked about the right length and Flintoff was spot on second time round, as Hauritz found.

Not since the Oval Test of 2005 had Flintoff taken a five-for and he badly wanted another. He was coming towards the end of a ten-over spell and I had to think about asking him to save some of his body and energy for the last three Tests of the series. The last ball of his tenth over was a no-ball to Siddle, called by Koertzen. Flintoff walked back to his mark, pounded in, bowled the ideal inswinger of fullish length, and the fifth wicket was his as he demolished Siddle's stumps. Flintoff sank to his knees, and the ground rose to him.

One wicket left until England's first victory at Lord's for 75 years. Swann to Johnson. After the fifth ball I brought the field in, except for deep square-leg: even if Johnson hit the last ball of the over for four, we could then have a go at Hilfenhaus. Swann speared in another of his quicker balls, like the one that beat North, except that Johnson was well down the wicket and yorked himself. The ball not only hit middle stump but took it out of the ground.

After all the speeches and media interviews and celebrations and sighs of relief and drinks, I slept well that night. As I went to sleep, all I could hear was 'the welcome sound' of Swann on wood.

14
TANTALISING

Our victory at Lord's came at a price. Kevin Pietersen, our best batsman, was ruled out of the rest of the series.

Before the game was over, it was pretty apparent that Pietersen would have to undergo some medical treatment. The only question was whether his right Achilles tendon would require short-term or long-term rehabilitation.

It was a physical injury with psychological effects. In the Lord's Test, Pietersen could not do his job; the injury did not so much affect his strokes as his setting off for a run afterwards, so he could not take quick singles for himself or his partner. As he lost confidence in the ability of his body to perform, he became distracted from the task of watching the ball.

The surgeon, flown in from Sweden, took one look at the Achilles tendon and said the option of full surgery with long-term rehab had to be taken, not the short-term one. After innings of 69 and 8, 32 and 44, we had lost our number four batsman who had not missed a Test since his debut in 2005.

As a captain I was worried by such a sad and potentially serious loss. Pietersen had been managing his injury for a long time and England's medical staff had planned to get him through the series. Statistically, he was our best batsman against Australia. The Ashes had always brought the best out of him from the moment he strutted out at Lord's for his Test debut and made a fifty in each innings as if he owned the place. In his 12 Tests against Australia Pietersen had averaged 50.

We were fortunate to have Ian Bell in reserve. It would have been bad if we had been forced to hand someone a Test debut, but Bell was chomping at the bit to return to the England Test team after seven months out of it, since the Kingston Test. And we decided to slot him into Pietersen's place at number four to minimise the disruptions to our side.

Five-Test series are a test of – among other things – the depth of cricketing talent in the countries involved. Australia had lost their most experienced pace bowler, Brett Lee, before the series began; now we had lost our best batsman. It was a piece of bad luck, but at least it was the one and only piece of bad luck that England had had so far.

For me, golf is the ultimate form of relaxation, and since taking over the England captaincy it has been all the more so. Figuring out why the ball is fading or drawing on a golf course leaves little space in my mind for other things to creep in, like the batting order, or the state of wickets, or team selection. They all have to go to the back of your mind for four or five hours on the golf course. Spending time with the kids is similar, but even when pottering around at home your mind can start wandering.

The day after the Lord's Test the England and Australia teams took part in a golf day at Stoke Poges organised by Sir Michael Parkinson, which I hope raised a lot of money for charity. The captains of both sides had pretty heavy heads. Nevertheless, we did reasonably well in the competition to hit a ball closest to the pin.

At one stage I hit a ball which was obviously the closest yet, and when I reached the hole I found to my delight that the person I had overtaken to take the lead was Ricky Ponting. I did not win the competition, however, because I was then overtaken.

Matthew Prior and Ian Bell play with a handicap of nine or ten. James Anderson is improving rapidly and has a handicap of six or seven. Paul Collingwood and I have a handicap of four at present and a fierce, intense, no-holds-barred rivalry. My one and only hole-in-one came in a tussle with Collingwood at Woburn. But, to my regret, I have to admit that he won the round in the end.

The day before the Edgbaston Test, at the press interview which every captain has to give according to ICC regulations, I was asked if the Australians had lost their aura. A few hours later everyone was talking about auras: they became the big issue. But I did not intend to create a stir, and I think there was an element of mischievous journalism involved in the uproar which ensued.

What happened was that I was asked if the Australians had the same aura as they had possessed in previous years, and I replied that it was fairly obvious that they had not. Simon Barnes in *The Times* dedicated a long article to an examination of the subject, mulling over whether an aura occurred in the person said to have it, or in the eye of the beholder. But effectively we defined it in a similar way: an aura is something that only occurs in established campaigners, in this case cricketers who have become outstanding.

So, by definition, this Australian team could not have an aura because so many of their players were starting out on their Test careers: without Lee, and Stuart Clark, only Ricky Ponting, Simon

Katich, Michael Hussey and Michael Clarke had played as many as 20 Tests. They had some very good players, they were still very hard to beat, but the Australian side of 2009 no longer had an aura. I did not think it was a very controversial statement. The day before the Third Test was a wet one, however, and there cannot have been much else to talk about apart from Andrew Flintoff's right knee.

So wet, in fact, that although the opening day began brightly, a heavy downpour before the start topped up Edgbaston's water-table and cost us most of the first day. It was not until half past four that I could walk out to toss and exchange team-sheets with Ponting. He won it for the first time in the series and must have had a few doubts before batting first after so much rain in the build-up to the match that Warwickshire's groundsman Steve Rouse had said the surface would be jelly. But Ponting could hardly have chosen to bowl first after the barrage of criticism he had received for doing that in the Edgbaston Test of 2005.

By 4.45 p.m. I was back in our dressing-room, after doing the post-toss interviews with television and radio, and getting ready to field. In came Steve Bernard, the Australian manager, and Jeff Crowe, the match referee. They said Brad Haddin had broken a finger in his left hand just after the toss, which was reminiscent of Glenn McGrath twisting his ankle just before the toss in 2005. McGrath, playing touch rugby on the outfield, had trodden on a ball which had been left in his path by, of all people, Haddin.

Crowe said the matter was in my hands: I could force Haddin to play because he had suffered the injury after the toss and the exchange of team-sheets. I asked Bernard and Crowe if they could let me have a couple of minutes for a quick chat with Andy Flower (it could not have been any longer because we were about to go out and field). We felt pretty strongly that allowing Australia to play their reserve wicket-keeper, Graham Manou, was the right thing to do. There have been occasions when reserve keepers have been allowed, and when they have not been allowed, but I think that everyone in our dressing-room realised – once they had got their heads around it – that it would have been a step too far if we had made Haddin play.

I went back to Bernard and Crowe and said yes, that was fine by us. They were thankful, and next morning Manou and the Australian coach Tim Nielsen also came in to say thanks. It was not a massive decision, because doing anything else would have sat uncomfortably with me, but they appreciated it; and the episode showed that the spirit between the teams was not as bad as some of the media had made out.

The decisive factor in the Edgbaston Test, so far as it went, was swing. In Australia's first innings the ball swung after about 30 overs, which was consistent with the batch of Dukes balls we had used to that stage of the 2009 season, although in the two May-time Tests against West Indies it had swung as early as 15 overs. You may remember that in the Lord's Test I had dared to open the bowling with Graeme Swann, partly on the basis that the new ball would not swing for the first few overs.

In Australia's second innings at Edgbaston, however, the ball did not swing – not when it was new, not after 30 overs. I have no idea why, only that we should have won the game if it had. When I started in the England team, Marcus Trescothick was in charge of polishing the ball, and any secrets tend to get passed on from generation to generation within the dressing-room. Now we had two people in charge of the ball-polishing, Paul Collingwood and James Anderson. But the reality is that there is only so much you can do.

For certain, you have to cover with saliva any abrasions on the shiny side of the ball which have been made by the pitch or the bat, then polish hard; and the lacquer has to come off one side of the ball. More than that is beyond me and my knowledge of science. The second morning, when the 30–over ball swung, felt very similar in terms of temperature and cloud-cover to the fifth morning, when another 30–over ball did not swing.

Australia scored 126 for one in the two-hour session that made up day one, which was not exactly the present which Anderson wanted for his twenty-seventh birthday. It was such an easy-paced pitch that we needed to be at our most disciplined, but we were not. The crowd, after being patient all through a sunny afternoon while the outfield slowly drained, got carried away when play eventually started at 5 p.m., and maybe we did too. It can be hard, after you have been stuck in a dressing-room for most of the day, to strike the right note. Some commentators blamed the wet run-ups for the bowlers being off target but I don't think that was much of an issue.

Australia had dropped Phil Hughes, after only two Tests in the series and five in his career, in favour of Shane Watson. Watson had made some runs in their practice game against Northamptonshire but he had batted at number three while Hughes opened, which made it seem like a late decision by Australia's selectors (their captain and coach had a voice only, not a vote). As an emergency opener, who had never batted higher than number six in a Test, Watson batted pretty well and put the wide balls away. The one wicket we got came when Swann trapped Simon Katich, who was trying to make up for lost time, in his opening over.

When we arrived at the ground on the second morning, we decided that we would be patient and bowl maidens. The ball was 30 overs old, in theory all ready to swing. I started the bowling with Graham Onions, at the City end, although he had taken eight wickets for Durham against Warwickshire earlier in the season from the Pavilion end. And a wonderful session ensued in which we took seven of Australia's wickets for 77 runs.

I wanted to start with Onions partly to give him some confidence after he had bowled three expensive overs on the opening day. I also had a feeling that he could get Ponting out, lbw or caught behind. My theory on Ponting was that he preferred balls that were bouncing over the height of the stumps; when the ball was bail-height or below he found it relatively difficult to judge what to play and what to leave. Onions is one of those bowlers who made it hard for the batsman to decide whether to play or leave. He is a bit like a souped-up version of Mark Ealham, who had played in the Edgbaston Test in 1997 when England took eight wickets in the opening session with swing, as we were soon to be reminded.

Onions is the ideal sort of bowler to captain. He is fiercely competitive; he hates losing at anything, even the football warm-ups. From the moment he came into the England side against West Indies he was a breath of fresh air and he carried the same effect through into the Ashes. He always wants the ball in his hand and to prove himself; and it is hard not to respond to someone who is so keen.

With his first ball of the second day, straight and skiddy, Onions trapped Watson. In bustled Hussey and he shouldered arms, just as he had in Australia's first innings at Lord's, the ball hitting his off stump. Normally Andrew Flintoff was needed to get the crowd going but not here. Apparently it was the first time in the Ashes, if not in the whole history of Test cricket, that someone had taken two wickets with the first two balls of the day. Soon afterwards Onions had Ponting caught behind, if not quite in the way I had intended, hooking at a bouncer.

The only real flaw in our cricket on that wonderful morning was a slip catch that went down. Clarke tried to withdraw his bat from a ball from Onions once he saw that it was not an inswinger, but instead he hit it off almost the middle of the bat to Flintoff at second slip at a speed which surprised him. I have to add that Edgbaston is not one of the best 'seeing grounds'.

Anderson followed up with a spell at the Pavilion end that was sensational, as good as the ones he had bowled in the Test at Chester-le-Street. He had to wait three or four overs before his first wicket came but in the process he was lining up Marcus North beautifully. Initially we thought we should go across North, then bring the odd ball back into him, but he was leaving about five out of six balls an over. So we switched to bringing the ball back into him on a regular basis, and got him with the one which left him. Matthew Prior dived in front of first slip with an outstretched left hand to spare me the trouble of catching it.

In the space of only 13 balls Anderson dismissed Michael Clarke,

North, Manou and Mitchell Johnson, who shouldered arms to his first ball. The Edgbaston crowd went wild, like they did for most of the four days in 2005. Anderson went wide of the crease for his outswinger to open up Manou, making him think it was going down legside, and hit his off stump. The magic was not quite the same after lunch, but Anderson took his fifth wicket when Peter Siddle somehow managed to outside-edge an inswinger, and Australia were all out for 263 on what was – taking away the overhead conditions – a very flat pitch.

Once we had recovered from the shock of losing Alastair Cook in Siddle's first over, I thought it was a bit like a one-day international in that the first 15 overs would be the easiest in which to score runs – in this case because the ball would not start swinging until after the first hour or so. Although I do not have a brilliant record at Edgbaston, I soon found it was a great wicket to bat on and that both back-foot and front-foot shots were low-risk.

In fact I like to think this was one of my best innings in terms of hitting the ball with the middle of my bat. I have seldom scored such a high percentage of my runs in the 'V' as I did in the 64 which I made before the close of the second day. Ben Hilfenhaus, well established by now as the steadiest of Ponting's pace bowlers, swung the new ball back into me and therefore straight-driving was a safe option. When Siddle pitched up, which was not too often, I put a couple away in the same direction; Ponting even posted a silly mid-off, like Michael Vaughan had done in 2005 to Matthew Hayden on this ground. Bad light ended play early – there were no floodlights, for the first time in this series – when we were 116 for two.

It was a shame having to start all over again two days later.

The forecast for Saturday had been terrible from the outset of the game, and so it proved: a thick blanket of rain-cloud stayed over the ground all morning, there was little wind to move it on, and Rouse was in despair because the water-table was so high that his super-soppers were having no impact. About half of the county grounds in England had installed new drainage during the previous winter or two, but Warwickshire were waiting to launch their multi-million pound redevelopment before doing it: all the heavy machinery on the outfield was going to make a mess of the ground, so this made sense. Still, Tests at Edgbaston usually have an incredible atmosphere and it would have been great to bat on such a flat wicket with all that support behind England. But Saturday's play was abandoned for the day as early as 2.30 p.m., and I went back to the team hotel to be with my wife and kids.

It was more than 36 hours later that I resumed my innings and those drives 'down the ground', as the Australians like to say, had become a distant memory. I was well aware of the need to go on but the Australians bowled tightly on the fourth morning and eventually I got a ball from Hilfenhaus which surprised me. The short balls had generally been there to cut but this one nipped back and bounced a bit more and I top-edged a cut to the keeper. That's a batsman's life for you: one good ball is all it takes to end your day.

At least it was good to see Bell settle into Pietersen's place with the first of what we hoped would be a series of telling contributions: he scored 53, almost exactly what Pietersen had averaged against Australia. As we were wobbling at 168 for five at lunch, and the ball was too (Johnson seemed happier with the old ball and bowled his steadiest spell of the series to date), we needed a partnership between Prior and Flintoff, and they delivered 89 in only 15 and a half overs.

Prior had caught everything that had come his way – and North's edge which was coming my way – and his batting was becoming increasingly assured. So assured that he was developing the Adam Gilchrist-like ability to reach 20 before blinking an eyelid. Flintoff began with some of his favourite front-foot drives when Ponting gave Watson a bowl, and soon we were all going down memory lane. It was the Edgbaston Test of 2005 again, and 'Fred' was taking the game to Australia, and the spectators were varying their songs about 'Matilda' and 'Your Gracious Queen' with 'Super, super Fred'.

After playing Flintoff in with some drive-balls, the Australians decided to bowl a bit shorter at him and at one point he scored five consecutive runs off his gloves – a four and a single – and, being Flintoff, he did it off only three deliveries. When Siddle had finished, Flintoff tucked into Nathan Hauritz, who had done considerably better than his many critics had prophesied. A six to mid-wicket off Hauritz – amazingly, it was reported to be Flintoff's twentieth six in Test cricket at Edgbaston, more than some of us score in a lifetime – took our score level with Australia's, and Flintoff's sweep for four next ball gave us the lead.

We scored 157 off 32 overs in the afternoon session (an extended one as we started the fourth day an hour late to allow for more drying up). Flintoff, much as the crowd wanted him to score his first century since 2005, was out before tea for 74 off 79 balls, caught at slip off an off-break that landed in Johnson's footmarks and bounced a lot. At the tea interval I told the players there was no need to up the gears too much; we had to keep being positive but there was no need to go crazy. I need not have bothered. The lower order felt it was their day, and they were exhilarating to watch.

Broad had some trouble against Siddle's bouncers early on but soon demonstrated what a valuable allround cricketer he is, even though he had taken only four wickets in the series to date. By reaching his fifty from only 62 balls he kept the pressure on Australia's pace bowlers and prevented the sudden growth of any auras. Swann swatted away merrily for 24 from only 20 balls and in the end we had a lead of 113, assembled at the healthy rate of four an over. And time to take two of their wickets before the close of day four: Katich – caught behind off Onions, driving at a full length – and Ponting.

The reception which the crowd gave Ponting as he walked out for his second innings became the subject of some discussion. Giles Clarke, the ECB chairman, was moved to write in the programme for the next Test at Headingley that Ponting, as one of the all-time greats, had 'earned the respect and courtesy of the crowd'. To me, it sounded largely like pantomime booing; it had been a long day in the sun, the bars had been worked to full capacity, and the Edgbaston crowd has never been prone to long periods of silent contemplation. It is also relevant that Ponting had received an ovation from the whole ground on the second morning when he had passed Allan Border's aggregate of Test runs and become Australia's leading scorer.

I think to some extent the absence of other experienced players from the Australian team channelled the crowd's attention towards

Ponting. If McGrath, Shane Warne and Matthew Hayden had been playing, they too would have copped several earfuls from the Edgbaston crowd and deflected some of the booing away from Ponting. If Brett Lee had been playing, instead of recovering from his rib injury, he would have aroused the crowd's attention on the fine-leg boundary and added to the pantomime atmosphere. Effectively, the point was being reinforced for me; Ponting had an aura, and maybe Lee, but the rest of his team did not.

After the game Ponting had no complaints. 'One of the memories I will take from Edgbaston will be the extraordinary noise. I am told that some people have been upset about the fact that some English fans were booing me, but I thought it was a terrific atmosphere to play in, and I loved every minute,' he said in his *Daily Telegraph* column. 'I have said for a long time that the Barmy Army are the best sporting crowd in the world. I don't care what sport you're talking about, or what country – they are unbelievably good supporters. There is never anything untoward. It is always good, light-hearted stuff, and when England have a sniff of winning, the volume goes up tenfold. They add a lot to the whole experience of the Ashes. The Edgbaston crowd were not the first to boo me this summer – but they were the loudest. Which makes sense, because Edgbaston is famous for being the bullring of English cricket. Whenever I walk out of the changing rooms I am half-expecting it. I'm thinking: "Right, let's get it out of the way, get the booing done, and then I'll start building my innings."' Those were the words of Australia's captain, not a whingeing Aussie.

We felt at the start of the last day, with 98 overs to be bowled to make up partly for lost time, that we had a chance of winning the game and going 2–0 up – if only the ball would swing. We already knew it would turn for Swann, but the ball had to swing as well if we were going to take Australia's last eight wickets in less than 70 overs and leave ourselves time to knock the target off. Draws in Ashes Tests had been relatively few in recent times, less than one per series on average.

We knew the ball would turn because of Swann's spell against Ponting on the fourth evening. After the booing had subsided, Swann had proceeded to bowl an exceptional over at him. Coming in from the City end and over the wicket, and aiming wide of the stumps at the footmarks made by Johnson, Swann landed every ball of an over in almost exactly the same place, but all with slightly different trajectories, degrees of spin and speeds.

I had taken Swann off in the first innings the moment Ponting had come in, but I felt that we could get him the second time round if Swann got the ball wide into the rough and drew him forward. The one gap in Ponting's great CV had been success in India and that had largely been down to India's offspinner Harbhajan Singh. I posted four men round the bat. If we could get Ponting and another wicket before the close, with Australia still behind, we would if nothing else take our momentum on to Headingley. And, after building up the pressure on Australia's captain ball by ball, as the climax of his wonderful over, Swann ripped one between his bat and front pad to hit middle-and-leg.

Ponting himself acknowledged afterwards that Swann's over was exceptional: he 'bowled a great over at me, in fact. It was a bit reminiscent of the last time we played at Edgbaston. On that occasion Andrew Flintoff bowled me one of the best overs I have faced in Test cricket. And while Swann's wasn't quite on the same plane, it was still pretty good.' High praise from the batsman who, at the time, was third only to Sachin Tendulkar and Brian Lara among all Test run-scorers.

But on the fifth day we could take no more than three of Australia's eight remaining wickets. The crowd tried to make an England victory happen, but the ball did not. Edgbaston was almost filled with spectators, taking advantage of cheaper last-day prices, but while they did everything they could to supply the right atmosphere to get the players going, they could not make the ball swing. Which was strange as the fifth morning felt much like the second morning, with a freshness in the wind.

The first session went all right as we took two wickets to give us four by lunch. After Flintoff had started from the Pavilion end and softened up Watson, hitting him twice with successive short balls, Anderson took over and had Watson edging a drive in his first over: 137 for three, Australia 24 ahead, shortly after midday.

Hussey took most of Flintoff's opening spell, sparing Watson some pain and punishment. Three consecutive balls from Flintoff to Hussey summed up our day, all of them just outside off stump; Hussey missed the first and third, and drove the second through the covers for four. Eventually, shortly before lunch, Broad came round the wicket and got Hussey in much the same way that he had dismissed Shivnarine Chanderpaul more than once, getting an outside edge from a defensive push.

With the wisdom of hindsight, I looked back to the beginning of Hussey's innings. He had come in on the fourth evening after being bowled first ball in his first innings (and apparently no Australian

batsman had been dismissed for a 'king pair' in an Ashes Test).
Onions, who knew Hussey from their Durham days, had bowled
a straight ball which Hussey had inside-edged on to his pad, it
ballooned up but Onions, following through and diving, could not
quite reach it. There had been a case for having a short-leg, who
would have had time to catch it, but in general I don't believe in
having a short-leg or 'bat-pad' on pitches without much pace in
them. At Lord's, where the ball did zip around, I used a short-leg
quite a lot but Edgbaston never had enough pace in it. How often
do you see a batsman caught by bat-pad off a pace bowler on a slow
wicket? As a captain you have to base your field on the likeliest
ways that you are going to get a batsman out; and if you have a
short-leg, you cannot have a fielder somewhere else.

Almost until the close, Clarke and North defied us in a sixth
wicket partnership of 185. The only chance came when I put Ravi
Bopara on and Clarke middled a pull straight at me at short mid-
wicket – one of those which either stick or not because there is no
time to react. We tried nearly everything but, whoever bowled it,
the ball would not swing, hard though Collingwood and Anderson
polished it. For sure, the ball we used in the second innings was a
softer one than the ball we used in the first.

There are different theories about different grounds. Mine is
that at Headingley, for instance, the ball swings when the clouds
are overhead and does not swing when the sun is shining. At Lord's,
on the other hand, the ball does not swing simply when the sky is
overcast – you need to have had some rain, and some moisture in
the ground and some humidity in the air, before it does.

The Third Test would no doubt have been the decisive game of the series if it had been played to a finish. England would either have gone 2–0 up with two to play, a pretty unassailable position in a damp summer, or else Australia would have levelled the series at 1–1 and gone into the last two Tests with the momentum on their side. But the rain, which had wiped out a third of the match at Edgbaston, had deferred the crunch until Headingley.

Before driving up to Leeds, on the day after the Edgbaston Test, I played a round of golf at The Belfry with Prior and our bowling coach Ottis Gibson. It was fantastic to play holes that had been immortalised by Ryder Cup battles, and a good way to walk off the stiffness from spending the last day and a third in the field. But there had been so much rain around the Midlands that the course was still pretty wet, and the standard of golf was similarly disappointing.

Still, in cricket and golf terms, we were one up with two to play.

15
THE MOST TESTING
OF TIMES

The Headrow in Leeds, with its grand Victorian buildings, makes a fine sight. But not, for preference, at 5 o'clock on the morning of an Ashes Test.

About 4.45 a.m. a massive intercom in my hotel room, of which I had not previously been aware, announced that we were all to stay in our rooms until further notice. This message was repeated continuously for about ten minutes. The announcement had started off by being incorporated into my dream before I realised it was for real.

My first conscious thought was that a terrorist attack was being launched – less than a year had passed since Mumbai. But, by the sound of things, not much was going on in our hotel. Then the most piercing fire alarm I have heard in my life went off in my room, followed by the announcement that we had to vacate the hotel.

We stayed outside for about half-an-hour in the Headrow and in the drizzle. Although it was the first morning of the Fourth Test, the England players did not say much to one another. I was mildly amazed to watch one hotel guest standing around in shorts and nothing else – no shirt, no shoes.

The fire alarm turned out not to be a false one. It was caused by someone who had put a towel on top of a lamp. The person responsible, so I believe, was not one of the England players or management. Our spin bowling coach Mushtaq Ahmed is the only one of our number who is normally awake at 5 a.m.

Eventually I went back to sleep, then woke up pretty groggy. But often during a Test match you do not get as much sleep as you want. Maybe you have your kids staying in the room who wake up early, or the excitement of what is to come keeps you awake. This disturbance was not ideal but it was not unusual. It might, however, have caused a few people to think of it as a bad omen, and this was not going to be our day.

There was nothing particularly lethargic about our warm-up football when we reached Headingley. There has been a lot of talk about why we play football on the morning of a Test, but most cricket teams around the world play a game that gets their legs moving and switches the players on; and from my experience football has always been the most popular. After England had a couple of injuries we implemented a no-tackling rule, and we will obviously have to look at the subject again if there are further injuries.

In any event, Matt Prior's back went into spasm as he went down the wing in our football game. About fifteen minutes before the toss was due to be made England's wicket-keeper was squirming around on the ground and barely able to move. With back spasms there is very little you can do except wait for them to work themselves out – that is what we had to do when Kevin Pietersen's back went into spasm when he was bowling during the one-day international in Barbados. Prior said later that it was the second of his career, the first having occurred the day before a game for Sussex.

While the medical staff took Prior into our dressing-room and tried to get him to move, our masseur Mark Saxby was hit square on the head. A ball designed to be a high catch for one of the Australian players had come into our zone by accident. So our medical staff had their hands full looking after Saxby as well. In the meantime I was out in the middle with Andy Flower and the chairman of selectors, Geoff Miller, trying to make some quick decisions in the event that Prior was unable to play.

If Prior could not play, would we have to change our original decision to play a specialist bowler instead of Andrew Flintoff who was injured? Who would be the wicket-keeper we called in as a replacement? As we might now have to play a specialist batsman instead of Flintoff, Jonathan Trott was in a state of flux. As Warwickshire's in-form batsman, who had played a couple of Twenty20 internationals for England in 2007, he had been called into the squad but had not expected to play after we had decided the day before on Steve Harmison to replace Andrew Flintoff.

Collingwood was not practising his batting and slip-fielding during this chaotic situation. He was doing some wicket-keeping drills in case he had to fill in for a while, as he had done when Prior had been injured during the Chester-le-Street Test against West Indies three months before. Speculation was rife about the composition of the England team for this decisive Test match, which was due to begin in half-an-hour.

Thanks to the Australians, we were able to delay the toss for ten minutes after they had okayed our request. Our agreement to let

Brad Haddin be replaced by Graham Manou after the toss in the previous Test had its reward. Those ten minutes allowed us to give Prior a fitness test which involved keeping wicket in the nets and some batting practice. I said to him before his test that he would have to be very confident about being fine by lunchtime on day one and being able to play a full part thereafter. And when he came back into the dressing-room Prior said he would be fine, so we were able to field the team we wanted.

That said, the team was not exactly the eleven that we wanted to play because Flintoff could not take part. In the practice session the previous day he had not been able to bowl more than 70 per cent of his maximum pace, and he was clearly struggling. His right knee was still very swollen after his 30 overs in the Edgbaston Test, which had ended on the Monday (the practice was on Thursday and the Fourth Test began on Friday). Indeed his knee looked more swollen than I had ever seen it.

In a meeting after the practice session Flintoff said the pace he had shown in the nets was all he had at that stage. During this meeting he had the chance to convince us that he was fit enough to last the game, but it was apparent he did not have sufficient confidence about getting through it. Adrenalin could have been a factor, and if Flintoff had said that adrenalin would have got him through then we would have considered it. Andy Flower and I consulted with the doctors, and with Flintoff, and decided that we would rest him for the Fourth Test and get him fit for The Oval.

We then had the perennially difficult decision of balancing the side in Flintoff's absence. One option was that we could go for the extra batsman in Trott – and play only three frontline seamers in James Anderson, Graham Onions and Stuart Broad. Not at Headingley, we thought, especially as we did not have anyone who could chip in with more than a couple of overs here and there as a fourth seamer. Neither Paul Collingwood nor Ravi Bopara had taken a wicket in the series, in fact it was a long time since Collingwood had taken a Test wicket and Bopara never had. Alternatively, we could play only five frontline batsmen, Prior at six, and five bowlers, which was not an ideal balance either.

The decision we came to was that we could just about cover for Flintoff's batting with Prior being so fluent at six, and Broad and Graeme Swann chipping in at seven and eight. But we could not cover for Flintoff's bowling if we had just three frontline seamers and Swann. Flintoff's hostility and bounce were essential ingredients, and they could be replaced by the similar attributes of Harmison, who had been in our squad for the Lord's and Edgbaston Tests. When we were seven wickets down by lunch on the first day, that decision looked like the wrong one, but replacing Flintoff with Harmison seemed the right one at the time.

At 10.40 I won a toss that I did not really want to win. Before Prior's injury I had told the team that I would not make the decision about whether to bat or bowl until nearer the time, to see what the overhead conditions were going to be at 11 o'clock. In favour of batting was the fact that the wicket looked drier than any previous pitch I had seen at Headingley and already had cracks in it before the start. But there had been overnight rain – drizzle at 5 a.m., as all the England players could testify – and there was a bit of moisture on the surface of the pitch and some freshness in the air.

By the time the match referee Ranjan Madugalle supervised the toss (he replaced Jeff Crowe for the last two Tests), the sun was breaking through and the forecast for the rest of the day was for more sunshine. If we could get through the first session, I felt, we would be able to make hay in the afternoon . . .

Headingley, like Edgbaston, is almost guaranteed to have a good atmosphere. Fancy dress day on the Saturday of a Test provides entertainment, even when you are in the field and the search for wickets is proving futile. Enough animals to stock a zoo turn up in addition to the usual array of pirates and nuns. In this series we had also become accustomed to the sight of groups of Australian supporters dressed in yellow taking up certain areas of the stands, like islands surrounded by a sea of England supporters. The banter between them had sounded as though it had been overwhelmingly good-natured, 'If you're one-nil up, stand up!' sang the England supporters, with the variation of 'If you're one-nil down, sit down!'

I had the pleasant memory of captaining England to victory at Headingley against Pakistan in 2006, even though Younis Khan and Mohammed Yousuf had put on a monstrous stand of 363 for the third wicket. Our win there had given England a 2-0 lead and, therefore, my first series win as captain. That game, and that partnership, had proved how different Headingley had become from the ground of legend. Up until the 1990s it had been very bowler-friendly with variable bounce and lots of seam movement.

Gradually Headingley had become more of a 'patience wicket'. And nobody had demonstrated this virtue more than the South African pair of Ashwell Prince and A.B. de Villiers the year before.

In the Pakistan Test of 2006 the sun had shone and it had been a high-scoring game, but in 2008 the only batsmen who had conquered the conditions had been Prince and de Villiers with their disciplined shot selection. They had left the ball very well and picked off our bowlers when they erred in line, and set up South Africa's victory in that game and the series.

During our practices before the Fourth Test against Australia we had to get used to the sight of two high cranes looming over the redevelopment at the Kirkstall Lane end. Yorkshire had gone into a partnership with Leeds Metropolitan University to extend the capacity of the ground and build a facility that would double as lecture halls for students and a new pavilion for the cricketers. There was a prize on offer for any batsman who could hit one of the cranes. They were a bit far away for me.

Why did we bat so badly? First of all, credit has to go to the four Australian bowlers. They applied pressure at both ends, whether it was Ben Hilfenhaus and Peter Siddle who opened their bowling, or Stuart Clark and Mitchell Johnson who backed them up. Clark immediately justified his selection in place of Nathan Hauritz and gave Ponting a degree of control which he had been missing at Lord's and Edgbaston, when we had assembled our first innings at 4 runs an over. All the maidens in our first innings, so far as it went, were bowled by Clark.

Secondly, driving was very difficult in that opening session. The ball stuck in the wicket and sat up with a tennis-ball bounce. Therefore the risk of edging the ball was high if you drove at the ball when it was short of a very full length, as I proceeded to demonstrate. Thirdly, with each wicket that fell on the first morning the pressure mounted on the next guy coming in, and we did not deal with that pressure as well as we should have done.

By the time the toss had finished and I had done three media interviews, I had eight or nine minutes to get ready, which is basically ten minutes less than usual in those circumstances. Some critics said that I should not have done those interviews. However, between one innings and the next, opening batsmen have to get ready in less than ten minutes. As a batsman, especially an opener, you have to get used to putting petty distractions out of your mind, indeed the more you can do that, the better player you are. The main thing which had disturbed me on this occasion was not the media interviews but thinking about what team we should play if Prior was unfit. It was not the rush to get ready but the amount of stuff that had been going on.

At 11 a.m. Hilfenhaus ran in from the Kirkstall Lane end, swung the first ball in, and I played all round it. I felt I was out first ball. So did the Australians, and some other people in the ground, but not Billy Bowden. I thought this reprieve was going to be a wake-up call – if not my first of the morning – and I was determined not to give the bowlers a second chance.

Before the game we had talked about the danger of driving early at Headingley because of the nature of the wicket with its tennis-ball bounce – all those lessons we had learned from Prince and de Villiers the year before. The most disappointing aspect of my dismissal therefore was getting out in exactly this way, edging a drive to third slip where Marcus North stuck out his right hand and clung on. I suppose this very fact that I got out driving when the ball was not full-length was a symptom of my mind not being completely switched on.

And so the pressure mounted on each incoming batsman. It soon became one of those nightmarish sessions that you sometimes get in cricket, when the roof falls in, when the gains that have come from days and weeks of hard work are lost in an hour. It was reminiscent of the First Test in Jamaica when we were all out for 51. There was no consolation in making precisely double that total here.

Bopara was caught in the gully off Hilfenhaus, who exemplified the steadiness required in the conditions. Bell got a fiery bouncer from Johnson which brushed his glove and was caught by Haddin. Cook was batting well at the other end but England were 39 for three, then 42 for four when Collingwood half-drove and was caught at second slip. Since Lord's, Ponting had reversed his habit of taking knee-high slip catches with his fingers pointing upwards and had caught everything.

Johnson seemed far more comfortable as first or second change, instead of having to take the new ball. When he did come on, he pitched a much fuller length than previously in the series, and as a result started to swing the ball more frequently. And there was always the threat of his bouncer – fast and hard to pick up because of his slingy action – to stop batsmen pushing forward to counter his newfound inswing.

For the second time that day the alarm bells were ringing as Collingwood and Cook were drawn forward by Clark's fullish length and edged catches behind the wicket. When Cook was out, we were 63 for five in the twenty-third over. Kevin Pietersen, as our best batsman, was being missed as sorely as he was feeling. About this time he was suffering an infection in the wound made during the surgery on his right Achilles tendon and needed to go back to hospital for treatment and antibiotics.

All of us in the first innings were dismissed by catches, and all of them came either behind or square of the wicket. Broad and Onions were the two dismissed square of the wicket, caught by Simon Katich, who moved back a few paces from his normal bat-pad position to take a clip by Broad off his legs just before lunch. The other eight of us were caught in the arc between wicket-keeper and gully .

Nobody could stay long enough with Prior, who again raced to 20 before blinking an eyelid, to give us even a semblance of a working total. No doubt he had been looking forward to resting his back until after teatime, but he had to walk out to bat in only the nineteenth over, fuelled by an injection, anti-inflammatories and physiotherapy. The crowd seemed to be ready to roar England on, but we could give them nothing to cheer in our 34 overs of batting. It was England's lowest total at Headingley for a hundred years; and to make matters even worse, James Anderson tweaked a hamstring in his left leg as he took a quick single to get off the mark.

Our game-plan for bowling was to do what the Australians had done, particularly Hilfenhaus and Clark – the same fullish length, pressure at both ends, and patience, rather than searching for magic wicket-taking balls. We made the best possible start – in the worst possible way. In his first over Harmison had Katich caught at backward short-leg off an unplayable ball that had all the hostility and bounce of Flintoff at his best. But it was a short ball, gloved away by Katich, and taking the first wicket in this way set an all too tempting example.

We also got caught up in the emotion of the moment. As players we had talked in the past about taking the emotion out of our cricket, but now we were so desperate to take quick wickets and get back into the game. We had been on top in the two previous Tests because Australia had not made a sizeable total in their first innings, and we had to stop them doing it here or else we would lose our 1-0 lead. The Australians – Shane Watson and Ponting – raced to 50 in the seventh over before we could take stock. In our first seven overs the Australians hit nine fours and a six with shots square of the wicket because we bowled so short.

A lot of credit has to go to Ponting for pulling off his game-plan. Nobody in world cricket could have put the short balls away so effectively as he did; one of those ten boundaries in the first seven overs was a six which he pulled over deep square-leg off the first ball of Onions' spell. The ball kept coming to him above stump-height and he was in his element with pulls, hooks, cuts and back-foot forces. He soon left Watson in his wake, but already Watson had helped to set the tone by putting away the first two balls of Australia's innings to third man, when Anderson – who was never himself after tweaking his left leg, hard as he tried – dragged the ball down.

Watson and Ponting put on 119 for the second wicket, and they faced only 157 balls in the process. After tea and towards the close we finally found the right lengths and took three wickets in 19 balls. The fact that all three wickets were lbw's gives some indication.

Broad took two of them – Ponting when he missed a clip to leg, and Mike Hussey when Broad angled a ball into him from round the wicket. When the second new ball came round, Broad added four more wickets to achieve his best Test figures.

Watson was the other lbw dismissal, when Onions beat him, though not before Australia's emergency opener had made his third fifty in a row. I did not know before the game that in a championship game for Durham at Headingley Onions had to bowl while Darren Lehmann had scored 339. In theory, as a wicket-to-wicket seamer who could find some swing at times, Onions was perfectly suited to Headingley but it turned out that it had not been one of his favourite grounds.

At 152 for four we felt we could still bowl Australia out for 250 and then we would still be in the game, even if a long way behind. This did not happen because Michael Clarke and North dug in, as they had on the last day at Edgbaston. Clarke was hit on the helmet on the first evening by Harmison which, like Katich's dismissal, was a temptation to give the batsman some more short stuff. Australia's vice-captain had also strained a stomach muscle during his hundred at Edgbaston which might have restricted his ability to duck the bouncers.

In the series to date North had been vulnerable at times early on if pressurised. When tied down at Lord's, he had got out pulling a ball that was not short enough and dragging on. When tied down in the first innings at Edgbaston, he had gone for a drive and been caught behind. But the 96 he had made in the second innings there gave him the confidence to hang in and bat through the pressure we applied on the first evening: North, after facing 40 balls at the crease, had scored only 3 runs. He showed the value of confidence in that it enables a batsman to be patient when playing himself in and the bowling is good. Both Clarke and North went into the Headingley Test with runs behind them earlier in the week, and when batsmen are in that sort of form you have to get them out; they do not give their innings away.

As the ball got older on the second morning, and stopped swinging, Clarke and North batted with ever more fluency. The first hour set the tone all right – they added 70 off 14 overs and that included a maiden by Swann. When we took the second new ball after lunch Australia had scored at 4 runs an over to reach 323 for five. North reached the hundred which brought him the man of the match award with a slog-sweep for six off Swann, while Clark was smacking us for 32 off 22 balls, including two successive pulls for six off Broad.

In the 32 overs we had in our second innings before the close we lost five wickets, and that did not even include a nightwatchman. Cook and I reached 58 without too much trouble, then a ball from Hilfenhaus broke the dry surface, cut in more than I expected and had me lbw. Bopara was out first ball, for the fifth time in the series to Hilfenhaus, to an inswinger which Hot Spot suggested he had got a nick on. Johnson, from the Pavilion end, then turned on his best spell of the series, swinging the odd ball in late to the right-hander (to dismiss Collingwood lbw), or away from the left-hander (to have Cook caught behind), and whipping in the occasional short ball (to have Bell caught at second slip). Somehow 58 for no wicket had become 82 for five by the close, and it would have been six down if North had caught Prior at third slip off the last ball of the day. It might even have been ten wickets down by the close, because Australia would have taken the extra half-hour and at the rate they were going they could have finished off our last four wickets in those eight overs.

When I returned to my hotel room I was as low as could be. Normally, after spending much of the last ten years of my life in hotels, what I look for in a room is a big bed with a firm mattress and a good shower, not one which just trickles out water. But these comforts did not count for much at that moment. We were 261 runs behind Australia with only Prior and the bowlers left, the forecast was fine and three days still remained.

Of course, this sort of experience was nothing new to England captains, from what I had heard. After an innings defeat in Australia Wally Hammond had got into a car in Brisbane and driven with a couple of players to Sydney without saying a word. A few years later, after leading England to an innings defeat in Brisbane, Len Hutton – who had been one of those couple of players – got into a car and drove to Sydney without saying a word. My Brisbane-to-Sydney moment came on that second evening in Leeds. I did not drive anywhere. I just sat in my hotel room. My second defeat as England captain was only a few hours away, and Australia would level the series at one-all.

Ruth had driven up from London after the game had started, enduring five hours on the motorway with the boys because of an accident. I am afraid my conversation with her was pretty non-existent. Watching mindless television did not help much either. Eventually she said that some people had been blown up in Afghanistan – they were the ones who had had a bad day. She was right. And time finally brings some perspective.

Next morning, on only the third day, Flower gave us a good talk. We were still 261 runs behind with only five wickets left, so this game was in all likelihood gone. But what happened on the third day here could have some effect on the Fifth Test at The Oval the following week, and we had to look on today as the start of that Oval Test. We had to leave the ball well, or play our shots well. Whatever we did, we had to make life as difficult as we could for Australia in the time remaining.

Prior initially, then Broad and Swann, responded brilliantly and took the game to the Australians. In the morning, when they bowled only 24 overs, England scored 163 runs for the loss of three wickets. Anderson went in the first over, and Prior not long afterwards, but then Broad and Swann added 108 for the eighth wicket from only 80 balls. They gave the crowd something to cheer about at last. They caused some bemusement on the Australians' faces.

Clark had looked very difficult to score off on the opening day but now he was pinged around the ground. Broad hit him for 16 in an over with four fours and went on to reach his fifty from only 42 balls. In Clark's next over Swann also hit him for 16, this time with three fours and two twos, and went on to reach his fifty from 53 balls. Broad did more than a passable impression of Graham Dilley flailing away at Headingley in 1981, even if it was a bit much to expect Swann to emulate Sir Ian Botham's 149 not out.

Only time would tell whether England's hitting would have an effect on the Australians in the Oval Test. But for a glorious hour or so our lower order had forced their bowlers to bowl short and wide, and their fielders had missed a couple of chances offered by

Broad. The match went past lunch before we were all out for 263 and lost by an innings and 80 runs.

We had a two-hour meeting back at the hotel on the Sunday afternoon before setting off for home. We had to apply closure to the Headingley Test, and a very good group discussion helped. It was one-all. We were still in the series. We had home advantage. And even if Pietersen would be unavailable for weeks if not months to come, Flintoff would be back for the decider at The Oval.

I probably felt slightly brighter when driving from Leeds to London that evening than some of my distinguished predecessors had done on the long road from Brisbane to Sydney.

16
THE MOST JOYFUL
OF TIMES

When I look back at my career, there have been a few challenges to overcome. The first was going into the Middlesex dressing-room as a naïve public schoolboy and having to prove myself: that was the first time outside my comfort zone. Then it was getting into the Middlesex first team; then captaining them at the age of 24; then getting into the England team, when the challenges started coming thick and fast. Or they did until I was dropped for the England tour of Sri Lanka in late 2007. Then came the Napier Test, where I made nought in my first innings and thought my international career was over.

With every obstacle that I have faced I have thought: can I do this? Everyone is scared about going outside his or her comfort zone for the simple reason that you don't know how you are going to react. But when I have had to go outside my comfort zone, I have been able to rise to the challenge and that has been hugely reassuring. What frustrates me though is that one of these big situations has to come along before I can get into the right mindset.

This Ashes series was the biggest challenge of my career. Purely on a batting level, one part of it was to come back from performing poorly in the 2006–7 series in Australia. Another part was the captaincy and all its demands amid the fanfare of expectation and scrutiny which comes with every Ashes series. By July 2009 I had an idea of what the captaincy was going to be like, but the challenge was still enormous. And now, with the series standing at 1–1 and England having no option but to win the final Test, the biggest match of my career was at hand.

It was a great relief to have ten days between the Fourth Test at Headingley and the Fifth at The Oval. Usually a week off between Tests entails some relaxation and not thinking about cricket, but before leaving Leeds I told the players that the forthcoming week was not about relaxing. This time it was about preparing ourselves for the game of our lives.

I could not get away from the job mentally. The selection dilemma lay heavily, along with how we were going to play at The Oval, and what I was going to tell the players. Throughout the series I had made sure that I didn't read any of the written media in case an article was distracting by being too complimentary or too critical. However, it was impossible not to know that the country was disappointed with our performance at Headingley and had written us off. I didn't sleep much. When I met with Andy Flower on the Thursday, a week before The Oval Test started, he was in a similar state. It was clear we had both had a very tough week.

Ruth and I were going to fly up to Scotland for a couple of days on the Friday but instead there was a selection meeting at Trent Bridge that I had to attend. It was decided there would be one casualty from Headingley and Ravi Bopara would sit out the final Test. I felt for him: he had done so many good things already this year, especially at home against West Indies, and he was most definitely a star of the future. But my experience of Ashes series was that, if you lost form, it was incredibly difficult to regain it because of the pressure that the Australians put on you. In 2006–7 I had been in a terrible state by the end.

As making a hundred at The Oval seemed to be too much to ask of Bopara (he made a double-hundred for Essex against Surrey instead), we needed a fresh mind and somebody who would be excited but not overwhelmed at starting his Test career in an Ashes decider. It was crucial, the selectors and I thought, that the replacement had to be in great form and know his game and not have any mental baggage. Clearly there were question-marks on that score about Mark Ramprakash, even though he had scored more than a hundred hundreds, one of them against Australia at The Oval; and there was the potential damage to our selection policy in picking someone who was 39. Marcus Trescothick had ruled himself out, and Robert Key had had an inconsistent season.

Only one man fitted all the criteria. And having seen Jonathan Trott at Headingley, he did not seem to be a guy who would be overawed by the big occasion. When I had told Trott he wasn't going to be making his debut in the Fourth Test, he looked genuinely distraught. This was a good sign, because some players would have been secretly relieved.

My wife and I finally went away to a hotel for the weekend after the selection meeting in Nottingham, when I finally put the Headingley Test to bed. I was now in some ways ready for the biggest game of my career.

Our first team meeting before The Oval Test was another golf day, in this case one organised by the Professional Cricketers' Association at Stoke Park. Coming as it did on the Monday, three days before the Fifth Test, the timing was not ideal, or so I thought at the time. But when I got there I saw the real benefits in meeting up again as a team in a relaxed environment away from the cricket, whereas normally we would have met up at a ground. A barbecue was held after the event, and the players were chatting about what they had been up to in the last few days, and Alastair Cook was gloating about Essex's championship win over Middlesex (after a declaration had set them a none too challenging target, I should add). There was general excitement at what was to come later in the week. Privately I had been worried that we would be shot to pieces after Headingley, but it now seemed that we were all in a decent place mentally. This was the real gain from having had our big meeting in the Leeds hotel on the afternoon that the Fourth Test ended: there was no more need to talk about it, and we had moved on.

Instead, during the build-up to The Oval, Andy Flower and I talked to the players about keeping it simple, doing the basics well, delivering skills under pressure, being 100 per cent sure of your game-plan, and enjoying the moment. These were the messages that we tried to convey. There was reassurance to be had in going back to basics, never mind the occasion and what happened if we won or lost. By the final practice session on Wednesday we were in as settled a state as possible, given the enormity of the match. We also had a fully fit squad (except for Kevin Pietersen who had his right foot in plaster) after Andrew Flintoff was declared fit for his final Test.

On that day before the game I had a coffee with Michael Vaughan. He said that I would soon see little signs of whether it was meant to be or not; and the biggest sign would come at 10.31 a.m. when I won the toss or lost it. I am not particularly superstitious, but I knew that winning the toss would play such an important part. It was the same when Vaughan won it at The Oval in 2005, so that England did not have to bat fourth against Shane Warne. The odd umpiring decision going your way, Vaughan said, or a freakish dismissal, would be other signs. By the end of my latte, at the back of mind, I felt there was a good chance I'd do well.

On the morning of the game Flintoff addressed us on The Oval outfield. Flower had asked him beforehand if he wanted to talk to the team before his final Test. This was partly designed so that we could all hear from someone who had 'been there and done that' in the Fifth Test of 2005. Also, this talk reintroduced Flintoff to the team after he had missed Headingley and showed them that he was ready to lead the bowling for one last time.

When Flintoff spoke about the game, he said there was to be no sentimentality. He told us that we had to do the job together, thanked the team for the support they had given him, and told us what we needed to do to win this last Test match. A lot of final talks before retirement have been emotional but, funnily enough, his was more of a battle-cry for what lay ahead. It was not saddening, it was inspiring.

Fred and I have never been really close because we have different interests. He once said we are chalk and cheese: he is a northern lad who likes a beer, I'm a straitlaced southerner. At slip we have spent days and weeks of our lives together – with him at second slip, me at first, and chatted about a lot of things, mainly not connected with cricket, like family stuff. But I think we came to a mutual respect about what we have each achieved. He knew what a tough job the England captaincy was after his experience of it, so he went out of his way to help when I became captain. I like to think I appreciated how hard it was to be an allrounder, especially one with the weight of the nation on his shoulders and knees, and how soul-destroying his periods of rehabilitation were for him.

In some ways Fred was difficult to captain, but that was mainly because of the media attention that was devoted to what he did, not because of what he did himself.

The media constantly wanted to know the state of his injuries; or, if he did something off the field that was not 100 per cent professional, they would comment endlessly about it. His joining the Indian Premier League was another massive talking-point. And therefore a lot of time had to be spent on thinking about what the effect of all this media coverage had upon the team. He could not be blamed; it was the celebrity that his magnificent performances had brought his way.

The Oval, in my opinion, has been the best cricket wicket in the country during my career. It has offered bounce to the seamers, and increasing turn to the spinners, and excellent value for shots to the batsmen. As the scene of Kevin Pietersen's momentous knock in 2005, it showed how attacking batting is possible even on day five.

As such, The Oval provides the perfect setting for a grand finale: the tall old pavilion, the gasometers, the distant view of the Houses of Parliament. Ashes series have traditionally ended at The Oval, and maybe that has been a factor in England's excellent record there: after several months on the road, Australian touring teams have been ready for home. Whether that is true or not, the Fifth Test at The Oval has often been decided by the ability to handle pressure as much as by the ability to handle the opposition's batting or bowling.

Several conspiracy theories were aired about the pitch for the final Test of 2009. A high-scoring draw or run-fest was clearly no good to us with the series standing at 1–1 and Australia holding the Ashes. Bill Gordon, Surrey's head groundsman, was left to decide how to prepare the wicket.

As spin is a factor towards the end of county matches at The Oval, we hoped to turn up and find a pitch that was drier than usual, and we did. But then came the dilemma of whether to select a second spinner or not. Monty Panesar had been struggling during his season for Northamptonshire before and after the Cardiff Test, and would have admitted himself that he was not in the best form. Steve Harmison, on the other hand, was having another fine season for Durham, pushing them towards the county championship for the second year running, and had the best record at The Oval of any of our bowlers. We thought the wicket would have some pace and bounce at least in the first innings. In the end we misjudged it, but not as badly as the Australians did, and the fact that we played only one spinner undermined the conspiracy theories.

At 10.15 a.m. on Thursday, 20 August it made a pleasant change to stand in the middle, practise my strokes – shadow-batting – and visualise my innings if we did bat first. No thoughts about back spasms, fire alarms and team selections to get in the way on this occasion. The football warm-up had gone without any incident or accident. Trott had fitted in so well that he scored with a fine individual goal from halfway on the right wing.

'Heads!' called Ricky Ponting.

The coin rolled a long way before Ranjan Madugalle picked it up, or at least it seemed to take a long time before he announced, 'Tails.' Words to the effect that we would have a bat did not take long to come out of my mouth. If we had lost the toss and bowled first, we would have had no option but to take a healthy first-innings lead in setting up a win.

Anyone who says luck is not one of the elements of success is way off the mark.

In 2005 a large number of little things went our way, like Gary Pratt bringing off his first direct-hit run-out of the season at Trent Bridge to dismiss Ponting. In 2009 I won four of the tosses. The two big tosses were at Lord's and The Oval, and Cardiff should have been massive too but we didn't take advantage of it. There was no great advantage in winning it at Edgbaston, as Ponting did, or at Headingley, as I did.

The first day of a Test match is often the one that is least remembered, but everyone who plays in it knows how important it is. The team that lands the first punch or two gains the initiative. In helping to do that on the first day here I have to say that the fact that I had been in this situation before at The Oval in 2005 was influential: on the opening day then I had scored 129. So I knew how the tone had to be set.

The complete contrast with Headingley continued when Ben

Hilfenhaus bowled the first over from the Vauxhall end. All series he had been right on the spot at the start of every spell: with his second ball of the second day at Lord's he had hit my off stump, with his first ball of the game at Headingley he had been very unlucky not to have dismissed me lbw. This time Hilfenhaus did not begin at his best: he had been the only one of the Australian bowlers not to play in their two-day practice game at Canterbury against the Lions. Brett Lee had played, and had bowled effectively enough and long enough for him to be seriously considered for a recall, especially on a dry pitch, which would have aided his reverse-swing. Peter Siddle, Mitchell Johnson, Stuart Clark and Nathan Hauritz had all played too, to keep them in form. But not Hilfenhaus.

And as an opening batsman it is such a pleasure to watch the first few balls go past without having to play them, especially if you are a traditional style of Test opener and want to assess the pace of the pitch rather than belt the first ball into the stand like Virender Sehwag. Hilfenhaus's first five balls went so far wide of off stump that they could all be safely left as I watched them through to the keeper. They were mostly on the way down as they reached Brad Haddin, confirming the pitch's essential slowness. The sixth ball I pushed towards extra-cover for a quick single off the mark. Nothing yet had dented the feeling that it was going to be our day.

Another factor in our favour was that Hilfenhaus swung the new ball less than at any time in the series, as well as allowing us to leave the ball: of his first 18 balls, Cook and I left ten of them. Siddle found his rhythm from the start and gave me a bouncer in his first over, which I ducked, but when he pitched short in his next over I was confident that I had gauged the pace of the wicket and pulled him, as did Cook in Siddle's next over. And just as everything was going smoothly, in the same over, Siddle drew Cook into a push outside off stump and he was caught at second slip: 12 for one wicket in the sixth over, and the sky was literally darkening.

Before Hilfenhaus had refound his rhythm – and he finished with 22 wickets in the series, the most on either side – I managed to get the momentum going our way at his expense. In his fourth over I square-cut one four and square-drove a wide half-volley for another and, when he overcompensated by bowling too straight, clipped a couple to make ten runs off the over; and as Hilfenhaus bowled two no-balls as well (he seemed troubled by the looseness of the footholds), we doubled the score in this one over. Another useful punch, even though drizzle soon began and the new Oval floodlights were briefly on.

I have to say that by now I was in the zone and felt brilliant; I knew what I was doing. After losing Cook, it was essential that Ian Bell and I got through to lunch. In such a situation you can't be distracted, you must think about your game-plan and what the bowlers are doing. For some reason I felt I was in such a good place.

Another turning-point came when Mitchell Johnson took over from Siddle at the Pavilion end. Ian Bell had started fluently and reached 13 at a run a ball, but when Johnson came on it became another game. Bell now had to dig deeper than he ever had before in his Test career, and he did.

Johnson's bouncer is so hard to pick up, especially for a right-hander: all through the series Bell and Paul Collingwood and Matt

Prior had struggled against it. For left-handed batsmen Johnson seemed to be much easier to score off: his slinginess might offer you something short outside off stump to cut, and anything angled into our bodies could be worked away legside. But right-handers had fewer scoring options when they had to cope with his lines: if they drove at the ball going across them they risked getting an outside edge, while the short ball came in at their ribcage. And as the series wore on, especially from Edgbaston onwards, our right-handers were increasingly worried about the ball that swung back into them.

Johnson's first three balls were bouncers. While the first was playable, the second two were laser-straight. Bell got a bat on the first of this pair – got a bat on it twice in fact as he did not know where the ball was as it came down – and gloved the second. It was the first time that I had seen Bell really struggle technically because he has a brilliant technique. But when we had a talk between overs during this spell by Johnson I was very reassured about how Bell was. He was ready to graft and did not care if he got hit a few times.

One of the keys to building a partnership, particularly when the bowling is at its most hostile and one batsman is right-handed and the other left, is rotating the strike. This Bell did with a quick single to mid-off at the start of Johnson's second over. I managed a couple of fours to leg in the rest of that over when Johnson pitched the ball up, and another four in his next over, and another in his next: so many more scoring options for the left-hander against him. The next time Johnson had more than the odd ball at Bell, Hilfenhaus was too deep at backward square-leg – rather than leg-slip – to catch the fend-off. Another turning-point.

We had spoken before the game about the significance of the first session, and to be 108 for one at lunch was not far off the perfect start. To a certain extent we had exorcised the demons of Headingley. A few boundaries are a good way of getting the crowd going, and thanks to the fast outfield I had hit ten fours in my fifty and Bell had scored seven fours in his 41 before lunch. I had a protein shake, lovingly prepared by our strength and conditioning expert, Hugh Bevan, and nibbled on some chicken, but an appetite is often missing when you are batting. I felt an enormous relief in the dressing-room at the interval, and perhaps in myself as well, which might have led me to switch off a bit mentally.

After lunch I was also distracted by thinking about whether the ball was reverse-swinging or not. When Stuart Clark bowled the first over afterwards I couldn't work out whether his swing was conventional or reverse. When Hilfenhaus – now right back in his groove – bowled at the Vauxhall end, I remembered the yorker that he had bowled to me before lunch and had swung a long way back in.

Everything in Hilfenhaus's action, when he bowled the ball that got me, suggested the ball was going to swing in again. But it didn't, and I nicked it. If ever there was a time *not* to make fifty and get out, this was it. But you can't think too much about batting otherwise it will drive you mad. Some days you can play and miss 25 times, nick a couple, and go on to a hundred. Sometimes, like this innings, you can make one mistake – and not a major mistake – and you are out. Batting defies logic. The lesson is don't beat yourself up about it and move on.

We reached 166 for two with comparative comfort from 42 overs. But as the ball aged, and Siddle found the right length, and

Hilfenhaus nibbled the ball around, and Marcus North made some of his off-breaks grip sharply, batting became more and more tricky. In the next eleven overs (the last eleven before tea), runs dried up – only 14 added – and we lost Collingwood just before the interval and Bell just afterwards. Some said that Bell should have gone on to score a hundred; I would say that his innings of 72, which banished the memory of his pair at The Oval in 2005, was huge for us.

Trott from the start of his debut innings showed his composure by patiently waiting for 12 balls before getting off the mark. He looked the part against pace and spin and it took a freakish dismissal to get rid of him for 41, when Simon Katich at bat-pad threw the stumps down. We were a little frustrated and disappointed to finish the day at 307 for eight. We had reinforced the importance of going big in the first innings. It was not a terrible score, but it was not a good one either, and we went to bed thinking we had missed out.

After finishing on 332 next morning, we knew we had to start well with the ball. And although we didn't take a wicket in the first session, we began pretty well. James Anderson, like Hilfenhaus, wasn't really suited to that sort of pitch because the ball skidded on and didn't swing when new. But he and Flintoff were difficult to score off, and the odd ball from Anderson – who was bowling from the Vauxhall end – looked as though it was going through the top in puffs of dust. So although Shane Watson and Katich finished the session with a few boundaries off Harmison and Graeme Swann, our dressing-room felt there was enough happening for the wickets to follow.

A rain break extended the lunch interval by almost an hour, until 2.30 p.m. When we resumed, I decided that although the Vauxhall end was better to bowl spin from – as North had shown – I wanted someone who could exploit the variable bounce. I went for Stuart Broad as he had more height than Anderson, while there was still some spin for Swann from the Pavilion end.

Broad produced one of the finest spells of bowling that I have seen during my involvement with the England side. He put the ball in the right area, he attacked the stumps, he had variable bounce, and the Australians were so worried about the two-paced nature of the pitch that they did not know whether to play forward or back. When Broad is bowling well, he is one of a rare breed of bowlers who can trouble a batsman with swing and bounce. There are genuine swing bowlers, and there are genuine hit-the-deck bowlers, but Broad can combine the two – which is why we will see him take five-wicket Test hauls often.

He looked threatening with every ball. After he had Watson lbw, the huge wicket was Ponting dragging a ball into his stumps – much as he had done against Broad at Lord's. You could almost sense how dispiriting it was for the Australian camp to see their captain trudging back, while the crowd were going wild as they got behind us. At that moment you felt it was going to take some special Australian batting for them to wrest the game back from us.

All through the series Mike Hussey had been unsure about where his off stump was. A couple of times he had been bowled off stump shouldering arms, and a couple of times he had nicked off. Having been forced by Broad into deciding whether to play or not, he hesitated a moment when an outswinger came down – an inswinger to the left-hander – and that hesitation was his downfall.

One of our talks before the game had been about how to bowl at Michael Clarke. He went into the game as the leading run-scorer in the series: in every match to date he had produced, with a couple of hundreds, a 90 and an 80. In the process we had noticed that his drives through the extra-cover region, while very crisp, were sometimes aerial. And as is so often the case when the game is going your way, he proceeded to hit his drive straight at Trott at short extra, putting Australia under even more pressure.

A late away-swinging yorker, which uprooted Brad Haddin's off stump, was probably the best ball of the lot in Broad's spell. Right through the session he bowled – another tribute to our strength and conditioning experts as well as him – for a spell that read: 12–1–37–5. With Swann chipping away from the Pavilion end, once the momentum was going our way the Australians were unable to deal with it. From 73 for no wicket, they went to 133 for eight at tea – one incredible session – and 160 all out.

When the Australians look back at this series, they will recognise that where they lost it was in three sessions: when we took six of their wickets at Lord's, when we took seven at Edgbaston, and when we took eight at The Oval, all of them in their first innings. In these three sessions we had some help from the conditions: at Edgbaston and Lord's the ball swung, while The Oval offered a wearing wicket and variable bounce.

Even so, it was surprising that so many wickets fell in such a short space of time, on the Friday afternoon at The Oval and the other two occasions. In Test matches you usually have to graft for wickets. Once they were in, the Australian batsmen scored far more hundreds than we did, eight to two, but they were more susceptible early on. Therefore in these three sessions, with the crowd behind us, we created a momentum, which they found difficult to contend with.

I was concerned about going into our second innings. The pitch was not playing well, 12 wickets had already fallen in the day and I was worried that our second innings would follow suit. All too soon we were 39 for three: Cook got a ball from North that turned a long way, Bell and Collingwood were caught at short-leg off Johnson's bouncer. People were saying that only 250 or 300 would be a big enough target, but I knew that the wicket was starting to lose pace. At the back of my mind, too, was the Old Trafford Test of 2008 against New Zealand. When they went into their second innings with a lead of 179, the New Zealanders thought they had enough, played some big shots and got out, and we knocked off 294 to win. This time I knew we had to get as many runs as possible so the Australians, when they batted a second time, had not a sniff of victory.

Trott and I made it through safely to the close of the second day on 58 for three. My game-plan was to play the ball as late as possible. There were still demons in the wicket but it was slowing down, so if you did not commit too early and played the ball late, the percentages were in your favour. Indeed the wicket was reminiscent of Chennai: a lot of turn for the spinners amid puffs of dust, but slow turn as it died. This allowed India to chase their record target and Australia to bat so well in the fourth innings here.

On the third morning we knew the Australians would come back hard and the first session would be pivotal: either they would take enough wickets to have a chance of winning or we would bat them out of the game. After the first half-hour it was evident that the demons were not as bad as many had thought, and I also took comfort from how well Trott was playing. His debut could to some extent be forgotten, given everything else that happened during that week at The Oval, but it was truly remarkable. It was not only the biggest match in most of our careers, but he also had the concerns of every debutant: how different is Test cricket from the first-class game and will I be able to cope? Yet he batted in such an assured way and had a clear game-plan for every bowler.

I hadn't come across Trott much at all before: a few games for Warwickshire against Middlesex, an England Lions game, and the warm-up match at Edgbaston in early July between Warwickshire and England. He had seemed confident in his ability, but you don't know what a player will be like when he makes his Test debut. Ashley Giles, as Warwickshire's coach and an England selector, was certain that Trott would cope, but the reality is that we didn't know. Selectors will take the plaudits for choosing Trott, and rightly so, but they selected him in the hope that he would deliver; it was the player himself who had to do it.

At the other end I also took comfort in having my favourite bat. Pietersen seems to have a different bat for every innings, but I am a little bit superstitious. The bat I used at The Oval had come out of retirement earlier in the series: I had used it in India and the West Indies, and it had been retired with five Test hundreds under its belt before the Cardiff Test. But as I scored only 30 and 17 with my

Man of the match Andrew Flintoff after bowling Nathan Hauritz at Lord's.

Special feelings for Andrew Flintoff and myself on the day when England beat Australia in a Lord's Test for the first time since 1934.

The Saturday of the Edgbaston Test when play was abandoned as early as 2.30 p.m. Who knows . . .

Shane Watson is trapped lbw by Graham Onions with the first ball of the second day at Edgbaston.

By taking another wicket with his second ball, that of Mike Hussey, Graham Onions found a niche in Ashes history.

James Anderson follows up the Onions offensive by trapping Mitchell Johnson lbw first ball.

Some excellent hitting by Andrew Flintoff gave England a sizeable first-innings lead at Edgbaston. Here he forces Nathan Hauritz, watched by Australia's reserve wicket-keeper Graham Manou.

Andrew Flintoff receives treatment on his right knee before the Headingley Test. He wanted to play. But discretion was the better part of valour.

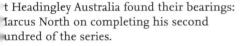

aconsistent, even erratic in the first half of the eries, but always capable of a magic ball: Mitchell Johnson at Headingley.

t Headingley Australia found their bearings: Marcus North on completing his second undred of the series.

At least somebody was happy after England had been dismissed for 102 at Headingley, In this case, Stuart Clark (left) and Peter Siddle.

Michael Clarke during his 93 at Headingley: his two stands of 150-plus with Marcus North helped to tip the series Australia's way after they had been 1–0 down.

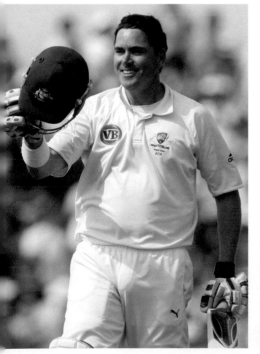

In the zone, with my favourite bat, in the Oval decider.

What a start: Jonathan Trott becomes the third England batsman in the last 100 years to make a century against Australia on his Test debut.

Man of the match at the Oval, Stuart Broad dismisses Shane Watson lbw.

piece of individual brilliance: Ricky Ponting run out by Andrew Flintoff's power-throw from
id-on at the Oval.

he moment that England regained the Ashes. We went so far out of our senses that I am about
 hug Graeme Swann.

We celebrate the fruits of all our teamwork in the summer of 2009.

The Ashes urn (a replica, I hasten to add) makes a nice change from a rattle or remote control. Ruth with Sam, while I hold Luca in the Oval dressing-room.

new one there, I went back to my old bat for the Lord's Test where it made its sixth hundred, and it promptly had to carry on for a few more games. It felt so comfortable, with exactly the right pick-up and weight, that I was not going to change it.

By the time I was caught at slip off one of North's off-breaks shortly before lunch, Trott and I had added 118 together and our lead was 329. In the afternoon we took the game out of Australia's hands. Partnering Trott, Flintoff in his last Test innings played a quick cameo of 22 from 18 balls. Broad followed his example, and Swann did some excellent hitting, especially against the second new ball, which really came off his bat.

Our lower order was a constant thorn in Australia's side: they allowed us to make bigger totals than our top-order batting would have suggested possible. Flintoff, Broad and Swann took the game to the Australian bowlers, often in Prior's company, and the four of them scored at a rate of over 70 runs per 100 balls, which none of the Australians could match (except Clark on the strength of a few hits at Headingley). In addition, Anderson and Panesar held on in Cardiff, and Anderson and Graham Onions had that record tenth wicket stand at Lord's.

For once, the declaration was not difficult to make. When our lead passed 450 I knew the target would be almost impossible to chase, but so much time was still left in the game that there was a value in snuffing out all Australian hopes of winning. By the time Trott was out – I was going to declare in any event at the end of that over – the Australians appeared demoralised. Their lack of celebrations at the fall of Trott's wicket showed they were mentally resigned and I knew we had this game by the scruff.

Still, it was going to be a war of attrition to take the last ten wickets. A target of 546 was nigh impossible but we knew the pitch was dying and balls, when edged, were not carrying to slip. Spin was substantial but slow. And on the third evening Australia raced to 80 for no wicket to remind us that the job was not yet done and they would not lie down and die.

On the fourth morning, a hot and sunny one, Flower talked to us in boxing terms. The Australians were the champions who held the belt and they would not let go of it unless we hit them and hit them until they could no longer stand up. Our early nerves were settled when Swann had Katich lbw with the same sort of straight-on ball that had got Devon Smith more than once, and Broad had Watson lbw for the second time in the match.

Ponting and Hussey, however, got the bit between their teeth and fought hard to reach lunch with only two wickets down. An hour after lunch they were still there and it was hard not to feel the frustrations of the crowd. Most spectators were hushed, with the odd comment of 'Come on, England!', and the nervous atmosphere started rubbing off on the players. We knew that victory was going to happen, but Ponting and Hussey were so assured.

In the end it took a piece of unbelievable, individual brilliance from Flintoff to prise open a gap. Hussey took a single to mid-on and Flintoff threw down the stumps at the far end with Ponting short of his ground. Technically he does not set himself on a good base, as our fielding coach wants the rest of us to do, but he has a great arm, and he sets the ball in motion on the right line, and in practice he hits the stumps as often as anyone.

On his last day in Test cricket Flintoff bowled tidily but his right knee obviously troubled him and the pitch did not suit his style of bowling. So the run-out was a fitting way of reminding everybody of why he had been such an important Test cricketer for England. The statistics bear out what Fred himself said before and after the game: that he was not a great player, as he averaged four or five too few with the bat and four or five too many with the ball.

But there were three reasons why Flintoff was so valuable. He had the rare ability to make something happen out of nothing. If he went in to bat when five or six wickets were down, he could instantly take the game to the opposition and knock their best bowlers out of the attack. In 2005 he often did that against Warne and Brett Lee.

Secondly, as a bowler, if there was nothing in the wicket or the conditions, Flintoff could burst open an end through his strength of will and body. One example was his over at Edgbaston in 2005 when he dismissed Justin Langer and Ponting and made us feel for the first time that we could win the series. Another was his spell at Jacques Kallis on the same ground in 2008, which culminated in his bowling Kallis with a reverse-outswinging yorker. The last example was his ten-over spell on the final morning at Lord's.

Thirdly, as a fielder, Flintoff could make a match-winning contribution. He had the best pair of hands of anyone I played with and made slip-catching look ridiculously easy. Or his strength of arm would lead to a run-out, as in the case of Ponting: not a textbook throw, but a round-arm throw, which never got above waist-height and pitched so close to the stumps that it could not bounce over them, and detonated off stump out of the ground.

Flintoff's performances, like this one, created the momentum off which other players could feed: and Swann and Harmison set to work with hope and energy renewed. Moreover, for one last time, Flintoff got the crowd going. He was a crowd favourite because the man in the street could feel that he had a lot in common with him. Fred would have a beer, and whack the ball as hard as he could, or run in and bowl as fast as he could: most people would like to play cricket in this manner, so he could stir the crowd into a frenzy. And never underestimate the effect on the opposition of such a crowd.

Bizarrely, one run-out followed another. Clarke, like Trott in his first innings, went down the pitch to an off-break and turned it to leg. On this occasion the ball ricocheted off Cook's foot at forward short-leg towards me at backward short-leg and my under-arm throw, after a television replay, was upheld. In ten minutes both of Australia's most dangerous batsmen were out in the most unexpected circumstances: a couple of those freakish dismissals that Vaughan had mentioned.

Swann had North stumped by Prior, which made a fitting end to the series for our wicket-keeper. Besides his batting, Prior did not miss a real chance behind the stumps. Working hard with Bruce French, he made sure our out-cricket was tidier than Australia's: they conceded almost twice as many runs in extras as we did in a series of small margins.

The end, when it came, was mercifully swift. After Haddin had chipped Swann a couple of times, I moved a bit deeper at mid-wicket and caught him there. It was then that I knew the Ashes were ours. When Harmison came into the attack, I said: 'There is not a huge amount in the wicket for you but still bowl as fast as you can because it's going to be very unpleasant for the batsmen.' Finally he had some reward for his efforts: first, Johnson caught at second slip by Collingwood after he had put down three slip chances – two of them very difficult – off Swann; then Siddle and Clark.

The last rites were administered by Swann with his eighth wicket of the match. After an incredible, career-saving century by Hussey, he prodded a catch off bat and pad to short-leg. Mayhem ensued. You don't imagine the moment when you win the Ashes in case the moment never happens. I didn't know whether to jump in the air or lie down or scream, so I hugged Swann instead. We were running round not knowing what to do with ourselves. When we came to our senses, we realised we had to do certain things like thank the umpires and our opponents, and there would be plenty of time to enjoy afterwards.

The celebrations were good. For those of us who had been there before, they were just as satisfying as in 2005. For the others it was a sample of just how special it is to win an Ashes series, especially when they are regained.

Amid the champagne and the beer, the tears and the joy, two important things happened. One was that our families came into the dressing-room for an hour and shared the moment. When we hadn't been there for them over the two previous months, they had been there for us all along. I owed so much to Ruth for picking me up after Headingley, and her words about Afghanistan and what a bad day really was. As a sort of reminder, I had worn a blue wristband in aid of 'Hope for Heroes', a charity for soldiers wounded in Afghanistan after the *Sun* had asked me to join it before the series.

Then we spent a couple of hours drinking with the Australians. It had not been like 2005 when we had shared a few beers after each Test. This was the first time that we had really socialised with them and talked. We came to realise just how special they thought an Ashes series was for them. North told me that he hadn't known what it would be like but it had been everything he had expected and more, and that it was such a great privilege to have been involved.

Rivalry at cricket between England and Australia is intense, and has been intense for more than a hundred years. Yet as we talked the evening away before going back to our hotel for more partying, I think every one of us understood that a strong bond existed between the two sides and countries. All 22 of us had been through an experience we would never forget for the rest of our lives.

ANDREW STRAUSS CAREER RECORD

Compiled by Victor Isaacs

NEW ZEALAND V ENGLAND
(3rd Test) At Napier 22–26 March 2008

England

A.N.Cook b Martin	2	– c McCullum b Patel		37
*M.P.Vaughan lbw b Southee	2	– c McCullum b Martin		4
A.J.Strauss c How b Southee	0	– c Bell b Patel		177
K.P.Pietersen c How b Southee	129	– c Taylor b Vettori		34
I.R.Bell c & b Elliott	9	– c Sinclair b Vettori		110
P.D.Collingwood c Elliott b Patel	30	– c & b Vettori		22
+T.R.Ambrose c Taylor b Patel	11	– c & b Vettori		31
S.C.J.Broad c McCullum b Southee	42	– not out		31
R.J.Sidebottom c Bell b Southee	14	– not out		12
M.S.Panesar b Martin	1			
J.M.Anderson not out	0			
l–b 9, w 3, n–b 1	13	l–b 3, w 1, n–b 5		9

1/4 2/4 3/4 4/36 5/125   253   1/5 2/77 3/140 4/327   (for 7 wkts dec) 467
6/147 7/208 8/240 9/253 10/253   5/361 6/424 7/425

Bowling: *First innings* – Martin 26–6–74–2; Southee 23.1–8–55–5; Elliott 10–2–27–1; Vettori 19–6–51–0; Patel 18–3–37–2. *Second innings* – Martin 18–2–60–1; Southee 24–5–84–0; Elliott 14–1–58–0; Patel 30.5–4–104–2; Vettori 45–6–158–4.

New Zealand

J.M.How c Strauss b Sidebottom	44	– lbw b Panesar		11
M.D.Bell lbw b Sidebottom	0	– c Broad b Panesar		69
S.P.Fleming c Collingwood b Sidebottom	59	– c Ambrose b Panesar		66
M.S.Sinclair c Broad b Sidebottom	7	– c Ambrose b Broad		6
R.L.Taylor c Ambrose b Broad	2	– c Collingwood b Panesar		74
G.D.Elliott c Ambrose b Sidebottom	6	– c Bell b Broad		4
+B.B.McCullum b Sidebottom	9	– b Panesar		42
*D.L.Vettori c Cook b Sidebottom	14	– c Ambrose b Anderson		43
T.G.Southee c Pietersen b Broad	5	(10) not out		77
J.S.Patel c Panesar b Broad	4	(9) c Broad b Panesar		18
C.S.Martin not out	4	– b Sidebottom		5
l–b 13, w 1	14	B 6, l–b 5, w 4, n–b 1		16

1/1 2/103 3/116 4/119 5/119   168   1/48 2/147 3/156 4/160   431
6/137 7/138 8/152 9/164 10/168   5/172 6/276 7/281 8/329 9/347 10/431

Bowling: *First innings* – Sidebottom 21.4–6–47–7; Anderson 7–1–54–0; Broad 17–3–54–3; Panesar 1–1–0–0; Collingwood 2–2–0–0. *Second innings* – Sidebottom 19.5–3–83–1; Anderson 17–2–99–1; Broad 32–10–78–2; Panesar 46–17–126–6; Collingwood 2–0–20–0; Pietersen 2–0–14–0.

Umpires: D.J.Harper and R.E.Koertzen

England won by 121 runs

ANDREW STRAUSS IN TEST CRICKET

Compiled by Victor Isaacs

Test Career Record (2004–2009)
– up to and including First Test v West Indies at Lord's 2009

M	I	NO	Runs	HS	Avge	S/R	100s	50s
61	113	5	4766	177	44.12	49.53	17	14

1. v New Zealand at Lord's 20–24 May 2004 – won by 7 wickets
Toss: New Zealand
New Zealand 386 & 336 (M.H.Richardson 101); England 441 (A.J.Strauss 112)
& 282–3 (N.Hussain 103*)

1st innings	c M.H.Richardson b D.L.Vettori	112
2nd innings	run out (C.L.Cairns)	83

Match highlights:
Named Man of the Match; 15th player to score a century on debut for England and 80th in all; fourth player to score a century on debut at Lord's.

2. v New Zealand at Headingley 3–7 June 2004 – won by 9 wickets
Toss: England
New Zealand 409 & 161; England 526 (M.E.Trescothick 132, G.O.Jones 100) & 45–1

1st innings	c D.R.Tuffey b D.L.Vettori	62
2nd innings	c N.J.Astle b D.R.Tuffey	10

3. v New Zealand at Trent Bridge 10–13 June 2004 – won by 4 wickets
Toss: New Zealand
New Zealand 384 (S.P.Fleming 117, S.B.Styris 108) & 218; England 319
(C.L.Cairns 5–79) & 284–6 (G.P.Thorpe 104*)

| 1st innings | c B.B.McCullum b C.L.Cairns | 0 |
| 2nd innings | lbw b C.L.Cairns | 6 |

4. v West Indies at Lord's 22–26 July 2004 – won by 210 runs
Toss: West Indies
England 568 (R.W.T.Key 221, A.J.Strauss 137, M.P.Vaughan 103) & 325–5dec
(M.P.Vaughan 101*); West Indies 416 (S.Chanderpaul 128*) & 267 (A.F.Giles 5–81)

| 1st innings | c R.D.Jacobs b O.A.C.Banks | 137 |
| 2nd innings | c R.R.Sarwan b P.T.Collins | 35 |

Match highlights:
Third player to score a century in his first two Lord's Test matches.

5. v West Indies at Edgbaston 29 July–1 August 2004 – won by 256 runs
Toss: England
England 566–9dec (A.Flintoff 167, M.E.Trescothick 105) & 248
(M.E.Trescothick 107, C.H.Gayle 5–34); West Indies 336 (R.R.Sarwan 139)
& 222 (A.F.Giles 5–57)

| 1st innings | c R.D.Jacobs b J.J.C.Lawson | 24 |
| 2nd innings | c R.D.Jacobs b J.J.C.Lawson | 5 |

6. v West Indies at Old Trafford 12–16 August 2004 – won by 7 wickets
Toss: West Indies
England 395–9 dec & 165; England (G.P.Thorpe 114, D.J.Bravo 6–55) & 231–3

| 1st innings | b D.J.Bravo | 90 |
| 2nd innings | c S.Chanderpaul b P.T.Collins | 12 |

7. v West Indies at The Oval 19–21 August 2004 – won by 10 wickets
Toss: England
England 470 & 4–0; West Indies 152 (S.J.Harmison 6–46) & 318 following on
(C.H.Gayle 105)

| 1st innings | c F.H.Edwards b J.J.C.Lawson | 14 |
| 2nd innings | not out | 0 |

8. v South Africa at Port Elizabeth 17–21 December 2004 – won by 7 wickets
Toss: South Africa
South Africa 337 (H.H.Dippenaar 110) & 229; England 425 (A.J.Strauss 126)
& 145–3

| 1st innings | c A.B.de Villiers b S.M.Pollock | 126 |
| 2nd innings | not out | 94 |

Match highlights:
*Named Man of the Match; eighth consecutive victory – an England record; seventh
player to score a century on debut in home and away Test matches.*

9. v South Africa at Durban 26–30 December 2004 – match drawn
    Toss: South Africa
    England 139 & 570–7 dec (A.J.Strauss 136, M.E.Trescothick 132, G.P.Thorpe
    118*); South Africa 332 (J.H.Kallis 162) & 290–8

| 1st innings | c M.Ntini b N.Boje | 25 |
| 2nd innings | c M.van Jaarsveld b M.Ntini | 136 |

10. v South Africa at Cape Town 2–6 January 2005 – lost by 196 runs
    Toss: South Africa
    South Africa 441 (J.H.Kallis 149) & 222–8 dec; England 163 (C.K.Langeveldt
    5–46) & 304

| 1st innings | b M.Ntini | 45 |
| 2nd innings | lbw b N.Boje | 39 |

Match highlights:
*Reached 1,000 Test runs during first innings score of 45; joint 17th fastest player
to reach that target (19 innings) and fourth-fastest Englishman (behind Sutcliffe,
Hutton and Hammond).*

11. v South Africa at Johannesburg 13–17 January 2005 – won by 77 runs
    Toss: England
    England 411–8 dec (A.J.Strauss 147) & 332–9 dec (M.E.Trescothick 180);
    South Africa 419 (H.H.Gibbs 161, M.J.Hoggard 5–144) & 247 (M.J.Hoggard
    7–61)

| 1st innings | c J.H.Kallis b S.M.Pollock | 147 |
| 2nd innings | c A.B.de Villiers b M.Ntini | 0 |

12. v South Africa at Centurion 21–25 January 2005 – match drawn
    Toss: England
    South Africa 247 & 296–6 dec (J.H.Kallis 136*, A.B.de Villiers 109); England
    359 (A.Nel 6–81) & 73–4

| 1st innings | c M.V.Boucher b A.Nel | 44 |
| 2nd innings | c J.H.Kallis b M.Ntini | 0 |

Match highlights:
Named Man of the Series for his three centuries.

13. v Bangladesh at Lord's 26–27 May 2005 – won by an innings and 261 runs
Toss: England
Bangladesh 108 & 159; England 528–3 dec (M.E.Trescothick 194,
M.P.Vaughan 120)

| 1st innings | lbw b Mashrafe Mortaza | 69 |

14. v Bangladesh at Riverside 3–5 June 2005 – won by an innings and 27 runs
Toss: England
Bangladesh 104 (S.J.Harmison 5–38) & 316 (M.J.Hoggard 5–73); England
447–3 dec (I.R.Bell 162*, M.E.Trescothick 151)

| 1st innings | lbw b Mashrafe Mortaza | 8 |

15. v Australia at Lord's 21–24 July 2005 – lost by 239 runs
Toss: Australia
Australia 190 (S.J.Harmison 5–38) & 384; England 155 (G.D.McGrath 5–53) & 180

| 1st innings | c S.K.Warne b G.D.McGrath | 2 |
| 2nd innings | c & b B.Lee | 37 |

16. v Australia at Edgbaston 4–7 August 2005 – won by 2 runs
Toss: Australia
England 407 & 182 (S.K.Warne 6–46); Australia 308 & 279

| 1st innings | b S.K.Warne | 48 |
| 2nd innings | b S.K.Warne | 6 |

17. v Australia at Old Trafford 11–15 August 2005 – match drawn
Toss: England
England 444 (M.P.Vaughan 166) & 280–6 dec (A.J.Strauss 106, G.D.McGrath
5–115); Australia 302 (S.P.Jones 6–53) & 371–9 (R.T.Ponting 156)

| 1st innings | b B.Lee | 6 |
| 2nd innings | c D.R.Martyn b G.D.McGrath | 106 |

18. v Australia at Trent Bridge 25–28 August 2005 – won by 3 wickets
Toss: England
England 444 (A.Flintoff 102) & 129–7; Australia 218 (S.P.Jones 5–44) & 387
following on

1st innings	c M.L.Hayden b S.K.Warne	35
2nd innings	c M.J.Clarke b S.K.Warne	23

19. v Australia at The Oval 8–12 September 2005 – match drawn
Toss: England
England 373 (A.J.Strauss 129, S.K.Warne 6–122) & 335 (K.P.Pietersen 158,
S.K.Warne 6–124); Australia 367 (J.L.Langer 105, M.L.Hayden 138, A.Flintoff
5–78) & 4–0

1st innings	c S.M.Katich b S.K.Warne	129
2nd innings	c S.M.Katich b S.K.Warne	1

20. v Pakistan at Multan 12–16 November 2005 – lost by 22 runs
Toss: Pakistan
Pakistan 274 & 341 (Salman Butt 122); England 418 (M.E.Trescothick 193)
& 175

1st innings	lbw b Mohammad Sami	9
2nd innings	c Hasan Raza b Danish Kaneria	23

21. v Pakistan at Faisalabad 20–24 November 2005 – match drawn
Toss: Pakistan
Pakistan 462 (Inzamam-ul-Haq 109) & 268–9 dec (Inzamam-ul-Haq 100*);
England 446 (I.R.Bell 115, K.P.Pietersen 100) & 164–6

1st innings	b Naved-ul-Hasan	12
2nd innings	b Naved-ul-Hasan	0

v Pakistan at Lahore 29 November–3 December 2005 – lost by an innings
and 100 runs
Toss: England
England 288 & 248 (Shoaib Akhtar 5–71); Pakistan 636–8 dec (Mohammad
Yousuf 223, Kamran Akmal 154)
STRAUSS DID NOT PLAY

22. v India at Nagpur 1–5 March 2006 – match drawn
Toss: England

England 393 (P.D.Collingwood 134*) & 297–3 dec (A.N.Cook 104*); India 323
(M.J.Hoggard 6–57) & 260–6 (W.Jaffer 100)

1st innings	c V.V.S.Laxman b S.Sreesanth	28
2nd innings	c M.S.Dhoni b I.K.Pathan	46

23. v India at Mohali 9–13 March 2006 – lost by 9 wickets
Toss: England
England 300 (A.Kumble 5–76) & 181; India 338 & 144–1

1st innings	c M.S.Dhoni b I.K.Pathan	18
2nd innings	c M.S.Dhoni b A.Kumble	13

24. v India at Mumbai 18–22 March 2006 – won by 212 runs
Toss: India
England 400 (A.J.Strauss 128) & 191; India 279 & 100 (S.D.Udal 4–14)

1st innings	c M.S.Dhoni b Harbhajan Singh	128
2nd innings	c M.S.Dhoni b M.M.Patel	4

25. v Sri Lanka at Lord's 11–15 May 2006 – match drawn
Toss: England
England 551–6 dec (K.P.Pietersen 158, M.E.Trescothick 106); Sri Lanka 192
& 537–9 following on (D.P.M.D.Jayawardene 119)

1st innings	c D.P.M.D.Jayawardene b M.Muralitharan	48

Match highlights:
*Reached 2,000 Test runs during his first innings score of 48; 10th fastest
Englishman to achieve this feat (47 innings).*

26. v Sri Lanka at Edgbaston 25–28 May 2006 – won by 6 wickets
Toss: Sri Lanka
Sri Lanka 141 & 231 (M.G.Vandort 105); England 295 (K.P.Pietersen 142,
M.Muralitharan 6–86) & 81–4

1st innings	run out (Samaraweera)	30
2nd innings	c D.P.M.D.Jayawardene b M.Muralitharan	16

27. v Sri Lanka at Trent Bridge 2–5 June 2006 – lost by 134 runs
Toss: Sri Lanka
Sri Lanka 231 & 322 (M.S.Panesar 5–78); England 229 & 190 (M.Muralitharan 8–70)

| 1st innings | b W.P.U.J.C.Vaas | 7 |
| 2nd innings | c D.P.M.D.Jayawardene b M.Muralitharan | 55 |

28. v Pakistan at Lord's 13–17 July 2006 – match drawn
Toss: England
England 528–9 dec (P.D.Collingwood 186, A.N.Cook 105, I.R.Bell 100*) &
296–8 dec (A.J.Strauss 128); Pakistan 445 (Mohammad Yousuf 202) & 214–4

| 1st innings | lbw b Abdul Razzaq | 30 |
| 2nd innings | c Imran Farhat b Danish Kaneria | 128 |

Match highlights:
*Test captain for the first time; the 77th Test captain for England; his 128 was the
highest score by an England captain on debut.*

29. v Pakistan at Old Trafford 27–29 July 2006 – won by an innings and 120 runs
Toss: Pakistan
Pakistan 119 (S.J.Harmison 6–19) & 222 (S.J.Harmison 5–57, M.S.Panesar
5–72); England 461–9 dec (A.N.Cook 127, I.R.Bell 106*)

| 1st innings | c Kamran Akmal b Abdul Razzaq | 42 |

Match highlights:
England captain.

30. v Pakistan at Headingley 4–8 August 2006 – won by 167 runs
Toss: England
England 515 (K.P.Pietersen 135, I.R.Bell 119, Umar Gul 5–123) & 345 (A.J.Strauss
116); Pakistan 538 (Mohammad Yousuf 192, Younis Khan 173) & 155

| 1st innings | c Younis Khan b Shahid Nazir | 36 |
| 2nd innings | c Kamran Akmal b Mohammad Sami | 116 |

Match highlights:
*England captain. Became the third fastest player to reach 10 Test centuries for
England (the others being Compton and Sutcliffe) and the eighth in Test history
(Bradman, Harvey, Walcott, Compton, Weekes, Sutcliffe and Morris).*

31. v Pakistan at The Oval 17–21 August 2006 – won by a concession
Toss: Pakistan
England 173 & 298–4; Pakistan 504 (Mohammad Yousuf 128)

1st innings	c Kamran Akmal b Mohammad Asif	38
2nd innings	lbw b Danish Kaneria	54

Match highlights:
England captain. Match was conceded by Pakistan at the tea interval on the fourth day.

32. v Australia at Brisbane 23–27 November 2006 – lost by 277 runs
Toss: Australia
Australia 602–9 dec (R.T.Ponting 192) & 202–1 dec (J.L.Langer 100*);
England 157 (G.D.McGrath 6–50) & 370

1st innings	c M.E.K.Hussey b G.D.McGrath	12
2nd innings	c sub (R.A.Broad) b S.R.Clark	11

33. v Australia at Adelaide 1–5 December 2006 – lost by 6 wickets
Toss: England
England 551–6 dec (P.D.Collingwood 206, K.P.Pietersen 158) & 129; Australia
513 (R.T.Ponting 142, M.J.Clarke 124, M.J.Hoggard 7–109) & 168–4

1st innings	c D.R.Martyn b S.R.Clark	14
2nd innings	c M.E.K.Hussey b S.K.Warne	34

34. v Australia at Perth 14–18 December 2006 – lost by 206 runs
Toss: Australia
Australia 244 (M.S.Panesar 5–92) & 527–5 dec (M.J.Clarke 135*, M.E.K.Hussey
103, A.C.Gilchrist 102*); England 215 & 350 (A.N.Cook 116)

1st innings	c A.C.Gilchrist b S.R.Clark	42
2nd innings	lbw b B.Lee	0

35. v Australia at Melbourne 26–28 December 2006 – lost by an innings and 99 runs
Toss: England
England 159 (S.K.Warne 5–39) & 161; Australia 419 (A.Symonds 156,
M.L.Hayden 153)

1st innings	b S.K.Warne	50
2nd innings	c A.C.Gilchrist b B.Lee	31

36. v Australia at Sydney 2–5 January 2007 – lost by 10 wickets
Toss: England
England 291 & 147; Australia 393 & 46–0

1st innings	c A.C.Gilchrist b B.Lee	29
2nd innings	lbw b S.R.Clark	24

Match highlights:
England lost the series 5–0, just the second time in England Test history.

37. v West Indies at Lord's 17–21 May 2007 – match drawn
Toss: West Indies
England 553–5 dec (A.N.Cook 105, P.D.Collingwood 111, I.R.Bell 109*,
M.J.Prior 126*) & 284–8dec
(K.P.Pietersen 109); West Indies 437 (M.S.Panesar 6–129) & 89–0

1st innings	c D.S.Smith b D.B-L.Powell	33
2nd innings	c R.S.Morton b C.D.Collymore	24

Match highlights:
England captain.

38. v West Indies at Headingley 25–28 May 2007 – won by an innings and 283 runs
Toss: England
England 570–7 dec (M.P.Vaughan 103, K.P.Pietersen 226); West Indies 146 &
141

1st innings	c D.Ramdin b D.B-L.Powell	15

39. v West Indies at Old Trafford 7–11 June 2007 – won by 60 runs
Toss: England
England 370 & 313 (A.N.Cook 106, D.J.G.Sammy 7–66); West Indies 229 & 394
(S.Chanderpaul 116, M.S.Panesar 6–137)

1st innings	lbw b J.E.Taylor	6
2nd innings	lbw b F.H.Edwards	0

40. v West Indies at Riverside 15–19 June 2007 – won by 7 wickets
Toss: England
West Indies 287 (S.Chanderpaul 136*, R.J.Sidebottom 5–88) & 222
(M.S.Panesar 5–46); England 400 (P.D.Collingwood 128, F.H.Edwards 5–112)
& 111–3

1st innings	c D.Ramdin b F.H.Edwards	77
2nd innings	b D.B-L.Powell	13

Notes:
Passed 9,000 First-class runs when he reached 7 in the first innings.
Also passed 3,000 Test runs when he reached 1 in the second innings.

41. v India at Lord's 19–23 July 2007 – match drawn
Toss: England
England 298 & 282 (K.P.Pietersen 134, R.P.Singh 5–59); India 201
(J.M.Anderson 5–42) & 282–9

1st innings	c R.Dravid b A.Kumble	96
2nd innings	c S.R.Tendulkar b Z.Khan	18

42. v India at Trent Bridge 27–31 July 2007 – lost by 7 wickets
Toss: India
England 198 & 355 (M.P.Vaughan 124, Z.Khan 5–75); India 481 & 73–3

1st innings	c S.R.Tendulkar b Z.Khan	4
2nd innings	c M.S.Dhoni b Z.Khan	55

43. v India at The Oval 9–13 August 2007 – match drawn
Toss: India
India 664 (A.Kumble 110*) & 180–6 dec; England 345 & 369–6
(K.P.Pietersen 101)

1st innings	c S.Sreesanth b Z.Khan	6
2nd innings	c V.V.S.Laxman b R.P.Singh	32

44. v New Zealand at Hamilton 5–9 March 2008 – lost by 189 runs
Toss: New Zealand
New Zealand 470 (L.R.P.L.Taylor 120) & 177–9 dec (R.J.Sidebottom 6–49);
England 348 & 110

1st innings	b D.L.Vettori	43
2nd innings	c B.B.McCullum b K.D.Mills	2

45. v New Zealand at Wellington 13–17 March 2008 – won by 126 runs
Toss: New Zealand
England 342 (T.R.Ambrose 102) & 293; New Zealand 198 (J.M.Anderson 5–73)
& 311 (R.J.Sidebottom 5–105)

1st innings	c M.S.Sinclair b K.D.Mills	8
2nd innings	lbw b J.D.P.Oram	44

46. v New Zealand at Napier 22–26 March 2008 – won by 121 runs
Toss: England
England 253 (K.P.Pietersen 129, T.G.Southee 5–55) & 467–7dec
(A.J.Strauss 177, I.R.Bell 110); New Zealand 168 (R.J.Sidebottom 7–47)
& 431 (M.S.Panesar 6–126)

| 1st innings | c J.M.How b T.G.Southee | 0 |
| 2nd innings | c M.D.Bell b J.S.Patel | 177 |

Notes:
Recorded his highest Test score and his highest First-class score in the second innings.
Also passed 10,000 First-class runs when he passed 117 in the second innings

47. v New Zealand at Lord's 15–19 May 2008 – match drawn
Toss: England
New Zealand 277 & 269–6 (J.D.P.Oram 101); England 319 (M.P.Vaughan 106,
D.L.Vettori 5–69)

| 1st innings | lbw b J.D.P.Oram | 63 |

Notes:
Passed 3,500 Test runs when he passed 3 in the first innings.

48. v New Zealand at Old Trafford 23–26 May 2008 – won by 6 wickets
Toss: New Zealand
New Zealand 381 (L.R.P.L.Taylor 154*) & 114 (M.S.Panesar 6–37); England 202
(D.L.Vettori 5–66) & 294–4 (A.J.Strauss 106)

| 1st innings | c B.B.McCullum b I.E.O'Brien | 60 |
| 2nd innings | c L.R.P.L.Taylor b I.E.O'Brien | 106 |

49. v New Zealand at Trent Bridge 5–8 June 2008 – won by an innings and 9 runs
Toss: New Zealand
England 364 (K.P.Pietersen 115); New Zealand 123 (J.M.Anderson 7–43) & 232
(R.J.Sidebottom 6–67)

| 1st innings | c L.R.P.L.Taylor b K.D.Mills | 37 |

50. v South Africa at Lord's 10–14 July 2008 – match drawn
Toss: South Africa
England 593–8dec (K.P.Pietersen 152, I.R.Bell 199); South Africa 247 (A.G.Prince
101) & 393–3dec (G.C.Smith 107, N.D.McKenzie 138, H.M.Amla 104*)

| 1st innings | lbw b M.Morkel | 44 |

Notes:
Became the 55th England player to play in 50 Tests.

51. v South Africa at Headingley 18–21 July 2008 – lost by 10 wickets
Toss: South Africa
England 203 & 327; South Africa 522 (A.G.Prince 149, A.B.de Villiers 174)
& 9–0

| 1st innings | c M.V.Boucher b M.Morkel | 27 |
| 2nd innings | c M.V.Boucher b M.Ntini | 0 |

52. v South Africa at Edgbaston 30 July–2 August 2008 – lost by 5 wickets
Toss: England
England 231 & 363 (P.D.Collingwood 135); South Africa 314 & 283–5
(G.C.Smith 154*)

| 1st innings | hit wicket b A.Nel | 20 |
| 2nd innings | c J.H.Kallis b M.Morkel | 25 |

53. v South Africa at The Oval 7–11 August 2008 – won by 6 wickets
Toss: South Africa
South Africa 194 & 318; England 316 (K.P.Pietersen 100, M.Ntini 5–94)
& 198–4

| 1st innings | c G.C.Smith b M.Ntini | 6 |
| 2nd innings | c G.C.Smith b P.L.Harris | 58 |

54. v India at Chennai 11–15 December 2008 – lost by 6 wickets
Toss: England
England 316 (A.J.Strauss 123) & 311–9dec (A.J.Strauss 108, P.D.Collingwood
108); India 241 & 387–4 (S.R.Tendulkar 103*)

| 1st innings | c and b A.Mishra | 123 |
| 2nd innings | c V.V.S.Laxman b Harbhajan Singh | 108 |

Notes:
Passed 4,000 Test runs when he reached 57 in the first innings.
Became the 11th English batsman to record two centuries in a Test match and the
first in India.

55. v India at Mohali 19–23 December 2008 – match drawn
Toss: India
India 453 (G.Gambhir 179, R.Dravid 136) & 251–7dec; England 302
(K.P.Pietersen 144) & 64–1

| 1st innings | lbw b Z.Khan | 0 |
| 2nd innings | not out | 21 |

56. v West Indies at Kingston 4–7 February 2009 – lost by an innings and 23 runs
Toss: England
England 318 & 51 (J.E.Taylor 5–11); West Indies 392 (C.H.Gayle 104,
R.R.Sarwan 107, S.C.J.Broad 5–85)

| 1st innings | c D.Ramdin b J.E.Taylor | 7 |
| 2nd innings | c D.Ramdin b J.E.Taylor | 9 |

Notes:
Was appointed full-time England captain prior to this series.

57. v West Indies at North Sound 13 February 2009 – match drawn
Toss: West Indies
England 7–0; West Indies did not bat

| 1st innings | not out | 6 |

Notes:
England captain.
Match was abandoned after just 10 balls due to the dangerously sandy outfield.

58. v West Indies at St Johns 15–19 February 2009 – match drawn
Toss: West Indies
England 566–9dec (A.J.Strauss 169, P.D.Collingwood 113) & 221–8dec; West
Indies 285 (G.P.Swann 5–57) & 370–9 (R.R.Sarwan 106)

| 1st innings | c and b F.H.Edwards | 169 |
| 2nd innings | c D.S.Smith b F.H.Edwards | 14 |

Notes:
England captain.

59. v West Indies at Bridgetown 26 February–2 March 2009 – match drawn
Toss: England

England 600–6dec (A.J.Strauss 142, R.S.Bopara 104) & 279–2dec
(A.N.Cook 139*); West Indies 749–9dec (R.R.Sarwan 291, D.Ramdin 166,
G.P.Swann 5–165)

1st innings	b D.B-L.Powell	142
2nd innings	b C.H.Gayle	38

Notes:
England captain.
Passed 4,500 Test runs when he reached 100 in the first innings
Also passed 12,000 First-class runs when he reached 21 in the second innings

60. v West Indies at Port-of-Spain 6–10 March 2009 – match drawn
Toss: England
England 546–6dec (A.J.Strauss 142, P.D.Collingwood 161, M.J.Prior 131*)
& 237–6dec (K.P.Pietersen 102); West Indies 544 (C.H.Gayle 102,
S.Chanderpaul 147*, B.P.Nash 109) & 114–8

1st innings	b F.H.Edwards	142
2nd innings	c and b C.H.Gayle	14

Notes:
England captain.

61. v West Indies at Lord's 6–8 May 2009 – won by 10 wickets
Toss: West Indies
England 377 (R.S.Bopara 143, F.H.Edwards 6–92) & 32–0; West Indies 152
(G.Onions 5–38) & 256

1st innings	c D.Ramdin b J.E.Taylor	16
2nd innings	not out	14

Notes:
England captain.

62. v West Indies at Chester–le–Street 14–18 May 2009 – won by an innings and
83 runs
Toss: England
England 569–6dec (A.N.Cook 160, R.S.Bopara 108); West Indies 310
(R.R.Sarwan 100, J.M.Anderson 5–87) & 176

1st innings	c D.Ramdin b C.H.Gayle	26

Notes:
England captain

63. v Australia at Cardiff 8–12 July 2009 – match drawn
Toss: England
England 435 & 252; Australia 674–6dec (S.M.Katich 122, R.T.Ponting 150,
M.J.North 125*, B.J.Haddin 121)

1st innings	c M.J.Clarke b M.G.Johnson	30
2nd innings	c B.J.Haddin b N.M.Hauritz	17

Notes:
England captain

64. v Australia at Lord's 16–20 July 2009 – won by 115 runs
Toss: England
England 425 (A.J.Strauss 161) & 311–6dec; Australia 215 & 406 (M.J.Clarke 136,
A.Flintoff 5–92)

1st innings	b B.W.Hilfenhaus	161
2nd innings	c M.J.Clarke b N.M.Hauritz	32

Notes:
*England captain. Passed 5,000 Test runs when he reached 161 in the England first
innings.*

65. v Australia at Edgbaston 30 July–3 August 2009 – match drawn
Toss: Australia
Australia 263 (J.M.Anderson 5–80) & 375–5 (M.J.Clarke 103*); England 376

1st innings	c G.A.Manou b B.W.Hilfenhaus	69

Notes:
England captain

66. v Australia at Headingley 7–9 August 2009 – lost by an innings and 80 runs
Toss: England
England 102 (P.M.Siddle 5–21) & 263 (M.G.Johnson 5–69); Australia 445
(M.J.North 110, S.C.J.Broad 6–91)

1st innings	c M.J.North b P.M.Siddle	3
2nd innings	lbw b B.W.Hilfenhaus	32

Notes:
England captain

67. v Australia at The Oval 20–23 August 2009 – won by 197 runs
Toss: England
England 332 & 373–9dec (I.J.L.Trott 119); Australia 160 (S.C.J.Broad 5–37) &
348 (M.E.K.Hussey 121)

1st innings	c B.J.Haddin b B.W.Hilfenhaus	55
2nd innings	c M.J.Clarke b M.J.North	75

Notes:
England captain.
*Won the England Man of the Series award and also the Compton–Miller Medal for
the Ashes Man of the Series.*

ANDREW STRAUSS IN ONE-DAY INTERNATIONAL CRICKET

Compiled by Victor Isaacs

One-Day International Career Record (2003/04–2008/09)

– up to and including West Indies at Gros Islet 2009

M	I	NO	Runs	HS	Avge	S/R	100s	50s
83	82	8	2443	152	33.01	76.70	3	15

1. v Sri Lanka at Dambulla 18 November 2003 – lost by 10 wickets
    Toss: England
    England 88 (46.1 overs); Sri Lanka 89–0 (13.5 overs)
    c & b K.A.D.M.Fernando   3   (9 balls)

    v Sri Lanka at Colombo (RPS) 21 November 2003 – match abandoned without a ball bowled

    v Sri Lanka at Colombo (RPS) 23 November 2003 – match abandoned without a ball bowled

2. v West Indies at Georgetown 18 April 2004 – won by 2 wickets
    Toss: England
    West Indies 156–5 (30 overs) (S.Chanderpaul 84); England 157–8 (29.3 overs)
    b D.J.Bravo   29   (46 balls; 5 fours)

3. v West Indies at Port-of-Spain 24 April 2004 – no result
    Toss: West Indies
    West Indies 57–2 (16 overs); England did not bat

    v West Indies at Port-of-Spain 25 April 2004 – match abandoned without a ball bowled v West Indies at St George's 28 April 2004 – match abandoned without a ball bowled

4. v West Indies at Gros Islet 1 May 2004 – lost by 5 wickets
    Toss: West Indies
    England 281–8 (50 overs) (M.E.Trescothick 130, A.Flintoff 59); West Indies 284–5 (48 overs) (R.R.Sarwan 73*)
    b M.Dillon   10   (16 balls; 1 four)

5. v West Indies at Gros Islet 2 May 2004 – lost by 4 wickets
    Toss: West Indies
    England 280–8 (50 overs) (M.P.Vaughan 67, A.J.Strauss 67); West Indies 282–6 (47.1 overs) (S.Chanderpaul 63, B.C.Lara 57)
    lbw b C.H.Gayle   67   (82 balls; 7 fours)

6. v West Indies at Bridgetown 5 May 2004 – won by 5 wickets
    Toss: England
    West Indies 261–6 (50 overs) (R.R.Sarwan 104*); England 262–5 (47.2 overs) (M.E.Trescothick 82, A.J.Strauss 66)
    b I.D.R.Bradshaw   66   (86 balls; 4 fours)

    v New Zealand at Old Trafford 24 June 2004 – match abandoned without a ball bowled

7. v West Indies at Trent Bridge 27 June 2004 – lost by 7 wickets
    Toss: West Indies
    England 147 (38.2 overs); West Indies 148–3 (32.2 overs) (C.H.Gayle 60*)
    c R.D.Jacobs b D.J.Bravo   43   (63 balls; 6 fours)

8. v New Zealand at Riverside 29 June 2004 – lost by 7 wickets
    Toss: New Zealand
    England 101 (32.5 overs) (J.E.C.Franklin 5–42); New Zealand 103–3 (17.2 overs)
    c J.D.P.Oram b J.E.C.Franklin   8   (29 balls)

9. v West Indies at Headingley 1 June 2004 – won by 7 wickets
    Toss: England
    West Indies 159 (40.1 overs); England 160–3 (22 overs) (M.E.Trescothick 55)
    not out   44   (37 balls; 9 fours)

10. v New Zealand at Bristol 4 July 2004 – lost by 6 wickets
    Toss: New Zealand
    England 237–7 (50 overs) (A.Flintoff 106, A.J.Strauss 61); New Zealand 241–4

(47.2 overs) (S.P.Fleming 99, H.J.H.Marshall 55, N.J.Astle 53)
c N.J.Astle b I.G.Butler   61   (86 balls; 7 fours)

11. v West Indies at Lord's 6 July 2004 – lost by 7 wickets
     Toss: West Indies
     England 237–7 (50 overs) (A.Flintoff 123, A.J.Strauss 100); West Indies 286–3
     (49.1 overs) (C.H.Gayle 132*, R.R.Sarwan 89)
     c D.J.Bravo b C.H.Gayle   100   (116 balls; 8 fours, 2 sixes)

12. v India at Trent Bridge 1 September 2004 – won by 7 wickets
     Toss: England
     India 170 (43.5 overs) (M.Kaif 50); England 171–3 (32.2 overs) (V.S.Solanki 52)
     not out   41   (52 balls; 6 fours)

13. v India at The Oval 3 September 2004 – won by 70 runs
     Toss: India
     England 307–5 (A.Flintoff 99, P.D.Collingwood 79*); India 237 (46.3 overs)
     (M.Kaif 51, D.Gough 4–50)
     c S.C.Ganguly b V.Sehwag   2   (9 balls)

14. v India at Lord's 5 September 2004 – lost by 23 runs
     Toss: India
     India 204 (49.3 overs) (S.C.Ganguly 90, R.Dravid 52, S.J.Harmison 4–22);
     England 181 (48.2 overs) (M.P.Vaughan 74)
     lbw b I.K.Pathan   2   (4 balls)

15. v Zimbabwe at Edgbaston 10 September 2004 – won by 152 runs
     Toss: Zimbabwe
     England 299–7 (50 overs) (P.D.Collingwood 80*, V.S.Solanki 62); Zimbabwe
     147 (39 overs)
     c T.Taibu b E.C.Rainsford   25   (30 balls; 2 fours)

16. v Sri Lanka at Rose Bowl 17 and 18 September 2004 – won by 49 runs
     (D/L)
     Toss: Sri Lanka
     England 251–7 (50 overs) (A.Flintoff 104, M.E.Trescothick 66); Sri Lanka
     95–5 (24 overs)
     run out (M.F.Maharoof)   7   (22 balls)

17. v Australia at Edgbaston 21 September 2004 – won by 6 wickets
     Toss: England
     Australia 259–9 (50 overs) (D.R.Martyn 65); England 262–4 (46.3 overs)

(M.P.Vaughan 86, M.E.Trescothick 81, A.J.Strauss 52*)
not out   52   (42 balls; 6 fours)

18.   v West Indies at The Oval 25 September 2004 – lost by 2 wickets
Toss: West Indies
England 217 (49.4 overs) (M.E.Trescothick 104); West Indies 218–8 (48.5 overs)
run out (D.J.Bravo)   18   (33 balls; 2 fours)

v Zimbabwe at Harare 26 November 2004 – match abandoned without a
ball bowled

19.   v Zimbabwe at Harare 28 November 2004 – won by 5 wickets
Toss: England
Zimbabwe 195 (49.3 overs) (E.Chigumbura 52); England 197–5 (47.4 overs)
(I.R.Bell 75, M.P.Vaughan 56)
c & b S.Matsikenyeri   8   (14 balls)

20.   v Zimbabwe at Harare 1 December 2004 – won by 161 runs
Toss: England
England 263–6 (50 overs) (K.P.Pietersen 77*, G.O.Jones 66); Zimbabwe 102
(36 overs) (A.G.Wharf 4–24)
b G.M.Ewing   33   (52 balls; 2 fours)

21.   v Zimbabwe at Bulawayo 4 December 2004 – won by 8 wickets
Toss: Zimbabwe
England 238–7 (50 overs) (S.Matsikenyeri 73, D.D.Ebrahim 65); England
239–2 (43.1 overs) (V.S.Solanki 100, M.P.Vaughan 54*, I.R.Bell 53)
not out   22   (34 balls; 2 fours)

22.   v Zimbabwe at Bulawayo 5 December 2004 – won by 74 runs
Toss: England
England 261–6 (50 overs) (M.P.Vaughan 90*, G.O.Jones 80); Zimbabwe 187
(48.4 overs) (H.Masakadza 66, D.Gough 4–34)
c E.Chigumbura b S.Matsikenyeri   17   (17 balls; 2 fours)

23.   v South Africa at Johannesburg 30 January 2005 – won by 26 runs (D/L)
Toss: England
South Africa 175–9 (50 overs); England 103–3 (25.1 overs)
c J.M.Kemp b A.Nel   15   (26 balls; 3 fours)

24.   v South Africa at Bloemfontein 2 February 2005 – match tied
Toss: South Africa

England 270–5 (50 overs) (K.P.Pietersen 108*); South Africa 270–8 (50 overs) (H.H.Gibbs 78, J.H.Kallis 63)
c M.V.Boucher b A.J.Hall   2   (9 balls)

25.   v South Africa at Port Elizabeth 4 February 2005 – lost by 3 wickets
Toss: England
England 267–8 (50 overs) (V.S.Solanki 66); South Africa 270–7 (49.1 overs) (G.C.Smith 105, H.H.Gibbs 50)
c A.G.Prince b S.M.Poolock   35   (40 balls; 3 fours)

26.   v South Africa at Cape Town 6 February 2005 – lost by 108 runs
Toss: England
South Africa 291–5 (50 overs) (H.H.Gibbs 100, J.H.Kallis 71, J.M.Kemp 57); England 183 (41.2 overs) (K.P.Pietersen 75)
c A.G.Prince b A.Nel   17   (25 balls; 2 fours)

27.   v South Africa at East London 9 February 2005 – lost by 7 runs
Toss: South Africa
South Africa 311–7 (50 overs) (G.C.Smith 115*, J.M.Kemp 80); England 304–8 (50 overs) (K.P.Pietersen 100*, M.P.Vaughan 70)
run out (M.V.Boucher)   20   (29 balls)

28.   v South Africa at Durban 11 February 2005 – no result
Toss: South Africa
South Africa 211 (46.3 overs) (H.H.Gibbs 118); England 7–2 (3.4 overs)
not out   0   (0 balls)

29.   v South Africa at Centurion 13 February 2005 – lost by 3 wickets
Toss: South Africa
England 240 (49.5 overs) (K.P.Pietersen 116); South Africa 241–7 (49 overs) (A.G.Prince 62*)
c M.V.Boucher b A.Nel   15   (35 balls; 2 fours)

30.   v Bangladesh at The Oval 16 June 2005 – won by 10 wickets
Toss: England
Bangladesh 190 (45.2 overs) (Aftab Ahmed 51, S.J.Harmison 4–39); England 192–0 (24.5 overs) (M.E.Trescothick 100*, A.J.Strauss 82*)
not out   82   (77 balls; 10 fours, 1 six)

31.   v Australia at Bristol 19 June 2005 – won by 3 wickets
Toss: Australia
Australia 252–9 (50 overs) (M.E.K.Hussey 84, S.J.Harmison 5–33); England

253–7 (47.3 overs) (K.P.Pietersen 91*, M.P.Vaughan 57)
b G.D.McGrath   16   (23 balls; 3 fours)

32.   v Bangladesh at Trent Bridge 21 June 2005 – won by 168 runs
Toss: England
England 391–4 (50 overs) (A.J.Strauss 152, P.D.Collingwood 112*,
M.E.Trescothick 85); Bangladesh 223 (45.2 overs) (Mohammad Ashraful 94,
Javed Omar 59, P.D.Collingwood 6–31, C.T.Tremlett 4–32)
lbw b Nazmul Hossain   152   (128 balls; 19 fours)

Match highlights:
Reached 1,000 runs in his 31st innings.

33.   v Australia at Riverside 23 June 2005 – lost by 57 runs
Toss: England
Australia 266–5 (50 overs) (A.Symonds 73, D.R.Martyn 68*); England 209–9
(50 overs)
b B.Lee   3   (13 balls)

34.   v Bangladesh at Headingley 26 June 2005 – won by 5 wickets
Toss: Bangladesh
Bangladesh 208–7 (50 overs) (Javed Omar 81, A.Flintoff 4–29); England 209–5
(38.5 overs) (A.J.Strauss 98)
b Manjural Islam Rana   98   (104 balls; 7 fours, 1 six)

Match highlights:
Named Man of the Match for the first time in one-day internationals.

35.   v Australia at Edgbaston 28 June 2005 – no result
Toss: Australia
Australia 261–9 (50 overs) (A.Symonds 74); England 37–1 (6 overs)
c J.N.Gillespie b G.D.McGrath   25   (18 balls; 5 fours)

36.   v Australia at Lord's 2 July 2005 – match tied
Toss: England
Australia 196 (48.5 overs) (M.E.K.Hussey 62*), England 196–9 (50 overs)
(G.O.Jones 71, P.D.Collingwood 53)
b B.Lee   2   (8 balls)

37.   v Australia at Headingley 7 July 2005 – won by 9 wickets
Toss: England
Australia 219–7 (50 overs) (P.D.Collingwood 4–34); England 221–1 (46 overs)

(M.E.Trescothick 104*, M.P.Vaughan 59*)
c A.C.Gilchrist b G.B.Hogg   41   (84 balls; 2 fours)

38.   v Australia at Lord's 10 July 2005 – lost by 7 wickets
Toss: Australia
England 223–8 (50 overs) (A.Flintoff 87, B.Lee 5–41); Australia 224–3 (44.2
overs) (R.T.Ponting 111)
b M.S.Kasprowicz   11   (25 balls; 1 four)

39.   v Australia at The Oval 12 July 2005 – lost by 8 wickets
Toss: Australia
England 228–7 (50 overs) (K.P.Pietersen 74, V.S.Solanki 53*); Australia 229–2
(34.5 overs) (A.C.Gilchrist 121*)
c A.C.Gilchrist b M.S.Kasprowicz   36   (50 balls; 5 fours)

40.   v Pakistan at Lahore 10 December 2005 – won by 42 runs
Toss: England
England 327–4 (50 overs) (A.J.Strauss 94, A.Flintoff 72*, K.P.Pietersen 56);
Pakistan 285 (46.5 overs) (Salman Butt 67, Younis Khan 60, Mohammad
Yousuf 59, Shoaib Malik 50)
c Salman Butt b Danish Kaneria   94   (98 balls; 6 fours)

Match highlights:
Named Man of the Match.

41.   v Pakistan at Lahore 12 December 2005 – lost by 7 wickets
Toss: England
England 230 (48.4 overs) (L.E.Plunkett 56, Shoaib Akhtar 5–53); Pakistan 231–3
(44 overs) (Kamran Akmal 102)
c Kamran Akmal b Shoaib Akhtar   0   (4 balls)

42.   v Pakistan at Karachi 15 December 2005 – lost by 165 runs
Toss: England
Pakistan 353–6 (50 overs) (Kamran Akmal 109, Mohammad Yousuf 68, Abdul
Razzaq 51*); England 188 (42 overs)
lbw b Mohammad Sami   23   (23 balls; 3 fours)

43.   v Pakistan at Rawalpindi 19 December 2005 – lost by 13 runs
Toss: Pakistan
Pakistan 210 (47.2 overs) (Inzamam-ul-Haq 81*); England 197 (48.1 overs)
lbw b Naved-ul-Hasam   0   (1 ball)

44. v Pakistan at Rawalpindi 21 December 2005 – won by 6 runs
Toss: England
England 206–9 (50 overs); Pakistan 200–9 (50 overs) (Yasir Hameed 57,
Mohammad Yousuf 54, J.M.Anderson 4–48)
st Kamran Akmal b Arshad Khan   26   (57 balls; 3 fours)

45. v India at Delhi 28 March 2006 – lost by 39 runs
Toss: England
India 203 (46.4 overs) (Kabir Ali 4–45); England 164 (38.1 overs) (Harbhajan
Singh 5–31)
c M.S.Dhoni b I.K.Pathan   o   (3 balls)

46. v India at Faridabad 31 March 2006 – lost by 4 wickets
Toss: England
England 226 (49.5 overs) (K.P.Pietersen 71, A.J.Strauss 61); India 230–6
(49 overs) (S.K.Raina 81*)
b R.R.Powar   61   (85 balls; 6 fours)

47. v India at Goa 3 April 2006 – lost by 49 runs
Toss: India
India 294–6 (50 overs) (Yuvraj Singh 103, S.K.Raina 61); England 245 (48.5
overs) (P.D.Collingwood 93, I.K.Pathan 4–51)
c M.S.Dhoni b I.K.Pathan   7   (13 balls; 1 four)

48. v India at Cochin 6 April 2006 – lost by 4 wickets
Toss: England
England 237 (48.4 overs) (K.P.Pietersen 77); India 238–6 (47.2 overs) (R.Dravid 65)
lbw b I.K.Pathan   7   (11 balls; 1 four)

   v India at Guwahati 9 April 2006 – match abandoned without a ball bowled

49. v India at Jamshedpur 12 April 2006 – won by 5 wickets
Toss: India
India 223 (48 overs) (M.S.Dhoni 96, R.R.Powar 54); England 227–5 (42.4 overs)
(A.J.Strauss 74*)
retired hurt   74   (85 balls; 10 fours)

Match highlights:
*First match as England captain; named Man of the Match; retired hurt at 74,
suffering from exhaustion.*

50. v India at Indore 15 April 2006 – lost by 7 wickets
Toss: India
England 288 (50 overs) (K.P.Pietersen 64, P.D.Collingwood 64, G.O.Jones
63, S.Sreesanth 6–55); India 289–3 (49.1 overs) (A.R.Uthappa 86, R.Dravid 69,
Yuvraj Singh 63*, S.K.Raina 53)
c K.D.Karthik b S.Sreesanth   25   (34 balls; 5 fours)

Match highlights:
England captain.

51. v Ireland at Belfast 13 June 2006 – won by 38 runs
Toss: England
England 301–7 (50 overs) (M.E.Trescothick 113, I.R.Bell 80); Ireland 263–9
(50 overs) (A.C.Botha 52)
c A.C.Botha b K.J.O'Brien   4   (13 balls; 1 four)

Match highlights:
England captain.

52. v Sri Lanka at Lord's 17 June 2006 – lost by 20 runs
Toss: England
Sri Lanka 257–9 (50 overs) (W.U.Tharanga 120); England 237–9 (50 overs)
(M.E.Trescothick 67, J.W.M.Dalrymple 67)
c K.C.Sangakkara b C.R.D.Fernando   12   (16 balls; 1 four)

Match highlights:
England captain.

53. v Sri Lanka at The Oval 20 June 2006 – lost by 46 runs
Toss: Sri Lanka
Sri Lanka 319–8 (50 overs) (S.T.Jayasuriya 122, D.P.M.D.Jayawardene
66, K.C.Sangakkara 61); England 273 (46.4 overs) (K.P.Pietersen 73,
P.D.Collingwood 56)
c M.Muralitharan b M.F.Maharoof   18   (23 balls; 2 fours)

Match highlights:
England captain.

54. v Sri Lanka at Riverside 24 June 2006 – lost by 8 wickets
Toss: England
England 261–7 (50 overs) (I.R.Bell 77); Sri Lanka 265–2 (42.2 overs)
(D.P.M.D.Jayawardene 126*, K.C.Sangakkara 58)

lbw b W.P.U.J.C.Vaas   32   (44 balls; 3 fours)

Match highlights:
England captain.

55.   v Sri Lanka at Old Trafford 28 June 2006 – lost by 33 runs
Toss: Sri Lanka
Sri Lanka 318–7 (50 overs) (D.P.M.D.Jayawardene 100, W.U.Tharanga 60,
M.F.Maharoof 58*); England 285 (48.4 overs) (A.J.Strauss 45)
c K.C.Sangakkara b T.M.Dilshan   45   (44 balls; 5 fours)

Match highlights:
England captain.

56.   v Sri Lanka at Headingley 1 July 2006 – lost by 8 wickets
Toss: England
England 321–7 (50 overs) (M.E.Trescothick 121, S.L.Malinga 4–44); Sri Lanka
324–2 (37.3 overs) (S.T.Jayasuriya 152, W.U.Tharanga 109)
c K.C.Sangakkara b S.L.Malinga   26   (32 balls; 1 four)

Match highlights:
England captain.

57.   v Pakistan at Cardiff 30 August 2006 – no result
Toss: Pakistan
England 202 (49.2 overs) (I.R.Bell 88); Pakistan 46–1 (7 overs)
c Shahid Afridi b Mohammad Asif   2   (14 balls)

Match highlights:
England captain.

58.   v Pakistan at Lord's 2 September 2006 – lost by 7 wickets (D/L)
Toss: Pakistan
England 166 (39.1 overs) (Shoaib Akhtar 4–28); Pakistan 169–3 (36.4 overs)
(Younis Khan 55)
c Kamran Akmal b Shoaib Akhtar   0   (1 ball)

Match highlights:
England captain.

59.   v Pakistan at Rose Bowl 5 September 2006 – lost by 2 wickets
Toss: Pakistan

England 271–9 (50 overs) (J.W.M.Dalrymple 62, P.D.Collingwood 61,
A.J.Strauss 50, Naved-ul-Hasan 4–57); Pakistan 274–8 (48.5 overs)
(Younis Khan 101, Mohammad Yousuf 60)
c Kamran Akmal b Abdul Razzaq   50   (46 balls; 8 fours)

Match highlights:
England captain.

60.   v Pakistan at Nottingham 8 September 2006 – won by 8 wickets
Toss: Pakistan
Pakistan 235–8 (50 overs) (Abdul Razzaq 75*); England 237–2 (46.2 overs)
(I.R.Bell 86*, A.J.Strauss 78)
b Mohammad Hafeez   78   (100 balls; 9 fours)

Match highlights:
England captain.

61.   v Pakistan at Edgbaston 10 September 2006 – won by 3 wickets
Toss: England
Pakistan 154–9 (50 overs); England 155–7 (31 overs)
c Kamran Akmal b Iftikhar Anjum   35   (41 balls; 8 fours)

Match highlights:
England captain.

62.   v India at Jaipur 15 October 2006 – lost by 4 wickets
Toss: India
England 125 (37 overs); India 126–6 (29.3 overs)
c R.Dravid b I.K.Pathan   10   (32 balls; 1 four)

63.   v Australia at Jaipur 21 October 2006 – lost by 6 wickets
Toss: Australia
England 169 (45 overs) (A.J.Strauss 56); Australia 170–4 (36.5 overs)
(D.R.Martyn 78)
c A.C.Gilchrist b A.Symonds   56   (90 balls; 6 fours)

64.   v West Indies at Ahmedabad 28 October 2006 – won by 3 wickets
Toss: West Indies
West Indies 272–4 (50 overs) (D.J.Bravo 112*, C.H.Gayle 101); England 276–7
(48.3 overs) (K.P.Pietersen 90*, A.J.Strauss 50, I.R.Bell 50)
b C.H.Gayle   50   (47 balls; 8 fours)

65. v Australia at Melbourne 12 January 2007 – lost by 8 wickets
Toss: England
England 242–8 (K.P.Pietersen 82); Australia 246–2 (45.2 overs) (R.T.Ponting
82*, A.C.Gilchrist 60, M.J.Clarke 57*)
c M.L.Hayden b N.W.Bracken   12   (20 balls; 1 four)

66. v New Zealand at Hobart 16 January 2007 – won by 3 wickets
Toss: New Zealand
New Zealand 205–9 (50 overs) (J.M.Anderson 4–42); England 206–7
(49.5 overs) (A.Flintoff 72*)
lbw b J.E.C.Franklin   28   (58 balls; 3 fours)

67. v Australia at Brisbane 19 January 2007 – lost by 4 wickets
Toss: England
England 155 (42 overs); Australia 156–6 (38.4 overs) (J.Lewis 4–36)
c B.J.Hodge b G.D.McGrath   18   (37 balls; 1 six)

68. v New Zealand at Adelaide 23 January 2007 – lost by 90 runs
Toss: New Zealand
New Zealand 210 (50 overs) (J.D.P.Oram 86, A.Flintoff 4–21); England 120
(37.5 overs) (D.L.Vettori 4–24)
lbw b J.E.C.Franklin   19   (33 balls; 3 fours)

69. v Australia at Adelaide 26 January 2007 – lost by 9 wickets
Toss: England
England 110 (34.3 overs) (M.G.Johnson 4–45); Australia 111–1 (24.3 overs)
(R.T.Ponting 51*)
c A.C.Gilchrist b M.G.Johnson   17   (32 balls; 2 fours)

70. v New Zealand at Perth 30 January 2007 – lost by 58 runs
Toss: New Zealand
New Zealand 318–7 (50 overs) (L.Vincent 76, R.L.Taylor 71, J.D.P.Oram 54*);
England 260–8 (50 overs) (E.C.Joyce 66)
st B.B.McCullum b D.L.Vettori   12   (20 balls)

71. v Australia at Sydney 2 February 2007 – won by 92 runs
Toss: England
England 292–7 (50 overs) (E.C.Joyce 107, I.R.Bell 51); Australia 200 (38.5 overs)
(M.L.Hayden 51)
c S.R.Clark b N.W.Bracken   26   (24 balls; 3 fours)

72. v Australia at New Zealand at Brisbane 6 February 2007 – won by 14
    runs
    Toss: England
    England 270–7 (50 overs) (P.D.Collingwood 106, A.J.Strauss 55, S.E.Bond
    4–46); New Zealand 256–8 (50 overs) (S.P.Fleming 106)
    b S.B.Styris   55   (63 balls; 3 fours, 1 six)

73. v Australia at Melbourne 9 February 2007 – won by 4 wickets
    Toss: Australia
    Australia 252 (48.3 overs) (M.L.Hayden 82, R.T.Ponting 75); England 253–6
    (49.3 overs) (P.D.Collingwood 120*, I.R.Bell 65)
    lbw b N.W.Bracken   0   (2 balls)

74. v Australia at Sydney 11 February 2007 – won by 34 runs (D/L)
    Toss: England
    England 246–8 (50 overs) (P.D.Collingwood 70); Australia 152–8 (27 overs)
    c A.C.Gilchrist b N.W.Bracken   6   (5 balls)

75. v Australia at St Peter's 8 April 2007 – lost by 7 wickets
    Toss: England
    England 247 (49.5 overs) (K.P.Pietersen 104, I.R.Bell 77); Australia 248–3
    (47.2 overs) (R.T.Ponting 86, M.J.Clarke 55*)
    b S.W.Tait   7   (10 balls)

76. v Bangladesh at Bridgetown 11 April 2007 – won by 4 wickets
    Toss: England
    Bangladesh 143 (37.2 overs) (Saqibul Hasan 57); England 147–6 (44.5 overs)
    lbw b Syed Rasel   23   (57 balls; 2 fours, 1 six)

77. v South Africa at Bridgetown 17 April 2007 – lost by 9 wickets
    Toss: England
    England 154 (48 overs) (A.J.Hall 5–18); South Africa 157–1 (19.2 overs)
    (G.C.Smith 89*)
    c G.C.Smith b J.H.Kallis   46   (67 balls, 2 fours, 1 six)

78. v West Indies at Bridgetown 21 April 2007 – won by 1 wicket
    Toss: England
    West Indies 300 (49.5 overs) (C.H.Gayle 79, D.S.Smith 61, M.N.Samuels 51);
    England 301–9 (49.5 overs) (K.P.Pietersen 100, M.P.Vaughan 79)
    c D.S.Smith b C.D.Collymore   7   (12 balls; 1 four)

79. v West Indies at Providence 20 March 2009 – won by 1 run (D/L method)
Toss: England
England 270–7 (50 overs) (O.A.Shah 62, P.D.Collingwood 69); West Indies
244–7 (46.2 overs) (L.M.P.Simmons 62, R.R.Sarwan 57)
c D.J.Bravo b D.B–L.Powell   15   (23 balls; 1 four)

Match highlights:
England captain.

80. v West Indies at Providence 22 March 2009 – lost by 21 runs
Toss: West Indies
West Indies 264–8 (50 overs) (R.R.Sarwan 74, S.Chanderpaul 112*); England
243 (48.2 overs) (A.J.Strauss 105)
b K.A.Pollard   105   (129 balls; 7 fours)

Match highlights:
England captain.

81. v West Indies at Bridgetown 27 March 2009 – lost by 8 wickets (D/L method)
Toss: West Indies
England 117 (41.3 overs) (D.J.Bravo 4–19); West Indies 117–2 (14.4 overs)
(C.H.Gayle 80)
c C.H.Gayle b F.H.Edwards   2   (18 balls)

Match highlights:
England captain.

82. v West Indies at Bridgetown 29 March 2009 – won by 9 wickets (D/L method)
Toss: England
West Indies 239–9 (50 overs) (D.J.Bravo 69); England 136–1 (18.3 overs)
(A.J.Strauss 79*)
not out   79   (61 balls; 9 fours, 1 six)

Match highlights:
England captain.

83. v West Indies at Gros Islet 3 April 2009 – won by 26 runs
Toss: England
England 172–5 (29 overs); West Indies 146 (28 overs) (A.Flintoff 5–19)
c D.J.Bravo b R.Rampaul   3   (4 balls)

Match highlights:
England captain.

84. v West Indies at Bristol 24 May 2009 – won by 6 wickets
Toss: England
West Indies 160 (38.3 overs) (D.J.Bravo 50, S.C.J.Broad 4–46); England 161–4
(36 overs)
c D.J.G.Sammy b J.E.Taylor   4   (16 balls)

Match highlights:
England captain.

85. v West Indies at Edgbaston 26 May 2009 – won by 58 runs
Toss: West Indies
England 328–7 (50 overs) (M.J.Prior 87, O.A.Shah 75, A.J.Strauss 52); West
Indies 270 (49.4 overs) (S.Chanderpaul 68)
st D.Ramdin b S.J.Benn   52   (66 balls)

Match highlights:
England captain.

ANDREW STRAUSS IN INTERNATIONAL TWENTY20 MATCHES

Compiled by Victor Isaacs

International Twenty20 Career Record (2005–2008/09)

– up to and including England v Pakistan in 2006

M	I	NO	Runs	HS	Avge	S/R	100s	50s
4	4	0	73	33	18.25	114.06	0	0

1. v Australia at Rose Bowl 13 June 2005 – won by 100 runs
    Toss: England
    England 179–8 (20 overs); Australia 79 (14.3 overs) (J.Lewis 4–24)
    b J.N.Gillespie   18   (16 balls; 1 four)

2. v Sri Lanka at Rose Bowl 15 June 2006 – lost by 2 runs
    Toss: Sri Lanka
    Sri Lanka 163 (20 overs) (P.D.Collingwood 4–22); England 161–5 (20 overs)
    (M.E.Trescothick 72)
    b C.R.D.Fernando   33   (21 balls; 6 fours)

3. v Pakistan at Bristol 28 August 2006 – lost by 5 wickets
    Toss: England
    England 144–7 (20 overs) (M.E.Trescothick 53); Pakistan 148–5 (17.5 overs)
    c Kamran Akmal b Mohammad Asif   0   (2 balls)

4. v West Indies at Port-of-Spain 15 March 2009 – lost by 6 wickets
    Toss: West Indies
    England 121 (19.1 overs); West Indies 123–4 (R.R.Sarwan 59)
    run out (S.Chanderpaul/D.J.G.Sammy)   22   (25 balls; 2 fours)

FULL CAREER RECORD:

First-class (1998-2009)
– upto and including England v Australia at The Oval 2009

M	I	NO	Runs	HS	Avge	100s	50s
181	321	16	13090	177	42.91	35	56

List-A (Limited Overs matches) (1997-2009)
– upto and including England v West Indies at Edgbaston 2009

M	I	NO	Runs	HS	Avge	100s	50s
206	199	14	5721	163	30.92	7	36

TEST CENTURIES

177	v New Zealand	Napier	2007/2008
169	v West Indies	St John's	2008/2009
161	v Australia	Lord's	2009
147	v South Africa	Johannesburg	2004/2005
142	v West Indies	Port of Spain	2008/2009
142	v West Indies	Bridgetown	2008/2009
137	v West Indies	Lord's	2004
136	v South Africa	Durban	2004/2005
129	v Australia	The Oval	2005
128	v Pakistan	Lord's	2006
128	v India	Mumbai	2005/2006
126	v South Africa	Port Elizabeth	2004/2005
123	v India	Chennai	2008/2009
116	v Pakistan	Leeds	2006
112	v New Zealand	Lord's	2004
108	v India	Chennai	2008/2009
106	v Australia	Old Trafford	2005
106	v New Zealand	Old Trafford	2008

THE ASHES 2009 SCORECARDS

Compiled by Victor Isaacs

ENGLAND V AUSTRALIA (1ST TEST)
At Cardiff 8–12 July 2009

England

*A.J.Strauss c Clarke b Johnson	30	– c Haddin b Hauritz	17
A.N.Cook c Hussey b Hilfenhaus	10	– lbw b Johnson	6
R.S.Bopara c Hughes b Johnson	35	– lbw b Hilfenhaus	1
K.P.Pietersen c Katich b Hauritz	69	– b Hilfenhaus	8
P.D.Collingwood c Haddin b Hilfenhaus	64	– c Hussey b Siddle	74
+M.J.Prior b Siddle	56	– c Clarke b Hauritz	14
A.Flintoff b Siddle	37	– c Ponting b Johnson	26
J.M.Anderson c Hussey b Hauritz	26	(10) not out	21
S.C.J.Broad b Johnson	19	(8) lbw b Hauritz	14
G.P.Swann not out	47	(9) lbw b Hilfenhaus	31
M.S.Panesar c Ponting b Hauritz	4	– not out	7
B 13, l–b 11, w 2, n–b 12	38	B 9, l–b 9, w 4, n–b 11	33

1/21 2/67 3/90 4/228   435   1/13 2/17 3/31 4/46 5/70   (for 9 wkts) 252
5/241 6/327 7/329 8/355 9/423 10/435   6/127 7/159 8/221 9/233

Bowling: *First innings* – Johnson 22–2–87–3; Hilfenhaus 27–5–77–2; Siddle 27–3–121–2; Hauritz 23.5–1–95–3; Clarke 5–0–20–0; Katich 2–0–11–0. *Second innings* – Johnson 22–4–44–2; Hilfenhaus 15–3–47–3; Siddle 18–2–51–1; Hauritz 37–12–63–3; Clarke 3–0–8–0; North 7–4–14–0; Katich 3–0–7–0.

Australia

P.J.Hughes c Prior b Flintoff	36
S.M.Katich lbw b Anderson	122
*R.T.Ponting b Panesar	150
M.E.K.Hussey c Prior b Anderson	3
M.J.Clarke c Prior b Broad	83
M.J.North not out	125
+B.J.Haddin c Bopara b Collingwood	121
M.G.Johnson	
N.M.Hauritz	
B.W.Hilfenhaus	
P.M.Siddle	
B 9, l–b 14, w 4, n–b 7	34

1/60 2/299 3/325 4/331   (for 6 wkts dec) 674
5/474 6/674

Bowling: *First innings* – Anderson 32–6–110–2; Broad 32–6–129–1; Swann 38–8–131–0; Flintoff 35–3–128–1; Panesar 35–4–115–1; Collingwood 9–0–38–1.

Umpires: Aleem Dar and B.R.Doctrove

Match drawn

ENGLAND V AUSTRALIA (2ND TEST)
At Lord's 17–20 July 2009

England

*A.J.Strauss b Hilfenhaus	161	– c Clarke b Hauritz		32
A.N.Cook lbw b Johnson	95	– lbw b Hauritz		32
R.S.Bopara lbw b Hilfenhaus	18	– c Katich b Hauritz		27
K.P.Pietersen c Haddin b Siddle	32	– c Haddin b Siddle		44
P.D.Collingwood c Siddle b Clarke	16	– c Haddin b Siddle		54
+M.J.Prior b Johnson	8	– run out		61
A.Flintoff c Ponting b Hilfenhaus	4	– not out		30
S.C.J.Broad b Hilfenhaus	16	– not out		0
G.P.Swann c Ponting b Siddle	4			
J.M.Anderson c Hussey b Johnson	29			
G.Onions not out	17			
B 15, l–b 2, n–b 8	25	B 16, l–b 9, w 1, n–b 5		31

1/196 2/222 3/267 4/302   425   1/61 2/74 3/147 4/174   (for 6 wkts dec) 311
5/317 6/333 7/364 8/370 9/378 10/425   5/260 6/311

Bowling: First innings – Hilfenhaus 31–12–103–4; Johnson 21.4–2–132–3; Siddle 20–1–76–2; Hauritz 8.3–1–26–0; North 16.3–2–59–0; Clarke 4–1–12–1. *Second innings* – Hilfenhaus 19–5–59–0; Johnson 17–2–68–0; Siddle 15.2–4–64–2; Hauritz 16–1–80–3; Clarke 4–0–15–0.

Australia

P.J.Hughes c Prior b Anderson	4	– c Strauss b Flintoff		17
S.M.Katich c Broad b Onions	48	– c Pietersen b Flintoff		6
*R.T.Ponting c Strauss b Anderson	2	– b Broad		38
M.E.K.Hussey b Flintoff	51	– c Collingwood b Swann		27
M.J.Clarke c Cook b Anderson	1	– b Swann		136
M.J.North b Anderson	0	– b Swann		6
+B.J.Haddin c Cook b Broad	28	– c Collingwood b Flintoff		80
M.G.Johnson c Cook b Broad	4	– b Swann		63
N.M.Hauritz c Collingwood b Onions	24	– b Flintoff		1
P.M.Siddle c Strauss b Onions	35	– b Flintoff		7
B.W.Hilfenhaus not out	6	– not out		4
B 4, l–b 6, n–b 2	12	B 5, l–b 8, n–b 8		21

1/4 2/10 3/103 4/111   215   1/17 2/34 3/78 4/120   406
5/111 6/139 7/148 8/152 9/196 10/215   5/128 6/313 7/356 8/363 9/388 10/406

Bowling: First innings – Anderson 21–5–55–4; Flintoff 12–4–27–1; Broad 18–1–78–2; Onions 11–1–41–3; Swann 1–0–4–0. *Second innings* – Anderson 21–4–86–0; Flintoff 27–4–92–5; Onions 9–0–50–0; Broad 16–3–49–1; Swann 28–3–87–4; Collingwood 6–1–29–0.

Umpires: B.R.Doctrove and R.E.Koertzen

England won by 115 runs

ENGLAND V AUSTRALIA (3RD TEST)
At Edgbaston 30 July–3 August 2009

Australia

S.R.Watson lbw b Onions	62	– c Prior b Anderson	53
S.M.Katich lbw b Swann	46	– c Prior b Onions	26
*R.T.Ponting c Prior b Onions	38	– b Swann	5
M.E.K.Hussey b Onions	0	– c Prior b Broad	64
M.J.Clarke lbw b Anderson	29	– not out	103
M.J.North c Prior b Anderson	12	– c Anderson b Broad	96
+G.A.Manou b Anderson	8	– not out	13
M.G.Johnson lbw b Anderson	0		
N.M.Hauritz not out	20		
P.M.Siddle c Prior b Anderson	13		
B.W.Hilfenhaus c Swann b Onions	20		
B 5, l–b 7, w 2, n–b 1	15	B 4, l–b 6, w 2, n–b 3	15

1/85 2/126 3/126 4/163   263   1/47 2/52 3/137 4/161 5/346   (for 5 wkts) 375
5/193 6/202 7/202 8/203 9/229 10/263

Bowling: *First innings* – Anderson 24–7–80–5; Flintoff 15–2–58–0; Onions 16.4–2–58–4; Broad 13–2–51–0; Swann 2–0–4–1. *Second innings* – Anderson 21–8–47–1; Flintoff 15–0–35–0; Onions 19–3–74–1; Swann 31–4–119–1; Broad 16–2–38–2; Bopara 8.2–1–44–0; Collingwood 2–0–8–0.

England

*A.J.Strauss c Manou b Hilfenhaus	69
A.N.Cook c Manou b Siddle	0
R.S.Bopara b Hilfenhaus	23
I.R.Bell lbw b Johnson	53
P.D.Collingwood c Ponting b Hilfenhaus	13
+M.J.Prior c sub b Siddle	41
A.Flintoff c Clarke b Hauritz	74
S.C.J.Broad c & b Siddle	55
G.P.Swann c North b Johnson	24
J.M.Anderson c Manou b Hilfenhaus	1
G.Onions not out	2
b 2, l–b 4, w 6, n–b 9	21

1/2 2/60 3/141 4/159   376
5/168 6/257 7/309 8/348 9/355 10/376

Bowling: *First innings* – Hilfenhaus 30–7–109–4; Siddle 21.3–3–89–3; Hauritz 18–2–57–1; Johnson 21–1–92–2; Watson 3–0–23–0.

Umpires: Aleem Dar and R.E.Koertzen

Match drawn

ENGLAND V AUSTRALIA (4TH TEST)
At Headingley 7–9 August 2009

England

*A.J.Strauss c North b Siddle	3	– lbw b Hilfenhaus		32
A.N.Cook c Clarke b Clark	30	– c Haddin b Johnson		30
R.S.Bopara c Hussey b Hilfenhaus	1	– lbw b Hilfenhaus		0
I.R.Bell c Haddin b Johnson	8	– c Ponting b Johnson		3
P.D.Collingwood c Ponting b Clark	0	– lbw b Johnson		4
+M.J.Prior not out	37	(7) c Haddin b Hilfenhaus		22
S.C.J.Broad c Katich b Clark	3	(8) c Watson b Siddle		61
G.P.Swann c Clark b Siddle	0	(9) c Haddin b Johnson		62
S.J.Harmison c Haddin b Siddle	0	(10) not out		19
J.M.Anderson c Haddin b Siddle	3	(6) c Ponting b Hilfenhaus		4
G.Onions c Katich b Siddle	0	– b Johnson		0
B 5, l–b 8, w 1, n–b 3	17	B 5, l–b 5, w 5, n–b 11		26

1/11 2/16 3/39 4/42   102   1/58 2/58 3/67 4/74   263
5/63 6/72 7/92 8/98 9/102 10/102   5/78 6/86 7/120 8/228 9/259 10/263

Bowling: *First innings* – Hilfenhaus 7–0–20–1; Siddle 9.5–0–21–5; Johnson 7–0–30–1; Clark 10–4–18–3. *Second innings* – Hilfenhaus 19–2–60–4; Siddle 12–2–50–1; Clark 11–1–74–0; Johnson 19.3–3–69–5.

Australia

S.R.Watson lbw b Onions	51
S.M.Katich c Bopara b Harmison	0
*R.T.Ponting lbw b Broad	78
M.E.K.Hussey lbw b Broad	10
M.J.Clarke lbw b Onions	93
M.J.North c Anderson b Broad	110
+B.J.Haddin c Bell b Harmison	14
M.G.Johnson c Bopara b Broad	27
P.M.Siddle b Broad	0
S.R.Clark b Broad	32
B.W.Hilfenhaus not out	0
B 9, l–b 14, w 4, n–b 3	30

1/14 2/133 3/140 4/151   445
5/303 6/323 7/393 8/394 9/440 10/445

Bowling: *First innings* – Anderson 18–3–89–0; Harmison 23–4–98–2; Onions 22–5–80–2; Broad 25.1–6–91–6; Swann 16–4–64–0.

Umpires: Asad Rauf and B.F.Bowden

Australia won by an innings and 80 runs

ENGLAND V AUSTRALIA (5TH TEST)
At The Oval 20–23 August 2009

England

*A.J.Strauss c Haddin b Hilfenhaus	55	– c Clarke b North		75
A.N.Cook c Ponting b Siddle	10	– c Clarke b North		9
I.R.Bell b Siddle	72	– c Katich b Johnson		4
P.D.Collingwood c Hussey b Siddle	24	– c Katich b Johnson		1
I.J.L.Trott run out (Katich)	41	– c North b Clark		119
+M.J.Prior c Watson b Johnson	18	– run out (Katich)		4
A.Flintoff c Haddin b Johnson	7	– c Siddle b North		22
S.C.J.Broad c Ponting b Hilfenhaus	37	– c Ponting b North		29
G.P.Swann c Haddin b Siddle	18	– c Haddin b Hilfenhaus		63
J.M.Anderson lbw b Hilfenhaus	0	– not out		15
S.J.Harmison not out	12			
B 12, l–b 5, w 3, n–b 18	38	B 1, l–b 15, w 7, n–b 9		32

1/12 2/114 3/176 4/181   332   1/27 2/34 3/39 4/157   (for 9 wkts dec) 373
5/229 6/247 7/268 8/307 9/308 10/332   5/168 6/200 7/243 8/333 9/373

Bowling: *First innings* – Hilfenhaus 21.5–5–71–3; Siddle 21–6–75–4; Clark 14–5–41–0; Johnson 15–0–69–2; North 14–3–33–0; Watson 5–0–26–0. *Second innings:* Hilfenhaus 11–1–58–1; Siddle 17–3–69–0; North 30–4–98–4; Johnson 17–1–60–2; Katich 5–2–9–0; Clark 12–2–43–1; Clarke 3–0–20–0.

Australia

S.R.Watson lbw b Broad	34	– lbw b Broad		40
S.M.Katich c Cook b Swann	50	– lbw b Swann		43
*R.T.Ponting b Broad	8	– run out (Flintoff)		66
M.E.K.Hussey lbw b Broad	0	– c Cook b Swann		121
M.J.Clarke c Trott b Broad	3	– run out (Strauss)		0
M.J.North lbw b Swann	8	– st Prior b Swann		10
+B.J.Haddin b Broad	1	– c Strauss b Swann		34
M.G.Johnson c Prior b Swann	11	– c Collingwood b Harmison		0
P.M.Siddle not out	26	– c Flintoff b Harmison		10
S.R.Clark c Cook b Swann	6	– c Cook b Harmison		0
B.W.Hilfenhaus b Flintoff	6	not out		4
B 1, l–b 5, nb 1	7	B 7, l–b 7, n–b 6		20

1/73 2/85 3/89 4/93   160   1/86 2/90 3/217 4/220   348
5/108 6/109 7/111 8/131 9/143 10/160   5/236 6/327 7/327 8/343 9/343 10/348

Bowling: *First innings* – Anderson 9–3–29–0; Flintoff 13.5–4–35–1; Swann 14–3–38–4; S.J.Harmison 4–1–15–0; Broad 12–1–37–5. *Second innings* – Anderson 12–2–46–0; Flintoff 11–1–42–0; S.J.Harmison 16–5–54–3; Swann 40.2–8–120–4; Broad 22–4–71–1; Collingwood 1–0–1–0.

Umpires: Asad Rauf and B.F.Bowden

England won by 197 runs

ASHES AVERAGES 2009 – ENGLAND

England batting averages

Player	Mat	Inns	NO	Runs	HS	Ave	BF	SR	100	50
IJL Trott	1	2	0	160	119	80.00	274	58.39	1	0
AJ Strauss	5	9	0	474	161	52.66	951	49.84	1	3
KP Pietersen	2	4	0	153	69	38.25	308	49.67	0	1
GP Swann	5	8	1	249	63	35.57	299	83.27	0	2
A Flintoff	4	7	1	200	74	33.33	275	72.72	0	1
MJ Prior	5	9	1	261	61	32.62	319	81.81	0	2
SJ Harmison	2	3	2	31	19*	31.00	46	67.39	0	0
SCJ Broad	5	9	1	234	61	29.25	322	72.67	0	2
IR Bell	3	5	0	140	72	28.00	296	47.29	0	2
PD Collingwood	5	9	0	250	74	27.77	615	40.65	0	3
AN Cook	5	9	0	222	95	24.66	426	52.11	0	1
JM Anderson	5	8	2	99	29	16.50	179	55.30	0	0
RS Bopara	4	7	0	105	35	15.00	228	46.05	0	0
MS Panesar	1	2	1	11	7*	11.00	52	21.15	0	0
G Onions	3	4	2	19	17*	9.50	51	37.25	0	0

England bowling averages

Player	Mat	Inns	Overs	Mdns	Runs	Wkts	BBI	BBM	Ave	Econ	SR	5	10	Ct	St
SCJ Broad	5	8	154.1	25	544	18	6/91	6/91	30.22	3.52	51.3	2	0	1	0
G Onions	3	5	77.4	11	303	10	4/58	5/132	30.30	3.90	46.6	0	0	0	0
SJ Harmison	2	3	43.0	10	167	5	3/54	3/69	33.40	3.88	51.6	0	0	0	0
GP Swann	5	8	170.2	30	567	14	4/38	8/158	40.50	3.32	73.0	0	0	1	0
JM Anderson	5	8	158.0	38	542	12	5/80	6/127	45.16	3.43	79.0	1	0	2	0
A Flintoff	4	7	128.5	18	417	8	5/92	6/119	52.12	3.23	96.6	1	0	1	0
PD Collingwood	5	4	18.0	1	76	1	1/38	1/38	76.00	4.22	108.0	0	0	4	0
MS Panesar	1	1	35.0	4	115	1	1/115	1/115	115.00	3.28	210.0	0	0	0	0
RS Bopara	4	1	8.2	1	44	0	–	–	–	5.28	–	0	0	3	0
IR Bell	3	–	–	–	–	–	–	–	–	–	–	–	–	1	0
AN Cook	5	–	–	–	–	–	–	–	–	–	–	–	–	7	0
KP Pietersen	2	–	–	–	–	–	–	–	–	–	–	–	–	1	0
MJ Prior	5	–	–	–	–	–	–	–	–	–	–	–	–	11	1
AJ Strauss	5	–	–	–	–	–	–	–	–	–	–	–	–	4	0
IJL Trott	1	–	–	–	–	–	–	–	–	–	–	–	–	1	0

ASHES AVERAGES 2009 – AUSTRALIA

Australia batting averages

Player	Mat	Inns	NO	Runs	HS	Ave	BF	SR	100	50
MJ Clarke	5	8	1	448	136	64.00	780	57.43	2	2
MJ North	5	8	1	367	125*	52.42	736	49.86	2	1
RT Ponting	5	8	0	385	150	48.12	581	66.26	1	2
SR Watson	3	5	0	240	62	48.00	437	54.91	0	3
BJ Haddin	4	6	0	278	121	46.33	400	69.50	1	1
SM Katich	5	8	0	341	122	42.62	633	53.87	1	1
MEK Hussey	5	8	0	276	121	34.50	577	47.83	1	2
NM Hauritz	3	3	1	45	24	22.50	91	49.45	0	0
GA Manou	1	2	1	21	13*	21.00	39	53.84	0	0
BW Hilfenhaus	5	6	4	40	20	20.00	81	49.38	0	0
PJ Hughes	2	3	0	57	36	19.00	97	58.76	0	0
PM Siddle	5	6	1	91	35	18.20	139	65.46	0	0
MG Johnson	5	6	0	105	63	17.50	169	62.13	0	1
SR Clark	2	3	0	38	32	12.66	31	122.58	0	0

Australia bowling averages

Player	Mat	Inns	Overs	Mdns	Runs	Wkts	BBI	BBM	Ave	Econ	SR	5	10	Ct	St
BW Hilfenhaus	5	9	180.5	40	604	22	4/60	5/80	27.45	3.34	49.3	0	0	0	0
PM Siddle	5	9	161.4	24	616	20	5/21	6/71	30.80	3.81	48.5	1	0	3	0
NM Hauritz	3	5	103.2	17	321	10	3/63	6/158	32.10	3.10	62.0	0	0	0	0
MG Johnson	5	9	162.1	15	651	20	5/69	6/99	32.55	4.01	48.6	1	0	0	0
SR Clark	2	4	47.0	12	176	4	3/18	3/92	44.00	3.74	70.5	0	0	0	0
MJ North	5	4	67.3	13	204	4	4/98	4/131	51.00	3.02	101.2	0	0	3	0
MJ Clarke	5	5	19.0	1	75	1	1/12	1/27	75.00	3.94	114.0	0	0	8	0
SM Katich	5	3	10.0	2	27	0	–	–	–	2.70	–	0	0	6	0
SR Watson	3	2	8.0	0	49	0	–	–	–	6.12	–	0	0	2	0
BJ Haddin	4	–	–	–	–	–	–	–	–	–	–	–	–	15	0
PJ Hughes	2	–	–	–	–	–	–	–	–	–	–	–	–	1	0
MEK Hussey	5	–	–	–	–	–	–	–	–	–	–	–	–	6	0
GA Manou	1	–	–	–	–	–	–	–	–	–	–	–	–	3	0
RT Ponting	5	–	–	–	–	–	–	–	–	–	–	–	–	11	0

INDEX